Ideology and Policy

The Political Uses of Doctrine
in the Soviet Union

Ideology and Policy

The Political Uses of Doctrine in the Soviet Union

Terry L. Thompson

Westview Press

BOULDER, SAN FRANCISCO, & LONDON

Westview Special Studies on the Soviet Union and Eastern Europe

Copyright © 1989 by Westview Press, Inc.

Published in 1989 in the United States of America by Westview Press, Inc., 5500 Central Avenue, Boulder, Colorado 80301, and in the United Kingdom by Westview Press, Inc., 13 Brunswick Centre, London WC1N 1AF, England

Library of Congress Cataloging-in-Publication Data
Thompson, Terry L.
  Ideology and policy: the political uses of doctrine in
the Soviet Union.
  (Westview special studies on the Soviet Union and
Eastern Europe)
  Bibliography: p.
  Includes index.
  1. Soviet Union—Politics and government—1953–1989.
2. Brezhnev, Leonid Il'ich, 1906–   . 3. Gorbachev,
Mikhail Sergeevich, 1931–   . I. Title. II. Series.
DK274.T53 1989   947.085   87-29533
ISBN 0-8133-7463-4

Printed and bound in the United States of America

The paper used in this publication meets the requirements of the American National Standard for Permanence of Paper for Printed Library Materials Z39.48-1984.

10   9   8   7   6   5   4   3   2   1

Contents

Preface

The role of ideology in the Soviet political system has been the subject of continuing debate. Most Western studies of the Soviet Union in the 1940s and 1950s assumed that Soviet policy was based on a theoretical framework derived from Marx and Lenin. Some analysts also believed that ideology was essential in the interaction between state and society; Soviet citizens were thought to be motivated by Marxism-Leninism. However, these assumptions began to change in the late 1960s. With few exceptions, students of the Soviet Union began to downplay the role of ideology, looking instead at pragmatism as the root cause of Soviet actions.

Gorbachev's wide-ranging reform program has led to new declarations that Soviet ideology is dead. Most analysts now assume that Gorbachev has abandoned theory in his effort to solve the problems confronting Soviet society and that his policies have no ideological underpinning. Some have suggested that the Gorbachev era heralds the end of communism as a viable political system. Nationality unrest has called into question the cohesiveness of the Soviet Empire, while the recent elections to the new Congress of People's Deputies demonstrate that the Soviet model of communist politics is indeed undergoing dramatic modifications.

Changes in the political system, however, do not have to reflect changes in the underlying principles. In this book I argue that ideology continues to be a central, if less visible, element in the formulation of Soviet policy. While pragmatism is clearly important for Gorbachev, as it has been for other leaders in the past, focusing attention exclusively on practical matters ignores the fundamental reality of the Soviet political system. Soviet leaders, after all, are by education and upbringing ideological politicians. They are the best products of the Leninist political system that evolved after the October Revolution. They have to be realistic in the development of specific policies, but they must also consider the ideological justification for and implications of their actions. This is not to say that Marxism-Leninism serves as a motivational force for the average Soviet citizen; in my view it has never served that purpose, despite the enthusiasm of its proponents.

The primary value of ideology in the Soviet Union is in communications among party members and, especially, those who would be party leaders. To build consensus and demonstrate their ability to rule, Soviet leaders must develop policy agendas within an acceptable theoretical framework. As the basis of this framework, ideology helps to shape political views among the elite and the party membership and serves as a catalyst in the building of leadership coalitions. It also provides a vehicle for communicating regime values to the population as a whole—a key role in a Leninist political system.

Analyzing the relationship between ideology and policy is a complex undertaking. What is eventually published as official ideology is most often the result of extended debate among party leaders and ideological specialists, debate that takes place largely behind the scenes in theoretical journals and seminars. Matching the ideology with specific policies is another complication, especially since ideological discussions frequently cross the boundary between domestic and foreign policy. Moreover, because the ideological dimension is not always evident in policy decisions, conclusions about the interrelationship between ideology and policy frequently can be drawn only by inference. The greatest difficulty, however, is to resolve a "chicken-or-egg" question: Does ideology determine policy or does the theoretical justification follow policy implementation?

This study addresses these issues by examining a cross section of policy areas over the past thirty-five years. It concentrates on several domestic policy areas (labor incentives, nationalities, political partici- pation, and CPSU policy) and one area of foreign policy (Sino-Soviet relations) that have been central to the policy agendas of Khrushchev, Brezhnev, and Gorbachev. Policies in each area are examined in light of their ideological justification. The main focus is the Brezhnev era and policies related to its ideological motto, *developed socialism*. One cannot hope to offer many conclusions about the Gorbachev era, even four years after Gorbachev came to power. Because of the dynamism of his regime, it has been difficult to determine when to conclude the discussion of ideology and policy under Gorbachev. I have generally used the Nineteenth Party Conference and the October 1988 Central Committee Plenum as the cut-off points for my analysis, although I have referred to several events that occurred in early 1989.

My research has benefited greatly from the comments and suggestions of Angela Stent, John Hardt, and Carl Linden. I am also grateful to Susan McEachern of Westview Press, whose informed nudging and patient support kept the project on track. I am most indebted to my family, Kathy, Jimmy, and Mark, who have been tolerant and supportive of the work that has taken so many hours that could have been spent with them.

Terry L. Thompson

1

Introduction

Soviet Ideology and Policy

In the Soviet political system, "ideology" in the broadest sense refers to the body of philosophical principles considered axiomatic in Marxism-Leninism. These principles (atheism, a theory of classes and class struggle, and the historical mission of the proletariat) are not subject to change and comprise the fundamental dogma of the ideology.[1] Although they form a common frame of reference and worldview for Soviet leaders, the principles of Marxism-Leninism are not generally evident in policy decisions that are focused on practical matters.

In contrast, the "normative" component of ideology is generally more visible. Highly flexible by nature, norms change in response to the values of the leader in power and the evolving needs of the political system. Ideology in this sense is more pragmatic and can be defined as "a reasonably coherent body of ideas concerning practical means of how to change and reform a society."[2] The normative component may therefore be termed the "official ideology" of a given regime. The official ideology forms the basis of doctrinal statements in the CPSU Party Program, the Soviet Constitution, and other programmatic documents and reflects the agreed-upon ideological framework for change. Throughout this book, "ideology" used without a modifier refers to the official ideology.

An examination of official ideology is critical to a thorough understanding of regimes in the Soviet Union and other Leninist states. Because Leninism contains very little practical guidance for post-revolutionary development, Leninist parties are forced to create their own policy guidelines appropriate to the conditions of their society and political system and consistent with leadership goals. However, because they are Leninist parties, they must justify their actions in the context of Marxism-Leninism. Ideological legitimation is thus as important as organizational or operational approaches in the formulation of policy.[3]

In their efforts to provide an ideological context for policy decisions, Soviet leaders have found the official ideology to be extremely flexible

1

and have modified it "creatively" (in Soviet terms) to justify their policies. Examples of such creativity abound. Stalin's reversal of the Leninist concept of a worldwide communist revolution with his notion of "socialism in one country" allowed him to direct more resources to the development of a Soviet industrial base and gave him a convenient pretext to discredit Trotsky and the "left opposition." Khrushchev, as part of his overall effort to broaden participatory opportunities in the Soviet political system and signal an end to Stalin's reign of terror, publicized the concepts of the "all-people's state" and "mature socialism." Brezhnev promoted the notion of "developed socialism" to support policies designed to overcome the problems created by Khrushchev's schemes and bolster Soviet prestige in the international communist movement. Gorbachev has abandoned developed socialism in his pursuit of far-reaching political and economic reforms to overcome the stagnation of the late Brezhnev era. Similar examples can be found in other Leninist systems.[4]

The historical record indicates that changes in official ideology most often follow rather than precede policy changes. Mature socialism, for example, was used predominantly in the last years of Khrushchev's regime, after his reform program had been implemented. Similarly, developed socialism was not incorporated into official ideology until 1971, well after the policy preferences of Leonid Brezhnev had become the basis of Soviet domestic and foreign policy. A similar phenomenon is occurring under Gorbachev. His policies so far have been justified in the broader context of "Leninism" and "socialism," although these are almost certainly temporary slogans that will last only until the Soviet ideological establishment can develop a new concept to encapsulate the theoretical basis of Gorbachev's campaign for *perestroika, demokratizatsiia, glasnost'*, and "new thinking."

The sequence of events (changes in official ideology follow changes in policy) does not indicate that Soviet leaders ignore ideology while they are consolidating power. Indeed, each Soviet leader since Lenin has felt compelled to justify his policy agenda in terms of theory, and the theoretical basis for his agenda is an important part of his authority-building strategy.[5] Typically it is the individual leader's ideological values rather than the official ideology that are most evident in the early stages of any regime. He may use the existing ideology as a point of departure, but he will express his own ideas in more general terms such as Leninism. Later, as his values become accepted into official ideology, he will use specific ideological formulations to convey the theoretical basis of his policy agenda.[6]

This is not a straightforward process, however, since no leader's beliefs, values, and habits are developed in isolation. To fully understand the relationship between individual values and ideology, we must consider the interaction between the leader's ideological values and the overall leadership consensus about the general direction of policy. This interaction is especially critical in the early stages of a new regime when the leadership may be in flux. Because the Soviet system lacks a consistent method of selecting new leaders, no General Secretary has yet come to power with absolute authority; such authority has had to be earned (or taken) over a period usually lasting for several years. To maintain support long enough to consolidate power, the General Secretary must offer both an agenda for change and a theoretical basis for that agenda that are within the parameters of the consensus of the party leadership. He may offer new ideas, even radical ones such as Gorbachev has done. But he must not stray too far from the general consensus that put him into power in the first place.[7] To be successful, a leader must express not only policy options but also ideological values that reflect what he believes is proper and legitimate and also what he thinks is possible.

The early years of Stalin's regime provide an illuminating case. After Lenin died, Stalin took the lead in expediting the publication of his works. Significantly, and unlike Trotsky and Zinoviev, Stalin did not publish his own collected works. He offered instead an interpretation of Leninism that established his legitimacy as an ideological as well as a political heir. In his struggle against Trotsky and Zinoviev, Stalin proposed what amounted to a revision of Lenin's ideas in his formula for "socialism in one country," but shrewdly proclaimed this notion to be consistent with Lenin's thought. He never rejected the traditional goal of worldwide revolution and was thus able to use the new formulation to defeat the leftists and justify redirecting resources to the domestic economy. Similarly, in 1928–1929 he joined Bukharin and other party leaders in advocating the collectivization of agriculture. He then seized upon the general attitude of crisis in the party to force the tempo of collectivization, eventually undermining the gradualist approach of Bukharin and the "right opposition." Stalin again justified his policy initiatives in terms of Leninism, implying that the emergency measures of War Communism provided both the policy precedent and the theoretical justification for his "revolution from above." Thus, Stalin plied a careful course for five years following Lenin's death. He offered new ideas in theory and policy that enhanced his authority, but maintained an overall frame of reference that was clearly Leninist. And he adroitly manipulated the leadership consensus regarding the need for policy changes to serve his own ends. Later, of course, after he had gained the dominant leadership position, the official ideology was modified to reflect the "inevitability" of Stalin's actions.[8]

The example of Stalin is consistent with the pattern described above: policy determines the substance of the official ideology, which is then used to justify policy and explain regime goals.⁹ This complex "dialectical" relationship between ideology and policy has been described most succinctly by Karl Mannheim in his seminal 1936 study of ideology:

> Theory arising out of a definitely social impulse clarifies the situation. And in the process of clarification reality undergoes a change. We thereby enter a new situation out of which a new theory emerges.¹⁰

While complex, the relationship between ideology and policy provides a tool for analyzing the Soviet political system. By examining a General Secretary's ideological values and policies, we can gain unique insights into his authority-building strategy, societal management program, and views on the existing institutions of the political system. By comparing his views with the overall leadership consensus expressed in the official ideology and other programmatic statements, we may also assess the General Secretary's influence in the development of that consensus. These dimensions of Soviet politics are important; despite glasnost and the extraordinary degree of candor under Gorbachev, we still know too little about them.

Ideology and Policy Under Brezhnev

Most of this book concerns the connection between ideology and policy in the Brezhnev period, an era that offers several advantages for such a study. Brezhnev's official ideology, developed socialism, has been described and commented on by countless Soviet writers. Moreover, developed socialism has distinct boundaries; it was officially accepted into Soviet ideology at the Twenty-fourth CPSU Congress in 1971 and was rejected by Gorbachev at the Twenty-seventh Congress in 1986. The policies associated with the ideology are readily identifiable and, more important, can be associated with Brezhnev's policy preferences, thus providing insight into how ideology was reshaped to reflect Brezhnev's own ideological values and agenda for change. Finally, because many of Brezhnev's policies have been targeted for revision by Gorbachev, an examination of the Brezhnev era provides a solid foundation for understanding the post-Brezhnev consensus within which Gorbachev's reform program has evolved.

Although it was not incorporated into official ideology until 1971, the concept of developed socialism originated in Eastern Europe in the mid-1960s and had been debated by Soviet ideological specialists since 1966. This debate focused on two critical issues of the post-Khrushchev era:

the need to reassert Soviet primacy within the international communist movement and the need to deal with the question of Stalinism. Both issues were consistent with Brezhnev's values and provide insight into his policy agenda. The origins and evolution of developed socialism are thus addressed in Chapter 2.

Chapters 3–6 examine the more visible dimensions of developed socialism that encompassed Soviet domestic policy and consisted of several doctrines relating to social, economic, and political development.[11] Chapter 3 addresses the use of material incentives as a tool in the development of the "new Soviet man." Chapter 4 discusses the "Soviet nation," defined as "a new historical community" uniting Soviet citizens across class and ethnic boundaries. Chapter 5 describes the "all-people's state," a concept used to publicize the expanded scope of political participation in Soviet society. Chapter 6 treats policy toward the Communist Party, focusing particularly on the "leading and guiding role" of the party that emerged as the key principle of developed socialism. All these concepts originated under Khrushchev and were included in the 1961 Party Program. They were not, however, identified as components of developed socialism until 1971, by which time they had been modified to reflect the policy preferences of the new regime and particularly of Leonid Brezhnev. Chapter 7 discusses the fate of the ideological and related policies of developed socialism in the interim regimes of Yurii Andropov and Konstantin Chernenko. Against this background, Chapter 8 addresses Gorbachev's ideological values and agenda for change.

Examining these policy areas helps clarify several roles for ideology in the Soviet political system, including: protecting the theoretical heritage and legitimacy of the Soviet leadership; discussing and debating policy options; and explaining and publicizing the regime's policy line after it has been decided upon.[12] These are extremely important functions in an "ideological" political system, which, in contrast to an "instrumental" system, requires a theoretical basis for all policies. Although to a certain extent any politician is driven by pragmatic concerns, in the Soviet context pragmatism by itself is an insufficient basis for action; policy must be based on ideology. This relationship is ingrained in the minds of the leaders, ideological and academic specialists and rank and file party workers. Ideology thus simultaneously provides a framework for establishing regime goals and sets limits on the policy options that can be considered.[13]

In the Brezhnev era, the need for ideology *to protect the theoretical heritage and legitimacy of the Soviet leadership* was very clear in a lengthy and intense debate about the concept of developed socialism itself. The focus of this debate was whether to declare developed socialism a new stage in socialist evolution. The need for such a debate was based on two equally important stimuli. First was the concern about Khrushchev's brash prediction in 1961 that communism would be achieved in the 1980s. Something had to be done to change this prediction, to show that progress toward communism was still being made but that its attainment was more than a few years away. Second, there was concern about China usurping the Soviet Union's leading role in the international communist movement. The competition between the USSR and China that followed Khrushchev's 1956 denunciation of Stalin—which undercut the USSR's claim as the world's leading socialist state—contributed greatly to the Sino-Soviet rift. When Brezhnev took over, Mao Zedong was perceived as a serious ideological threat since he was one of the founders of the Chinese Communist Party, in contrast to his Soviet counterparts who were a generation removed from Lenin.

Mao's Great Leap Forward in 1958 had been at least partly designed as an ideological challenge to the Soviets, not in the least because it was almost certainly modeled on Stalin's "Great Leap" in the collectivization of agriculture. Although tension had eased subsequently, it was exacerbated in 1966 with the launching of the Great Proletarian Cultural Revolution, which again challenged the Soviet ideological and political model. Many Soviet ideologists believed that the Chinese ideological threat could be overcome by declaring a new stage of socialism, one that the Soviet Union had attained but the Chinese had not. In this way not only could the Soviets retain ideological supremacy, they could presumably regain prestige among other communist and communist-leaning nations.

Somewhat surprisingly, however, the esoteric and deeply theoretical discussion about a new stage of socialism soon turned into a emotionally charged argument about the most sensitive topic in Soviet history: Stalinism. Although there was no mention of Stalin in any of the programmatic documents of developed socialism, the need to resolve this issue was evident throughout the debate conducted in party and specialist journals. Strong feelings were expressed, both pro and con, on Stalin's role in Soviet history, and a wide-ranging discussion of Stalinism was evident throughout the first several years of Brezhnev's leadership. This debate ended abruptly in early 1968, however, because of the need for ideological unity in support of the threat to Soviet hegemony over Eastern Europe caused by the Dubcek reforms in Czechoslovakia.

It is important to note that the Stalin question emerged in the Brezhnev period and was tied directly to the broader question of the theoretical legitimacy of the regime. As discussed in Chapter 2, there were many specialists who urged the establishment of a clear division between Stalin's regime and the post-Stalin era. These specialists believed it was essential to officially recognize Stalin as an aberration in the evolution of socialism. Their views, however, were rejected by the ideological establishment and, ultimately, by Brezhnev himself. This is not to say that Brezhnev, Suslov, and other leaders of the time were "Stalinists." They were clearly products of the Stalinist system and supported continuation of some Stalinist policies, such as centralized planning. But they did not follow Stalin's methods of terror and fear as the basis for their authority. They chose rather to ignore the question of Stalin's role in terms of theory, probably because they worried that their own authority could be undermined by denouncing their former leader. The Stalin question thus remained in the background during the Brezhnev period, emerging again when Gorbachev came to power. His advocacy of glasnost with its attendant emphasis on clarifying the historical record about Stalin indicates he is seeking different sources of legitimacy for his policies.

The role of *ideology in debating policy options* in the Brezhnev era is evident in almost every issue area addressed in this book. Debates among party leaders, specialists, academics, and others were a characteristic feature of the Brezhnev regime and served as an important barometer of specialist and party opinion on regime policies.[14] The use of ideology as the framework for these debates was especially clear on the sensitive questions of Stalinism and the nationalities issue. It was least apparent in the area of party policy. Ideological discussions were subdued but still important in the areas of incentives policy and political participation.

These debates provided insight not only into the development of policy, but also into the evolution and meaning of important ideological terms. With the exception of developed socialism, the ideological components of the official ideology under Brezhnev were identical to those in the 1961 Party Program, suggesting a great deal of continuity between Khrushchev and Brezhnev. But Brezhnev's use of these terms in some cases differed greatly from Khrushchev's. For example, Brezhnev's "all-people's state" emphasized CPSU control over the political participation of Soviet citizens in the administration of the state. This definition contrasted dramatically with the near spontaneous political participation advocated by Khrushchev. Similarly, the "leading and guiding role" of the CPSU was central to the official ideology under both Khrushchev and Brezhnev. Brezhnev, however, applied this precept much more consistently than did Khrushchev, especially in the area of party admissions policy. On the other hand, the concept of the "Soviet nation" was used by both men in much the same way to signal advocacy of Russifying and assimilationist nationality policies. Even developed socialism, the only new term associated with the official ideology under

Brezhnev, was frequently used synonymously with the "mature socialism" first mentioned by Khrushchev. Yet, as is clear from the distinctions between the policies advocated by the two leaders, in practice the concepts of developed and mature socialism frequently diverged.

Thus, the use of ideological concepts to debate policy options and the subsequent redefinition of these concepts to reflect new policy decisions provide insights into the ideology-policy relationship under Brezhnev and help determine general trends in the policy making strategies of the Brezhnev regime.[15]

The third, and most visible, role of ideology under Brezhnev was to *communicate and explain the regime's policy decisions* to the masses and, more important, to party officials at all levels. To be effective, party workers had to incorporate the new or revised ideological concepts into their discussions with each other and with the population at large. The use of common terminology is vital to an ideological political system. Alfred Meyer has termed this aspect of ideology the "language of politics," which performs three critical functions. The first is to provide a frame of reference for all Soviet citizens with which to view daily events. Second, ideology helps define the citizen's rights and duties. Third, it serves as a "code of communications" within the political system and helps to affirm the legitimacy of the regime. Under Brezhnev, all these uses were apparent in Soviet ideological pronouncements and programmatic documents after the adoption of developed socialism in 1971. In what Meyer has termed the "post-hoc rationalization of policies," ideology in this role was used to place policy decisions in a theoretical context, to explain them to the masses and party workers alike.[16]

To say that ideology is used to convey regime policy, however, is not the same as saying that ideology alone can influence or convince the masses. Those who have argued that ideology is no longer effective in persuading Soviet citizens are certainly correct.[17] But it is arguable that Soviet ideology ever played such a role. Ideology, once codified in party documents, is used to *explain* the direction of policy. As described in countless *Pravda* editorials, it is up to the media and party workers—using ideology and other rationale—to *convince* Soviet citizens to comply with regime policies and support regime goals. This message has been repeated by Gorbachev, who has called for improvements in the party's ideological work among the masses. But Gorbachev clearly has no illusions about the ability of ideological slogans to convince the masses to participate in perestroika.

Thus, ideology is used to illustrate the theoretical continuity of the Soviet system since Lenin and to debate and subsequently to explain policies adopted by the regime in power. Brezhnev, in acknowledging the critical link between ideology and policy, went one step further. To frame his policy preferences in a suitable ideological context and set himself apart from his predecessors, he used the concept "Leninism" to explain and garner support for his political agenda.

Brezhnev's Leninist Course

Brezhnev's "Leninism" does not refer only to the fact that he titled his collected works *On a Leninist Course (Leninskim Kursom)* or that he often spoke of the "return to Leninist norms." Khrushchev, after all, had used the same phrase. But Khrushchev's version of Leninism, or "pseudo-Leninism," was in many ways a radical departure from ideas contained in Lenin's works.[18] Moreover, his interpretation of Lenin was not in accord with the consensus of his peers in the leadership.

Brezhnev set out to reverse Khrushchev's interpretation of Lenin. In the broadest terms, Brezhnev's ideological values and political agenda were based on a rejection of the "cult of personality" leadership style adopted by both Stalin and Khrushchev. Although Khrushchev had explicitly rejected Stalin's personality cult in his 1956 secret speech, in the end he established his own *kul't lichnosti*. Reacting to his predecessor, Brezhnev advocated a rejuvenation of the institutions of the Soviet political system, particularly the CPSU. His advocacy of an enhanced role for the party and a return to more traditional forms of party organization was the main theme he used in the struggle with Aleksei Kosygin for the top leadership job. Even when a Brezhnev cult became apparent in 1976–77 with his elevation to the rank of Marshal of the Soviet Union and to the position of Chairman of the USSR Supreme Soviet, the ceremonial "presidency" of the Soviet Union, he continued to champion the institutions of the Soviet political system. In addition to his initial rejection of the cult of personality leadership style, Brezhnev presented other ideological values in the context of Leninism. These included: the reassertion of the primacy of the Soviet Union in the international communist movement; a preference for the balanced application of material and "moral" (non-material) incentives to stimulate productivity; an assimilationist approach to the nationalities issue; and a fundamental conviction of the primacy of the CPSU in the Soviet political system. As will be demonstrated in the chapters that follow, Brezhnev was more successful in some areas than others in implementing policies corresponding to his values. But his ideological values and agenda for political change remained generally consistent. Designed to overcome the excesses of both Stalin and Khrushchev, Brezhnev's political agenda had as its theoretical basis the reestablishment of the continuity with Leninist ideas that in many ways had been broken by his two predecessors.

Brezhnev strongly identified his views with those of Lenin throughout his tenure as General Secretary, frequently referring to the "ideas of Lenin" in his speeches. His use of Leninism as the framework for his policy preferences was most evident in his speech to the Twenty-fourth CPSU Congress in 1971, coinciding with the adoption of developed socialism into official ideology and signalling Brezhnev's rise to power.

Noting that Lenin's picture graced the new party documents CPSU members would receive in 1972–73, Brezhnev described the central role of Leninism in party thought and action:

> Leninism as an eternally living, developing doctrine was, is, and will be in the center of the party's ideological life and at the basis of all of its revolutionary-transformational activity. Turning to the ideological heritage of V. I. Lenin, the party sees its most important task finding solutions to current problems of communist construction on the basis of Leninist ideas and Leninist methodology.[19]

Having further discussed the value of Marxism-Leninism in overcoming both the cult of personality (Stalin) and subjectivist mistakes (Khrushchev), Brezhnev went on to provide the clearest link between his policies and Lenin's thought. In describing the party's approach in developing the new five-year plan, Brezhnev added: "The main task of the party and all of its organizations is to mobilize the masses for the struggle to fulfill assigned tasks, and to unite more closely the entire nation on a *Leninist platform of communist construction.*"[20]

Although he was addressing economic policy in this instance, the notion of a "Leninist platform of communist construction" accurately sums up Brezhnev's overall ideological and political agenda. By explicitly associating his policies with those of Lenin—especially those calling for increased party control over the economic and political system—Brezhnev presented a credible and acceptable platform in his efforts to gain the dominant leadership position. Obviously this is not a platform in exactly the same sense the concept is used in Western politics. In the Soviet system a platform can be described as the policy preferences of a single individual rather than of an entire political party, although the experience of the post-Stalin era has shown that these preferences cannot differ significantly from the consensus of the party leadership. As was evident with Brezhnev, a leader's policy preferences are shaped both by his desires to change certain aspects of the political situation and by the acceptability of these changes to the overall leadership. Although Brezhnev was not a candidate for election in the Western sense of the word, he did have to convince the majority of the leadership that his policies would be successful, particularly when juxtaposed against the reformist initiatives sponsored by Kosygin. Brezhnev accomplished this by overtly and consistently justifying his policies with the ideological authority of Lenin.[21]

Of course, it is difficult to say to what extent Brezhnev actually believed in the Leninism that informed his own words and those written about him. A cynical view would hold that Brezhnev (or any other Soviet leader) had no ideological values, that he simply mouthed the words of his ideological specialists and speechwriters. But the example of Gorbachev suggests otherwise. As Gorbachev has demonstrated abundantly in his first four years in power, the top leader clearly does have the latitude to express his own ideological values through his agenda for change. Brezhnev, too, presented an agenda for change based on his ideological values, although on a much quieter and more limited scale and with quite different dimensions.

Based on a thorough reading of Brezhnev's works, a strong case could be made that he did in fact believe in Leninism, that it was an integral part of his ideological beliefs. But the essential point in examining the relationship between his ideology and policy is that he *used* Leninism as the theoretical underpinning for an agenda for change designed to overcome the negative effects of Stalin and Khrushchev. This was essential for Brezhnev, who had to offer a different approach than Kosygin to retain credibility among his peers and remain in the running for the top leadership post. He chose to support the overall economic reforms sponsored by Kosygin, but he offered something more. By presenting a policy set that had irrefutable theoretical underpinnings in contrast to Kosygin's more practical approach, he established himself as a more traditional and thus more acceptable alternative.

Clearly, discussing Brezhnev's approach to ideology and policy in terms of Leninism does not explain all aspects of his political behavior. His performance, like that of any political leader, depended on circumstances, personalities and many other aspects of the political situation not subject to his control. But viewing Brezhnev's rise to the dominant leadership position in terms of his use of Leninism to express his ideological values does provide useful insights into his authority-building strategy. All Soviet leaders refer to Lenin's statements and philosophy to serve many needs. Indeed, any Soviet leader not referring to Lenin's works could not survive for long. But for Brezhnev, Leninism was something more. The concept for him was an important and effective tool to secure power and build authority because it provided an indisputable theoretical basis for his political agenda. More than simply referring to Lenin, Brezhnev continually wrapped himself in Lenin's mantle throughout his tenure as General Secretary.

Early in his regime, his references to Lenin may have helped him overcome the disadvantages of a policy program that was more conservative and less well-defined that Kosygin's reform agenda. In the end, however, Brezhnev's Leninism turned out to be more of a liability than an asset. The widening gap between his ideological statements and the reality of the Soviet political and economic system in the last years of his regime undermined his authority and gave a hollow ring to his statements on Lenin. Moreover, his lack of strong, Leninist leadership over the party in the late 1970s led to the growth of widespread corruption and cynicism not only in the population at large, but also (and more significantly) within the party itself. The combination of the loss of the party's authority among the population and Brezhnev's loss of credibility with the party rank and file eventually made a mockery of his use of Lenin and set the stage for radical change after his departure.[22]

Gorbachev's Leninism

The utility of Leninism to provide an ideological basis for policy has been underscored by Gorbachev's frequent references to Lenin to express his own ideological values and policy agenda (discussed in Chapter 8). Gorbachev, however, has chosen a different set of Lenin's ideas to justify his reform program. Whereas Brezhnev concentrated on the aspect of Leninism that emphasized control through a strong and elite party, Gorbachev has focused instead on Lenin's approach to practical economic and political problems in the immediate post-revolutionary period when the political situation in the country was still highly dynamic and control of the political system by the Communist Party was still in doubt. Like Lenin, Gorbachev has sought to compromise on certain ideological principles to gain practical results. To buttress his support for compromise he frequently refers to the crisis conditions that have arisen in the Soviet Union as the result of years of mismanagement, implicitly comparing the situation in the USSR today with that confronting Lenin in the aftermath of the October Revolution. Ironically, this is the same tack used by Stalin to force the tempo of collectivization and industrialization.

Gorbachev, of course, does not draw this parallel. In describing the sources of perestroika, he asserts that it was the neglect of Lenin's ideas in the years following his death that led to the current situation. "The specific situation in the country," he notes, "made us accept forms and methods of socialist construction corresponding to the historical conditions. But those forms were canonized, idealized, and turned into dogma. Hence the emasculated image of socialism, the exaggerated centralism in management, the neglect for the rich variety of human interests, the underestimation of the active part people play in public life, and the pronounced egalitarian tendencies." The answer to these problems, in Gorbachev's view, is to return to Lenin's teachings. "A drastic change must be made in social and political thought," he proclaims. "And here we must learn from Lenin. He had the rare ability to sense at the right time the need for radical changes, for a reassessment of values, for a revision of theoretical directives and political slogans."[23]

Gorbachev's Lenin is not Brezhnev's Lenin. Gorbachev is not only looking for justification for his policies in Lenin's voluminous writings, which was the basic approach used by Brezhnev. He is also using the example of Lenin the revolutionary politician who had to figure out ways of adapting to a continually changing situation. Gorbachev implies that he is as adroit as Lenin in coming up with the right answer at the right time to maintain his own position and the authority of the party, that he is the type of revolutionary leader needed at a time of economic, political, and moral crisis. There are clearly risks involved for Gorbachev in attempting to identify himself so closely with Lenin. If he has to modify Lenin's ideas too much to justify his reform agenda, his use of Lenin as a model will turn into a mockery just as Brezhnev's did. A greater risk lies in overreliance on Lenin, who has been criticized in the Soviet press for his moral relativism and his policies that restricted rather than encouraged political freedom.[24] But Gorbachev may expect the forcefulness of his personality and his demonstrated leadership ability to outweigh those risks. Certainly he relies on Lenin's work as the ideological underpinning for perestroika.

The pains taken by both Brezhnev and Gorbachev to describe the ideological roots of their policy programs in the works of Lenin is not surprising. Soviet leaders must refer to Lenin's thoughts in order to establish their credibility and maintain the legitimacy of the CPSU as the ruling party. In one sense it may seem a weakness of the Soviet system that leaders decades removed from the founder must rely on his writings for the theoretical justification of their societal management programs. But in a more fundamental way the continuing reliance on Lenin is a strength, and gives the Soviet leadership a measure of continuity not found in other political systems. Although Lenin wrote on many subjects and his writings may be interpreted in different ways by different leaders, these leaders are still obligated to stay within the Leninist frame of reference in developing policies to fit changing situations. Their use of Lenin therefore reveals a great deal about their ideological values and the overall direction of their policy programs.

Notes

1. For a comprehensive study of Soviet Marxism, see James P. Scanlan, *Marxism in the USSR: A Critical Survey of Current Soviet Thought* (Ithaca: Cornell University Press, 1985). For a brief examination of the philosophical principles,

see Joseph M. Bochenski, "The Three Components of Soviet Ideology," *Studies in Soviet Thought II* 1 (March 1962), pp. 7–11.

2. Carl J. Friedrich and Zbigniew K. Brzezinski, *Totalitarian Dictatorship and Autocracy*, 2d ed. rev. Carl J. Friedrich (New York: Frederick A. Praeger, 1965), p. 88.

3. Clement H. Moore, "The Single Party as Source of Legitimacy," in Samuel P. Huntington and Clement H. Moore, eds., *Authoritarian Politics in Modern Society: The Dynamics of Established One-Party Systems* (New York: Basic Books, Inc., 1970), p. 55. Also see Richard Lowenthal, "The Ruling Party in a Mature Society" in Mark G. Field, ed., *Social Consequences of Modernization* (Baltimore: Johns Hopkins Press, 1976), p. 81.

4. For example, "socialism with a human face," based on the humanistic aspects of Lenin's work, was the slogan used for Alexander Dubcek's 1968 liberalization program in Czechoslovakia; and "Mao Zedong thought" was the ideological basis for the Chinese Great Leap Forward and the Great Proletarian Cultural Revolution.

5. See the insightful and highly original discussion of authority-building in chapter one of George Breslauer's book, *Khrushchev and Brezhnev as Leaders: Building Authority in Soviet Politics* (London: George Allen & Unwin, 1982). Breslauer, however, does not include ideology as a dimension in authority-building.

6. Soviet leaders thus fit Robert Putnam's description of an ideological politican as one who "focuses on general principles rather than specific details, who reasons deductively rather than inductively, who . . . stresses the role of 'ideas' in politics." The ideological politician also relies on his "beliefs, values, and habits." Robert D. Putnam, "Studying Elite Political Culture: The Case of 'Ideology,'" *American Political Science Review* (September 1971), pp. 652 and 657.

7. I argue in Chapter 8 that many of Gorbachev's proposals are within the post-Brezhnev consensus for change, and are not, therefore, as radical as they are sometimes portrayed.

8. Sources for this paragraph include: Robert H. McNeal, *Stalin: Man and Ruler* (New York: New York University Press, 1988), pp. 85–108 and 124–132; Robert Conquest, *The Harvest of Sorrow: Soviet Collectivization and the Terror-Famine* (New York: Oxford University Press, 1986, pp. 77–116; and Adam Ulam, *Stalin: The Man and His Era* (New York: Viking Press, 1973), pp. 234–321.

9. The same situation exists after a leader has firmly established power, but at that time it is more difficult to distinguish the individual leader's values from the official ideology, which has been changed to incorporate the leader's values. For an illustration of how the leader's values can differ from the official ideology later in the regime, see the discussion on Brezhnev's nationality policy in Chapter 4. For an insightful discussion of the role of values in leadership politics in general, see Philip E. Jacob, "The Influence of Values in Political Integration," in Philip E. Jacob and James V. Toscano, eds., *The Integration of Political Communities* (Philadelphia: J. B. Lippincott Company, 1964), p. 211.

10. Karl Mannheim, *Ideology and Utopia* (New York: Harcourt, Brace and Company, 1936), p. 112.

11. For an excellent discussion of the political and ideological implications of developed socialism, see Alfred B. Evans, Jr., "Developed Socialism in Soviet Ideology," *Soviet Studies* 24 (July 1977), pp. 409–28. See also his "Social Transformation in Developed Socialism: Recent Trends in Soviet Ideology," *Co-existence* 17 (April 1980), pp. 58–81. Donald Kelley has also discussed the implications of developed socialism. See Donald R. Kelley, "Developed Socialism: A Political Formula for the Brezhnev Era," in Jim Seroka and Maurice D. Simon, eds., *Developed Socialism in the Soviet Bloc: Political Theory and Political Reality* (Boulder, Colorado: Westview Press, 1982), pp. 3–20. See also Kelley's book, *The Politics of Developed Socialism: The Soviet Union as a Post-Industrial State* (New York: Greenwood Press, 1986). Kelley (pp. 15–33) provides an excellent overview of the "scientific-technical revolution" (NTR in Russian) that was an important dimension of the doctrines of developed socialism. The NTR is not examined in my study, primarily because the general focus is on political and social issues. A secondary reason is the difficulty of tracing policies related to the doctrinal description of the NTR. It is easy to say that Brezhnev advocated growth and improvement in Soviet science and technology; it is more difficult to find policies that were implemented to actually meet this goal.

12. For a more general discussion of the roles played by ideology in the Soviet political system, see Kelley, *Politics of Developed Socialism*, pp. 4–13, and Alfred G. Meyer, "The Functions of Ideology in the Soviet Political System," *Soviet Studies* 17 (January 1966), pp. 273–285.

13. On the distinction between ideological and instrumental political systems, see Zbigniew K. Brzezinski and Samuel P. Huntington, *Political Power: USA/ USSR*, (New York: The Viking Press, 1965), pp. 56 and 71–76.

14. See the highly informative discussion on policy debates in Jerry F. Hough and Merle Fainsod, *How the Soviet Union is Governed* (Cambridge: Harvard University Press, 1979), pp. 285–293.

15. What I am describing is close to what Donald Kelley has called the "operational code" function of doctrine, which "both sets the boundaries of political battle and subtly alters the established notions about the legitimacy and continuity of party rule." See Kelley, *Politics of Developed Socialism*, p. 201. The term "operational code" was coined by Nathan Leites in the 1940s. See the discussion of Leites' work in Alexander L. George, "The 'Operational Code': A Neglected Approach to the Study of Political Leaders and Decision-Making," in Erik P. Hoffman and Frederic J. Fleron, Jr., eds., *The Conduct of Soviet Foreign Policy*, 2d ed. (New York: Aldine Publishing Company, 1980), pp. 165–190.

16. See Meyer, "The Functions of Ideology in the Soviet Political System," pp. 276–80.

17. For three opinions about the waning role of ideology in the Soviet system, see: Richard Lowenthal, "Development vs. Utopia in Communist Policy," in *Change in Communist Systems*, ed. Chalmers Johnson (Stanford: Stanford University Press, 1970), pp. 33–116; Robert C. Tucker, "Swollen State, Spent Society: Stalin's Legacy to Brezhnev's Russia," *Foreign Affairs* 60 (Winter 1981/2), pp. 431–434; and Robert V. Daniels, "The Ideological Vector," *Soviet Studies* 18 (July 1966), pp. 71–73.

18. For a useful discussion of Khrushchev's modifications to Leninism, see Carl A. Linden, *The Soviet Party-State: The Politics of Ideocratic Despotism* (New York: Praeger Publishers, 1983), pp. 115–135. On Khrushchev's pseudo-Leninism, see Frederick C. Barghoorn, "Soviet Russia: Orthodoxy and Adaptiveness," in Lucian W. Pye and Sidney Verba, eds., *Political Culture and Political Development* (Princeton: Princeton University Press, 1965), pp. 510–511. William Zimmerman argues that Khrushchev rejected Leninism as a guide to action. See his *Soviet Perspectives on International Relations, 1956-1967* (Princeton: Princeton University Press, 1973), p. 290.

19. L. I. Brezhnev, *Leninskim Kursom*, 8 vols. (Moscow: Politicheskaia Literatura, 1970–1981), vol 3, pp. 302 and 309.

20. Ibid., pp. 310 and 313 (emphasis added).

21. Alfred Meyer's study remains the best description of Lenin's ideology and policy. See Alfred G. Meyer, *Leninism* (Cambridge, Massachusetts: Harvard University Press, 1957).

22. See Chapter 7 for a discussion of the post-Brezhnev consensus that developed as a result of these circumstances.

23. Mikhail Gorbachev, *Perestroika: New Thinking for Our Country and the World* (New York: Harper & Row, 1987), pp. 45 and 48.

24. See the discussion in Thomas Sherlock, "Politics and History Under Gorbachev," *Problems of Communism* 37 (May-August 1988), pp. 39–41.

2

Origins and Evolution of Developed Socialism

According to the Soviet definition, "developed socialism" (*razvitoi sotsializm*) is the second stage in the transition from socialism to communism, and was attained by the USSR in the "early 1960s" and in certain countries of Eastern Europe by the "mid-1970s."[1] In contrast to this explanation, the published record reveals quite a different chronology. Although most Soviet writers have used "developed" socialism synonymously with "mature" socialism, introduced by Khrushchev at the Twenty-second CPSU Congress in 1961, the USSR was not said to be a "developed socialist society" by any of its leaders until Leonid Brezhnev first used the term in his 1967 speech on the fiftieth anniversary of the October Revolution. Moreover, despite the Soviet claim that developed socialism originated in the USSR, the concept in fact originated in Eastern Europe and this was the context in which it was introduced into the Soviet ideological vocabulary.

Although it did not officially become a component of Soviet ideology until the Twenty-fourth CPSU Congress in 1971, developed socialism was introduced in the mid-1960s as part of a coordinated Soviet attempt to restore the primacy of the USSR in the world communist movement that had been lost in the aftermath of Khrushchev's denunciation of Stalin in his secret speech to the Twentieth Party Congress in 1956. The turmoil in the communist movement in the subsequent eight years led to a serious erosion of Soviet authority and prestige, which threatened Soviet economic and political interests in Eastern Europe and elsewhere. The introduction of developed socialism was part of a concerted effort by the Brezhnev leadership to reestablish Soviet dominance over an

A previous version of this essay was published in Terry L. Thompson and Richard Sheldon, eds., *Soviet Society and Culture: Essays in Honor of Vera S. Dunham* (Westview Press, 1988), pp. 206–235.

increasingly rebellious communist community. The adoption of the concept into official ideology in 1971 reflected the Soviet perception that this dominance had been restored.

Besides its importance in Soviet foreign policy, developed socialism was also crucial to another key policy goal: distancing the Brezhnev regime from that of both Khrushchev and Stalin. This became clear in a debate about developed socialism conducted by Soviet ideological specialists in the late-1960s, after the concept had been introduced into the Soviet ideological vocabulary but before it was accepted as a component of official ideology. While it comes as no surprise that the regime that ousted Khrushchev in 1964 wanted to distance itself as much as possible from his policies, it is noteworthy that a need to distance the Brezhnev leadership from Stalin's policies was so strongly perceived. Yet that is the clear implication of much of the debate about whether to declare developed socialism a new stage in socialist evolution.

Developed socialism thus arose from the post-Khrushchev leadership consensus concerning the dual need to reestablish Soviet control over world communism and deal with the question of Stalin.[2] Brezhnev adopted the concept as the ideological component of his authority-building strategy. Later, when it became part of the official ideology, developed socialism came to be regarded as a "political formula" to identify the goals and management style of the Brezhnev regime.[3] Its evolution from the subject of debate to its acceptance into official ideology provides an illuminating example of the complex relationship between ideology and policy in the USSR.

Reasserting Soviet Primacy

The need to reestablish Soviet primacy in the world communist movement arose from the disarray that had characterized the communist world under Khrushchev. Even before his 1956 denunciation of Stalin, Khrushchev had encouraged diversity among communist leaders by replacing much of the former political dependence on Stalin with a system of semi-autonomous institutional and economic arrangements including the Warsaw Pact and a revitalized Council for Mutual Economic Assistance (CMEA). The abolition of the Cominform in 1956 was another measure designed to remove the essence of Stalinist control over Eastern Europe.[4] Besides rejecting Stalin's legacy in his secret speech, Khrushchev made a second important ideological concession in his open speech to the Twentieth Congress when he acknowledged that power could be attained through other than revolutionary means. This had the effect of implicitly renouncing the Leninist maxim that communists must come to power through the use of force.[5] Despite efforts by prominent Soviet ideologists like Mikhail Suslov and Boris Ponomarev to maintain Soviet primacy after the 1956 Party Congress,[6] the combined effect of Khrushchev's de-Stalinizing policies and his relaxation of traditional ideological demands created too much strain on communist leaderships accustomed to the iron rule of Stalin. These dramatic changes in Soviet ideology and policy led to the East German, Polish, and Hungarian events of 1956.[7]

Fears about the possible effects of the loss of Soviet authority were soon confirmed by Chinese efforts to "reconstruct a center" in the communist movement. This was significant especially in Eastern Europe where Wladyslaw Gomulka and Todor Zhivkov attempted to use Chinese ideological authority to develop policies to increase their independence from Moscow.[8] Although the Chinese did intervene to affirm Soviet primacy at the 1957 Moscow conference of communist parties, Mao Zedong the next year launched the Great Leap Forward, designed to end Soviet ideological, economic, and military domination of the PRC. The worst aspect of the Great Leap from the Soviet perspective was its emphasis on people's communes as the foundation for communist construction. Not only did this fly in the face of the Soviet approach to communism through industrialization, it also contained the implicit promise that the PRC would become the first country to attain communism.[9]

The Soviet response to the Great Leap was provided in the speeches to the Twenty-first "Extraordinary" CPSU Congress in 1959. Designated the "Congress of the Builders of Communism," this meeting was devoted exclusively to discussions of the Seven-Year Plan, which was designed to put the USSR on the threshold of communism. Documents from the congress emphasized heavy industry as the only possible basis for communist construction. This provided a vivid contrast to the Chinese notion of building communism on the basis of an agrarian economy. The anti-Chinese message was reinforced by statements at the congress stressing the integral relationship between industrial development and Marxism-Leninism.[10] The tension created by the ideological conflict was further exacerbated later in 1959 after the Chinese rejected a Soviet proposal that would have given the USSR broader control over the Chinese military in return for increased assistance in the development of Chinese nuclear capabilities.[11]

The Sino-Soviet split became public knowledge in 1960 and, together with Khrushchev's failure to reach agreement with the US over the rearmament of West Germany and the deteriorating state of US-Soviet relations in general, led to a decline in Soviet prestige and authority. This was emphasized at the 1960 Budapest Communist Conference at which the Chinese position regarding the non-peaceful transition to socialism was accepted, contradicting Khrushchev's 1956 revision of this notion. This action, in Richard Lowenthal's words, "conferred legitimacy on the de facto existence of two centers" of international communism in Moscow and Beijing.[12] The Budapest conference also signalled the beginning of open polemics between China and the Soviet Union and led to the complete abandonment of Soviet military and technical aid to the PRC. Taking full advantage of their newly gained prestige, the Chinese rubbed salt into Soviet wounds by establishing "Maoist" parties in certain Third World countries.[13]

The Soviet response to this challenge to their international authority was unveiled at the Twenty-second CPSU Congress in 1961. Renewing the social Darwinist argument first advanced against the Chinese at the Twenty-first Congress, Soviet ideologists expounded on the distinction between primitive and advanced societies to demonstrate that the USSR was by definition farther ahead on the road to communism. In his main speech to the congress, Khrushchev stressed particularly the contrast between Soviet and Chinese societies, proclaiming that all classes hostile to socialism had been eliminated in the USSR. He added that the "dictatorship of the proletariat" had evolved into an "all-people's state" where millions of ordinary Soviet citizens were participating in the daily tasks of administration and government.[14] Articles published after the Party Congress concentrated on other differences between Soviet and Chinese societies, addressing particularly the "Asiatic mode of production" characteristic of repressive oriental societies. The purpose of these discussions was to indicate that the PRC not only was not advancing towards communism but was in fact regressing to a more primitive form of society.[15] The Chinese countered these charges by condemning the Soviet "treason" against Marxism-Leninism. Mao himself responded to the concept of the all-people's state, declaring that the dictatorship of the proletariat would have to be continued for "five to ten generations or one or several centuries" in order to prevent the formation of new exploiting classes that would inevitably result from abandoning proletarian government.[16]

By the mid-1960s, what had begun as an ideological debate between Moscow and Beijing became a dispute about important policy issues. The lack of Soviet nuclear assistance still perturbed the Chinese, who criticized the Soviets severely for signing the Nuclear Test Ban Treaty in 1963.[17] The question of support to the North Vietnamese in their intensifying struggle with the United States also became a key policy concern for both countries, especially the USSR. This was crucial in terms of the broader ideological question regarding Soviet primacy in the communist movement: if the Soviets were to regain control of world communism, they would have to provide assistance to a communist regime engaged in a shooting conflict with the United States. But the provision of such assistance could not be taken for granted, particularly in light of the dismal performance of the Soviet Navy in the Cuban crisis—thus precluding supply of North Vietnam by sea—and the close relationship Beijing enjoyed with Hanoi.[18] The Soviet Union would have to secure a land route through China if there were to be any possibility of providing the quantity of supplies required by North Vietnam.[19]

By the time of Khrushchev's removal from power in October 1964, the continuing dispute on these key issues and the large doses of ideological venom being exchanged by Moscow and Beijing made it clear that international communism had lost its former solidarity. The Sino-Soviet rift had led not only to the "decolonization" of communist states and parties, but had also provided the basis for increasing polycentrism.[20] To say, however, that superior Soviet economic and military strength would have prevented any Chinese attempt to claim leadership of the communist movement misses the essential point.[21] The important thing was that ideological disagreement had delayed the attainment of a critical strategic objective—gaining a Soviet foothold in Southeast Asia. From Moscow's perspective, this set a worrisome precedent; Soviet loss of ideological (and, therefore, political) control over other communist countries could lead to similar setbacks in the future.

The initial response of the Brezhnev regime to the crisis over Vietnam was to initiate a conciliatory policy toward the Chinese.[22] Ideological polemics were suspended and a series of meetings was held with Chinese leaders. Kosygin's trips to Hanoi, Beijing, and Pyongyang in February 1965 were announced as part of an ongoing effort to achieve agreement over the question of unified communist support to North Vietnam.[23] The Soviet initiative evidently had the desired effect, for by March the Chinese had granted the minimal transit rights necessary for the Soviets to begin shipping supplies to Hanoi.[24] This agreement was followed by a positive sign from the Soviets that relations should continue to improve. In April, Serge D. Lapin, Deputy Foreign Minister and a career diplomat, replaced Stepan V. Chervonenko, a Khrushchev appointee with no previous diplomatic experience, as ambassador to Beijing.[25] Other signs that relations were improving included the resumption of Sino-Soviet trade negotiations and the resolution of details leading to the resumption of technical cooperation between the two countries.[26] These actions were nowhere near the magnitude of Gorbachev's opening to China twenty years later (see Chapter 8), but in 1965 they were signficant, representing a clear departure from Soviet policy of the preceding eight years.

However, the renewed cordiality between the two countries was short-lived. The US escalation in Vietnam in mid-1965 led to increased tension once again and forced the Soviets to press China for direct intervention into the war, or at a minimum, for the use of Chinese bases to expedite Soviet resupply of the North Vietnamese by air. The internal conflict over this issue among the Chinese leadership was evidently intense, with a strong pro-Soviet group backing Moscow's proposals and threatening Mao's position. Stalling on a decision for over six months, Mao eventually chose neither to intervene in Vietnam nor to grant the Soviet request for bases. In 1966, he launched the Cultural Revolution, presumably in order to consolidate his power within the Chinese leadership.[27] His decision signalled to the Soviets that further rapprochement was out of the question.

Although the Soviet Union remained officially cordial in public statements to and about the Chinese during this period (perhaps indicating that the Soviets hoped for continued improvement despite the Cultural Revolution), by mid-1965 subtle criticism was again being directed towards Beijing. Buried in *Pravda* articles on the 45th anniversary of Lenin's "Left Wing Communism," the 30th anniversary of the Seventh Comintern Congress, the 50th anniversary of the Zimmerwald Conference and other obscure dates in communist history, this criticism contained appeals for unity and warnings against diversity.[28] A year later, however, when the Cultural Revolution began, Soviet comments became more direct and more blunt. The Soviets revealed, for example, that the Chinese had twice (in November 1964 and February 1965) rejected a broad program for normalizing relations.[29] As the rift between the two communist powers widened once more, Soviet hostility was openly stated in the press, where Chinese attempts to replace Lenin's thoughts with the ideas of Mao Zedong were attacked and ridiculed.[30]

It was against this background of renewed Sino-Soviet hostility that developed socialism was introduced into Soviet ideology. In a December 1966 *Pravda* article, Fedor Burlatskii described developed socialism as it had been presented by the Bulgarians and Hungarians at their respective party congresses. He also discussed similar statements made by the East Germans, Poles, and Czechs. (Burlatskii neglected to point out that the concept of developed socialism had been introduced much earlier, in June 1960 at a plenum of the Czechoslovak CP Central Committee and had been adopted by other East European parties.)[31]

Generalizing from the statements of the Bulgarians and Hungarians and from the experience of the Soviet Union, Burlatskii presented four characteristics of a developed socialist society. Developed socialism provided for the creation of an *economy* that answered the demands of the scientific-technical revolution and allowed for greater labor productivity than capitalism. It also called for raising the level of agricultural production to that of industry, thus providing greater satisfaction of the needs of the population. *Socially*, a developed socialist society was characterized by a strengthened role of the working class, by the unity of all peoples, and by interpersonal relations built on camaraderie and socialist morality. *Politically,* a developed socialist society was led by the party operating on scientific principles of leadership. It also featured much greater participation by the masses in the administration of governmental affairs. *Ideologically,* a strengthened and unified world view based on Marxism-Leninism was the salient feature of developed socialism.

Concentrating on East European economic development, Burlatskii established the basis for the discussion concerning developed socialism as it evolved during the next five years: to extol the virtues of Soviet-style economic development based on industry while rejecting the Chinese model based on agriculture. To reinforce the distinction between Soviet and Chinese approaches to economic and societal development, most countries of Eastern Europe were said to be aligned with the Soviet Union in taking the path of industrialization. Equating developed socialism with the "complete construction of socialism" (*polnoe postroenie sotsializma*), Burlatskii asserted that despite some differences these countries had all been engaged in a broad process of economic reform similar to that underway in the USSR. They had also been involved in developing new socio-political relationships resulting from the economic reforms.[32] Burlatskii pointed out that this was the natural progression of socialist evolution. Chinese efforts to skip the "scientific" stages of historical development were therefore destined to fail. The flaw in the Chinese approach (evident in the Cultural Revolution) was that it emphasized only the political aspects of societal development, creating an imbalance in the entire set of political, economic, and social relationships inherent in any society. In contrast, developed socialism was to be a long period of the "all-around development of socialist society," affecting not only politics but economics and culture as well.[33]

Developed socialism was thus the latest iteration of the arguments presented against the Chinese at the Twenty-first and Twenty-second CPSU Congresses. Directed this time against Mao and the Cultural Revolution, the contrast between Soviet and East European industrialized society and Chinese agrarian society was the same that had been used previously to discredit both the Great Leap Forward in 1958 and Chinese attempts at claiming supremacy after the Budapest conference in 1960.

After Burlatskii reopened this argument, Soviet specialists added new elements to address specific characteristics of the Cultural Revolution. Academician T. Khachaturov accused Mao of establishing a "barracks regime" and predicted that the results of the Soviet 1966-70 Five Year Plan would fully justify the scientific, industrial type of development favored by the USSR.[34] Others contrasted the role of the CPSU and the growth of social democracy in the Soviet Union with the authoritarian nature of Mao's regime. The USSR and other countries that had completed the transition to socialism and "had begun or were beginning to build a developed socialist society" were utilizing the creative abilities of their citizens to build a more democratic system. The state apparatus and the party were the most important institutions for teaching citizens the values and methods of democracy and thus could not be undermined as they had been under Mao.[35]

The threads of the economic and social relations aspects of the societal development argument were tied together by Vladislav Kelle, who later became an important advocate of developed socialism. Chief of the Historical Materialism Section of the Institute of Philosophy in the Academy of Sciences, Kelle criticized Mao for "ignoring the objective conditions and laws of societal development," and for "throwing the country far back into the past in economic and social terms." The most dangerous aspect of Mao's actions, Kelle pointed out, was that they were intended to lead to a new "essential stage in the development of socialist social relations," and to serve as a "model for other socialist countries to follow." But, as Soviet experience with agricultural communes after the October Revolution had demonstrated, "socialist production relations cannot be developed on a backward material-technical base." The USSR had learned from this experience and had moved forward to a level characterized by higher economic productivity and increasingly democratic social relations.[36] Restating the same argument a year later, Kh. Momdzhian placed the contrast between the Soviet and Chinese approaches in ideological perspective by asserting that "communism can only be built on the basis of the achievements of developed socialism." He added that "any voluntaristic attempts to jump through the essential stages of historical progress will invariably end in defeat."[37]

Thus, developed socialism was described by Soviet ideologists as a logical step in the evolution of socialist societies. Based on industrial development and a corresponding improvement in social relations, developed socialism was defined as a *necessary* stage in socialist development. It could therefore not be skipped, as the Chinese had attempted to do in the Cultural Revolution. More than simply revisiting the Sino-Soviet ideological dispute of the late 1950s, use of developed socialism—especially the key point that the Soviet Union was the first to attain this necessary stage of development—reflected a concerted Soviet effort to reestablish political and ideological primacy within the world communist movement.

As part of this effort, and directly connected to the ideological and policy struggle with China, the Brezhnev regime also began to revitalize economic and political ties with Eastern Europe. One of the first steps taken by the new regime was to renew bilateral treaties and initiate a series of joint meetings. Soviet treaties of friendship were signed with Bulgaria and Hungary in 1967. An important meeting emphasizing communist unity was held in Karlovy Vary, Czechoslovakia the same year.[38] Unity was the main issue in all such meetings, and was the only item on the published agenda for the Moscow International Communist Conference originally scheduled for December 1968, but subsequently postponed until June 1969. The implicit goal of using this conference to reestablish Soviet primacy was broadly hinted at many times in the Soviet press, beginning with the original call for a conference in 1967.[39] The measures taken towards Eastern Europe, in other words, were part of the overall Soviet effort to reestablish dominance in world communism that was signalled most visibly by the use of developed socialism to discredit the Chinese.

One of the most important tactics in the Soviet drive to reassert its authority as the center of the communist world was the revitalization of *Problemy Mira i Sotsializma (PMS)*, the Prague-based theoretical journal established after the 1958 World Communist Conference.[40] Georgii P. Frantsov[41] was sent to Prague as Chief Editor of *PMS* in 1964. Under his leadership, the journal became an important forum for discussions about developed socialism. However, problems soon emerged with the whole notion of developed socialism. This was not because of difficulties created by the Chinese, but because of disagreement within the Soviet ideological establishment itself. Although developed socialism was eventually acknowledged as a new stage in Marxism-Leninism, it was not until after a thorough debate by some of the most powerful figures in the Soviet ideological hierarchy.[42]

The Ideological Debate

The central issue in the debate over developed socialism was whether to declare a new stage of communist evolution. Party leaders and ideological specialists in favor of developed socialism generally agreed that a new stage of Soviet development had already begun, dating its origins between 1956–61, or in other words between Khrushchev's denunciation of Stalin and the adoption of the 1961 Party Program. Those opposed to creating a new stage based their arguments on the writings of Marx and Lenin, objecting to any alteration either to Marx's two stages of communism or Lenin's naming these stages "socialism" and "communism."[43]

More than an esoteric dispute about ideology, however, this was in fact a debate about the proper role of Stalin in the historical and political development of the USSR. Those supporting developed socialism saw in the concept a chance to separate the Stalinist period from the post-Stalin era, thereby emphasizing the return to normalcy in the Khrushchev and Brezhnev periods.[44] Opponents of developed socialism saw no such boundary, insisting rather on maintaining the continuity of all regimes since Lenin. What began as an attempt to counter the Chinese and to shore up the Soviet position in the international communist movement had suddenly turned into a discussion of the most sensitive topic in Soviet history.[45]

Despite Burlatskii's explanation of developed socialism and the increasing use of the term by East European leaders (notably Walter Ulbricht[46]), Soviet ideologists in the late 1960s were slow to adopt "developed socialism." Other phrases were instead applied to the "current stage of communist construction." As used at the Twenty-third CPSU Congress and elsewhere, these phrases ranged from the Khrushchevian "mature socialism" and "all-out building of communism" to the awkward "stage of building the material-technical basis of communism" and the bland "building the new society."[47] It was clear from the frequent criticism of ideological decline under Khrushchev that the new regime wanted to distance itself from its immediate predecessor. Presumably this meant abandoning "mature socialism" and the "all-out building of communism," both of which were used extensively during the last years of Khrushchev's rule. But these terms continued to be used because no viable alternative was available. Specialists writing about ideology were thus caught between the need to reflect "creatively" on the policies of the new regime and the demand to maintain continuity with established doctrine. It was crucial, in other words, to stress the progress made by Brezhnev while at the same time demonstrating that official ideology had remained constant since Lenin.

The discussion regarding stages of socialism was divided between two schools of thought. The first, emphasizing the de-Stalinizing programs of Khrushchev and Brezhnev, was represented by specialists like Mikhail Iovchuk, Chief of the Historical Philosophy Section of the Institute of Philosophy of the USSR Academy of Sciences. Iovchuk distinguished four stages of socialism. The first, "the birth of socialist ideology and the formation of proletarian class consciousness under socialism," began in Russia during the industrial riots of 1895–96 and continued until the October Revolution. The second stage, "the development of class consciousness," included the transformation of the Soviet economy from capitalism to socialism and lasted until the "mid-1930s." The third stage, "the beginning of the transition to communism," covered the period 1936–55. This was followed by the fourth or "current stage," the "transition to the all-out building of communism." His periodization thus separated the Khrushchev and Stalin periods, in effect using

Khrushchev's 1956 secret speech as the dividing line between the two. He made no distinction between the Khrushchev and Brezhnev regimes, presumably because he wrote his article at about the time the new leadership was coming to power.[48]

Rikhard Kosolapov, former Chief Editor of *Kommunist* and an early and important advocate of developed socialism, also favored four stages of socialism. Writing in 1979 after the original debate on developed socialism had ended, he placed the beginning of the fourth stage in the "late 1960s," roughly coinciding with the initial use of developed socialism by Brezhnev in 1967 (see below), but disregarding the similarity between "developed" and "mature" socialism.[49] The latest versions of this periodization have placed the origins of the developed or mature stage of socialism in the early 1960s in the USSR and in the early 1970s in some countries of Eastern Europe. This approach, which links the Khrushchev and Brezhnev regimes, ignores the discussions on developed socialism that occurred in Eastern Europe in the 1960s and avoids mentioning that the concept in fact originated there. Most important, however, was that those wanting to declare developed socialism a new stage in Soviet socialist development agreed on a general periodization that distinguished between Stalin's era and the post-Stalin period.

The second school of thought on socialist evolution ascribed no importance to the distinction between the Stalin and post-Stalin eras, much less to that between Khrushchev and Brezhnev. Spokesmen for this approach emphasized instead the integrity of Marxism-Leninism from its inception. This view, which is more of a refinement of the standard Soviet definition of socialism than a new periodization, made no allowance for temporary social, political or economic changes of any kind. Grigorii Glezerman, for example, Assistant Head of the Central Committee's Academy of Social Sciences, delineated only three stages of socialist development. The first, "the creation of the foundations of a socialist economy," presumably began with the October Revolution and ended in the "early 1930s." The second stage, "the victory of socialism," was attained in the "late 1930s." Glezerman's third phase, "the consolidation of socialism," began at the end of the 1930s and, taken together with the two earlier periods, formed the complete stage of socialism. In other words, according to Glezerman, socialism was a "long stage of societal development" that was still in progress when he wrote about it in 1970.[50]

Glezerman was supported in this approach by P. N. Fedoseev, Director of the Central Committee's Institute of Marxism-Leninism (IML) from 1967–71 and the most vocal opponent of developed socialism. Writing in 1968, Fedoseev especially agreed that "socialism, as foreseen by the classicists of Marxism-Leninism and as practical experience has shown, is not a brief stage on the road to communism, but a separate, comparatively lengthy stage of development."[51] Fedoseev's opposition to developed socialism was the most aggressive, and the fact that he continued to oppose the concept after Brezhnev himself used it in 1967 indicates the strength of his convictions, even if it casts doubt about his political judgment.

As is clear from these two approaches to the periodization of Soviet socialist experience, the central question in the debate about a new stage of socialism was whether to acknowledge in theory Khrushchev's denunciation of Stalin, since this would be the necessary result of proclaiming a stage of socialism beginning in the 1950s or 1960s. Ideologists in favor of developed socialism were openly critical of Stalin. Iovchuk, for example, asserted that Stalin's thesis on the intensification of the class struggle that accompanied attainment of higher levels of social development caused a "basic distortion" in the proper Marxist-Leninist understanding of society. This distortion in turn had caused increased "ideological suspicion," "timidity" and the "absence of conflict theory" in the arts and sciences. The result of this combination was the eventual stagnation of scientific and artistic creativity.[52]

In contrast, specialists who opposed introducing a new stage of socialism were less dogmatic in their judgment of Stalin and openly defended Stalin in their ideological statements. F. Konstantinov, for example, formerly Chief Editor of *Kommunist* and from 1962–67 Director of the Institute of Philosophy in the USSR Academy of Sciences, was especially defensive on the question of Stalinism. He justified Stalin's actions as inevitable in the face of the tremendous opposition threatening to undermine the regime. According to Konstantinov, resistance came neither from enemies of the party nor from Stalin's personal enemies. It came instead from "anti-Leninists" who refused to recognize the notion of "socialism in one country," which Konstantinov claimed to be a doctrine of Lenin's. He went on in a remarkable piece of self-criticism to place the blame for Stalin's excesses on the party's "theoretical and philosophical cadres":

The enemies of Leninism attacked fully armed. They had to be defeated theoretically in front of the people and the working class. Who did this? The party and its theoretical and philosophical cadres. Could this possibly have been done better, with fewer victims and at a lower cost? Yes, it is possible. But we were the first, and we had no models or historical examples. We were not free to choose the time frame for either industrialization or collectivization. In terms of industrial development, we had to cover ground in ten years that others had covered in one hundred. Without struggling against dogmatism and various forms of revisionism, including philosophical revisionism, our Soviet country could not have achieved the victory of socialism.[53]

Konstantinov was apparently saying that he had once supported an important ideological revision—socialism in one country—only to see it used as the theoretical underpinning for the purges of the 1930s and Stalin's other excesses. He was therefore opposed to any major changes in socialist theory, implicitly warning about possible negative ramifications that could return to haunt ideological specialists who had developed the theory in the first place.[54]

The debate about developed socialism and the break with Stalinism it implied was conducted not only by individual specialists but by ideological institutions as well. The chief protagonists at this level were Frantsov's *PMS* in Prague and Fedoseev's IML in Moscow. Under Frantsov, *PMS* became a forum for advocates of developed socialism, particularly as it had evolved in Eastern Europe. Members of the Bulgarian and East German party central committees and politburos contributed numerous articles on the evolution of developed socialism and on the characteristics of this stage of communist development.[55] Frantsov personally supported the concept in a November 1967 *Pravda* article in which the USSR and "a group of other socialist countries" were said to have attained developed socialism.[56] This article and a companion piece in *Voprosy Filosofii* coincided with the initial use of developed socialism by Brezhnev in his 1967 speech on the fiftieth anniversary of the October Revolution, suggesting that this celebration was used by proponents of the new concept to orchestrate a "media blitz" on developed socialism.[57]

Brezhnev's initial use of developed socialism suggests that the position advocated by *PMS* was supported by at least some of Brezhnev's speechwriters in the Central Committee secretariat, one of whom may have been Kosolapov.[58] In his speech, Brezhnev implicitly addressed the ideological conflict with the Chinese, particularly the social relations aspect. As Khrushchev had done at the Twenty-second Party Congress, Brezhnev asserted that improved social relations in the Soviet Union had led to the growth of social democracy and creation of the "all-people's state" which had superceded the "dictatorship of the proletariat." He also touched on the internal Soviet debate on developed socialism. Providing support for those in favor of proclaiming a new stage of socialism, Brezhnev stated that communism could only be built on the basis of developed socialism. He also noted that developed socialism had already been achieved in the USSR, confirming that this was in accordance with the outline for development set forth in the 1961 Party Program. The last point was especially noteworthy since it placed

Brezhnev's full authority on the side of those using developed socialism as an ideological framework to acknowledge the break with Stalin.[59]

Despite Brezhnev's endorsement, Fedoseev and others in the ideological establishment remained opposed to the concept. Fedoseev's opposition was the most important because of the increased power that had been given to IML on ideological issues in 1967–1968.[60] Fedoseev's (and IML's) main objection against creating a new stage of socialism was that this would alter the very foundations of Marxist-Leninist thought. Such a major change should be reserved for truly epochal discoveries, not those made "every year," but those "fundamentally transforming our ideas about reality."[61] The fact that he published this argument in *PMS* in 1967, at the same time the journal was publishing many articles supporting developed socialism, strongly implied that he considered the socioeconomic and political developments associated with the new stage of socialism to be unworthy of recognition in official ideology.

Brezhnev's use of developed socialism did have some impact on Fedoseev, however. Several months later, he offered what amounted to a counterproposal by suggesting that the term "Leninism" be used to describe the current stage of socialist development. This idea first appeared in the theses prepared by IML for the 150th anniversary of the birth of Karl Marx, celebrated in April 1968. These theses were presented to demonstrate the "greatness of the scientific achievement" of Lenin's contributions to Marxism.[62] In a follow-up article entitled "Leninism is the Marxism of the 20th Century," Fedoseev repeated much of what had been stated in the theses, emphasizing strongly that the current stage of development should be called simply "Leninism."[63] The fact that the characteristics of Leninism as he described it—a strengthened material-technical base, increased social democracy, improved class and nationality relations, and further development of the new man—were identical to those offered by advocates of developed socialism indicated that Fedoseev had no quarrel with the substance of the new stage, only with its name.

In terms of the debate on developed socialism, the title "Leninism" was attractive for two reasons. First, it would credit the founder of the Soviet state with any and all ideological variations from Marxism, a position that could not be readily challenged. Second, it would preclude discussion of the sensitive issue of Stalinism. By lumping the entire Soviet experience under this rubric, the question of Stalin's, Khrushchev's, Brezhnev's or any other leader's contributions to ideology would become secondary. Moreover, the problem of how to deal with Stalin in terms of theory would disappear as there would no longer be any need to subdivide the "comparatively lengthy stage of development" that had begun with the October Revolution. Such an approach would also be consistent with Fedoseev's argument for reserving new labels for truly epochal changes.

Fedoseev's position was implicitly supported by Mikhail Suslov, in a way similar to that in which Brezhnev supported Frantsov and *PMS* in his fiftieth anniversary speech. In his 1968 speech on the 150th anniversary of Marx's birth, Suslov emphasized that the Soviet Union was in the process of "building communism," adding that "we now understand the path to communism more clearly." Agreeing that socialism should be considered "an entire historical period in the development of communist society," he implied that developed socialism could not be treated as a new stage between socialism and communism. At best it was a subphase of socialism. In a unique departure from previous periodizations, Suslov placed the beginnings of developed socialism in the 1930s and 1940s and pointed to the development of Soviet industry, the struggle for existence during the capitalist encirclement, and the fight against the Nazis in World War II as the formative elements. In his comprehensive approach to socialist evolution, Suslov used developed socialism in a more general way than those arguing whether it should be considered a new stage of socialist development. Most important, however, Suslov's approach eliminated the requirement for dealing with the question of Stalin by implicitly ascribing the origins of the concept to Stalin himself.[64]

Suslov's speech was the last major contribution in the debate over developed socialism. By mid-1968, ideological specialists on both sides of the issue had redirected their efforts towards events in Czechoslovakia. Those who formerly wrote descriptions of developed socialism switched to broader discussions of communist theory in general to emphasize the need for unity. Iovchuk contributed an article criticizing both pluralist tendencies among Marxist parties and theories of convergence being offered by Western specialists.[65] I. Pomelov, who in early 1967 had described the increasing democratization of developed socialist society, was in July 1968 more concerned about delineating the "essential characteristics and principles of socialism inherent in the new society in all socialist countries."[66] Similarly, Professor S. M. Kovalev, who in 1966 had been one of the first to refer to a "developed socialist economy," examined in late 1968 the "counter-revolutionary" situation in Czechoslovakia and fully justified the "fraternal assistance" of Soviet troops to protect the integrity of socialism. In a separate article he provided perhaps the most succinct theoretical justification for the Brezhnev Doctrine:

> The people of socialist countries and communist parties indisputably have the freedom and must have the freedom for determining the paths of development for their country. However, their decision must not cause

damage either to socialism in their own country or to the fundamental
interests of other socialist countries or the international workers' movement
in general in the struggle to achieve socialism.[67]

The end of the discussion on developed socialism was accompanied
by a tightening of the ideological reins in general. The strongest evidence
that a crackdown was underway was Frantsov's removal from the Chief
Editor's job at *PMS* and transfer back to Moscow, probably in 1968,
where he became Fedoseev's deputy at IML. The subject of developed
socialism was not addressed under the new editor of *PMS*, K. Zarodov,
until immediately prior to the Twenty-fourth CPSU Congress in 1971
when developed socialism became part of official Soviet ideology. Frantsov
subsequently published a *mea culpa* in *Pravda* when he called for a
unified socialist ideology that could be directed against bourgeois ideologists using Czechoslovakia as an example of the deterioration of
Marxism-Leninism. In contrast to his earlier encouragement of discussions
on the various paths to socialism, Frantsov now claimed that the Soviet
experience contained "general rules" that must be followed by any
country building socialism.[68]

Soviet Primacy Restored

Developed socialism reappeared in Soviet ideological literature in 1969
to signal Soviet perceptions of their renewed authority after Czechoslovakia. There was no evidence of the previous ideological debate, suggesting that the question about recognizing a new stage of communist
development had been put to rest.[69] Moreover, the debate about Stalinism
that had evolved from the discussion on developed socialism disappeared
from the pages of Soviet ideological and party journals. The primary
use of developed socialism at this time was to call attention to the
enhanced Soviet position with respect to both China and Eastern Europe
as well as to signal an end to Soviet tolerance of ideological diversity.
Although Soviet gains were to be eventually undermined in the mid-
1970s by the more dangerous diversity represented by Eurocommunism,
in 1969–1970 the Soviets were confident that their prestige and authority
among world communists had been restored.[70]

Reflecting this confidence, Soviet policy towards Eastern Europe and
China in the years immediately following the invasion of Czechoslovakia
was characterized by increasing power and self-assurance. Having cau-
terized the wound opened by ideological reform in Prague, the Soviets
attempted to take advantage of their gains in Eastern Europe by pursuing
a greater degree of economic integration than had previously been
possible. Specific bilateral agreements on the production of key industrial

goods were followed by several CMEA executive sessions emphasizing the need for overall coordination of economic planning and, in 1971, by publication of the CMEA Comprehensive Program for economic development.[71] Similar progress was made in the struggle with China, whose failed attempt to gain influence in Eastern Europe after the invasion of Czechoslovakia had been compounded by the embarrassing defeat of Chinese troops by the Soviets at the Ussuri River clashes in early 1969. The subsequent Soviet military build-up along the Sino-Soviet border had the intended effect of bringing the Chinese to the negotiating table. The obvious tilt in the correlation of forces towards the USSR after these events resulted in Chinese abandonment of their claim to leadership of world communism.[72] The Soviets began to publicize their enhanced authority at the June 1969 Conference of the International Communist Movement held in Moscow. In his speech, Brezhnev pointed with pride to the impressive achievements of the USSR and to its status as a world power. Criticizing the Chinese severely for supporting the imperialists in time of crisis, he accused Beijing of causing a split in communist unity through its great power chauvinism and attempts to gain hegemony over world communism. He directed his strongest criticism at the decisions of the Ninth Plenum of the Chinese Communist Party, held in April 1969, where the Chinese had declared that the thoughts of Mao Zedong should be considered the "Marxism-Leninism of the contemporary epoch." Brezhnev pledged that the USSR would conduct a "decisive struggle against the divisive policies of Beijing" and against the PRC's "great power pretensions" in foreign policy.[73] Despite the strong case made by Brezhnev, however, any Soviet hopes that the conference would expel Beijing from the communist movement were dashed when participants— including the East Europeans—refused to deal with the Chinese problem.[74] Instead, the conference focused on unity in general, on economic cooperation between CMEA members, and on threats to the integrity of socialist ideology. It was in the latter that developed socialism received its most important justification.

Although Brezhnev mentioned developed socialism only once in his speech to the conference, it was significant both in terms of the revitalized Soviet international position and the former Soviet ideological debate. Echoing the societal development argument previously advanced against the Chinese as well as the earlier *PMS* discussions on developed socialism, Brezhnev claimed that, "during the decade of the 1960s, many fraternal countries completed construction of the foundations of socialism and began to build a developed socialist society." Later in his speech, he discussed the dangers of revisionism and, in a clear reference to Czechoslovakia, asserted that no matter what problems any single country might encounter during the transition to socialism, "no difficulties could or can alter the general principles of socialist development."[75] In his emphasis on advanced societal development and ideological conformity, Brezhnev thus revealed the new Soviet formula for developed socialism: the concept would be applied to underline the unity of the USSR and Eastern Europe (vs. China), and ideological purity would be maintained by Moscow—by force if necessary. In terms of Soviet-East European relations, developed socialism thus became the theoretical underpinning of what Sarah Terry has termed "a revamped strategy of alliance management" that became evident in the early 1970s.[76]

The political undertone implied by the need for unity among communists was abundantly clear in the new emphasis on developed socialism. Brezhnev stressed this in a separate article describing the events leading up to the conference:

> The task of erecting a barricade in the path of the centrifugal aspirations in the communist movement and of achieving a strengthening of unity in the ranks of fraternal parties had become urgent. Marxist-Leninist parties therefore opened the struggle for unity in the communist movement in all directions and on the broadest front.[77]

The renewed urgency attached to the need for unity was reflected in appeals for increased cooperation between ideological specialists in all socialist countries and in a second media blitz in all major Soviet theoretical journals. As one tactic in the new campaign, East European leaders were again encouraged in the months preceding and following the June 1969 conference to describe the achievements of their "developed socialist" societies.[78] In a significant development regarding the origins of the concept, Soviet and East German ideologists announced in July 1969 that they had agreed on "all questions of the theory and practice of socialist and communist construction," acknowledging implicitly that despite the fact East Germany in 1967 had already published a developed socialist constitution, the USSR would be credited as the first country to actually achieve developed socialism.[79] *Pravda* readers who had not been following ideological developments would not recognize that the Soviets had in fact appropriated the concept of developed socialism from the East Germans, the Hungarians, and the Czechs.

Other Soviet specialists responded to Brezhnev's appeal by addressing the need for unity and describing the dangers of diversity. For example, Professor Teodor I. Oizerman of Moscow State University discussed the Chinese and Yugoslav revisions of Marxism-Leninism in an article attacking the notion that there could be more than one version of official doctrine. There could be no more "various Marxisms," said Oizerman, "than there could be various physics."[80] Kh. Momdzhian, an early supporter of developed socialism, cautioned against using the concept of "models" of socialism in discussing measures taken by separate countries in building socialism since this was basically a Western notion that disguised efforts to destroy the unity of international communism.[81] Mikhail Iovchuk pointed out that the 1969 conference was meant to clarify the situation regarding alternative approaches to Marxism, so that there really should be no further need to discuss the issue.[82] Suslov compared the current situation with that facing Lenin, and strongly implied that Lenin's struggle against populists, legal Marxists, Mensheviks, Social Revolutionaries, anarchists, Trotskyites, right opportunists, national deviationists, and others was being repeated in the Soviet campaign against revisionism. By unifying the communist movement with one ideology, Suslov implied, Brezhnev could duplicate Lenin's success in dealing with diversity.[83]

While not faced with quite the broad diversity that confronted Lenin, Brezhnev did have to contend with "democratic socialism," "socialism with a human face," "market socialism," "Maoism," and others. (There were also Western analytic notions to consider, such as "totalitarianism" and "convergence.") As is clear from the space devoted to descriptions of these variations in the most authoritative Soviet book on developed socialism, the problems and tensions created within the communist movement by alternatives to official Soviet ideology provided an important justification for using the "new stage of socialism" (i.e. developed socialism) as a unifying element that once again focused attention on the USSR as the center of communism.[84]

After 1969, developed socialism continued to signify the unity of communism under Moscow's ideological mantle. The Soviets were apparently confident that after more than a decade of turmoil since Khrushchev's denunciation of Stalin, the communist movement had been brought back into Soviet control and that the unity of theory and practice demanded in Marxist-Leninist political systems had been restored. As the prestige and authority of the USSR continued to grow, due in part to the "defeat of US imperialism in Vietnam,"[85] developed socialism was used increasingly to identify the Soviet Union as the leader of world communism. Developed socialism was proclaimed as the "new stage of socialist development" at the Twenty-fourth CPSU Congress in 1971[86] and Soviet ideologists began to claim the concept as their own. A "Manifesto of Developed Socialism" was published in conjunction with the Twenty-fifth CPSU Congress in 1976, proclaiming the USSR as the first socialist country to achieve developed socialism and codifying the major domestic and foreign policies associated with the new stage.[87]

Decline of Developed Socialism

Despite Soviet optimism, however, and despite a temporary increase in Soviet prestige, subsequent developments in Europe had by the mid-1970s begun to bring the degree of Soviet control over other communist parties into doubt. As described by Richard Lowenthal, Jiri Valenta, and others, the invasion of Czechoslovakia led eventually to a sharp decline in the international authority of the CPSU, especially among West European communist parties. In the long term, in fact, the invasion of Czechoslovakia had done as much damage to the unity of the communist movement as Khrushchev's secret speech, and with more important repercussions. While Khrushchev had tarnished Stalin's image and exposed the Soviet system to intense scrutiny, the move against Czechoslovakia had damaged severely, perhaps irreparably, the broader notion of "Leninism" that had served as the central element in the Soviet model of socialism. The subsequent rejection of the Soviet model by the Spanish and Italian communist parties (termed by Lowenthal the "withering away of Leninism") demonstrated the full extent of the damage.[88]

The challenges posed by the West European parties threatened to affect communist regimes in Eastern Europe as well. The appeals from East European leaders to Moscow to expel the Eurocommunist parties from the communist movement indicated the gravity with which they viewed this situation.[89] The overall extent of the decline in Soviet authority was revealed at the 1976 World Communist Conference, the documents of which emphasized voluntary cooperation and non-interference by communist parties instead of focusing on the leading role of the CPSU. The failure of the 1971 CMEA Comprehensive Program also became evident by 1976, adding another blow to Soviet prestige.[90] And, while the Soviets had attempted to shore-up the theoretical foundations of its relations with East European countries, they complicated this situation by supporting new attempts at economic reform. These signalled approval for more independent efforts on the part of bloc allies.[91] The cumulative result of these events was to erode the unity so widely proclaimed by the Soviets during the early 1970s. By the late 1970s, this unity had become a "facade" that obscured increasing diversity and independence within the communist movement.[92] In this sense, developed socialism had become a rather hollow symbol of Soviet authority.

By the end of the 1970s developed socialism had clearly lost its utility as a term synonymous with Soviet control of international communism. It still had some value as a "political formula" to describe the aspirations of the Brezhnev regime within the USSR.[93] It also provided a convenient label for the current stage of Soviet development that proved useful in forestalling the advent of communism so brashly predicted by Khrushchev for 1980. The continued use of the term by Brezhnev's immediate successors—modified slightly to "perfecting developed socialism"—may also reflect its perceived usefulness to connote the continuing de-Stalinization of Soviet society. But Soviet hopes for developed socialism as the ideological manifestation of renewed Soviet control over international communism, evident in the evolution of the concept in the late 1960s, have clearly not been realized. The invasion of Czechoslovakia, the lingering effects of Khrushchev's secret speech, and the invasion of Afghanistan in 1979 have combined to ensure that the Soviets will almost certainly not soon regain the dominance among world communists they enjoyed prior to 1956.

The outright rejection of developed socialism by Gorbachev suggests that a new ideological formula is being developed to serve as the theoretical basis for his reform program (see Chapter 8). While this formula will certainly maintain continuity with the de-Stalinizing policies of Khrushchev and Brezhnev, it will not contain any references to the USSR as the center of the world communist movement. As part of Gorbachev's overall reform program, the Soviet Union is now portrayed as more or less an equal partner in the communist movement. While such new thinking is always subject to reinterpretation, especially in the event of backlash to Gorbachev's policies, it appears that the Soviets are content to treat developed socialism as an historical concept appropriate to the Brezhnev era, when the stated Soviet policy regarding international communism was quite different.[94]

Notes

1. *Bol'shaia Sovetskaia Ehntsiklopediia*, 3rd ed., s.v. "Sotsializm" by L. I. Abalkin, pp. 222–26. See especially the subsection entitled "Ehtapy Razvitiia S.," pp. 224–5.

2. This interpretation is at odds with that of Alfred Evans and James Scanlan, both of whom argue that the main thrust of developed socialism was to postpone the advent of communism which Khrushchev predicted would occur by 1980. See Alfred B. Evans, Jr., "Developed Socialism in Soviet Ideology," *Soviet Studies* 24 (July 1977), pp. 409–428, and James P. Scanlan, *Marxism in the USSR: A Critical Survey of Current Soviet Thought* (Ithaca: Cornell University Press, 1985), pp. 239–240. Evans previously agreed about the political value of developed socialism. Recently, however, he has pointed out that the concept's previous value was diminished by the economic slowdown of the 1970s. See footnote 93.

3. Donald R. Kelley, *The Politics of Developed Socialism* (New York: Greenwood Press, 1986), p. 13.

4. Zbigniew K. Brzezinski, *The Soviet Bloc: Unity and Conflict*, Revised ed. (Cambridge, Massachusetts: Harvard University Press, 1967), pp. 159–70. See also Robert L. Hutchings, *Soviet-East European Relations: Consolidation and Conflict, 1968–1980* (Madison: University of Wisconsin Press, 1983), pp. 15–29.

5. Richard Lowenthal, *World Communism: The Disintegration of a Secular Faith* (New York: Oxford University Press, 1964), p. 38. Also see his article, "Moscow and the 'Eurocommunists'," *Problems of Communism* 27 (July-August 1978), p. 39.

6. See M. A. Suslov, *Na Putiakh Stroitel'stva Kommunizma*, 2 vols. (Moscow: Politicheskaia Literatura, 1977), vol. 1, p. 243. (Hereafter referred to as *Na Putiakh*.) For a statement regarding Ponomarev, see Brzezinski, *Soviet Bloc*, p. 310.

7. The secret speech also had negative repercussions on the nascent West European Communist Parties. See J. W. Friend, "The Roots of Autonomy in West European Communism," *Problems of Communism* 29 (September-October 1980), p. 33.

8. Brzezinski, *Soviet Bloc*, pp. 271 and 295–302.

9. For discussions of the Great Leap Forward, see Franz Schurman, *Ideology and Organization in Communist China* (Berkeley, California: University of California Press, 1966), p. 74, and Richard C. Thornton, *China: A Political History, 1917–80* (Boulder, Colorado: Westview Press, 1982), p. 250. For a more detailed study, see Roderick MacFarquhar, *The Origins of the Cultural Revolution, 2: The Great Leap Forward, 1958–1960* (New York: Columbia University Press, 1983).

10. Lowenthal, *World Communism*, pp. 135–7.

11. In response to this rejection, the Soviets cancelled their military assistance agreement of 1957, proposed that a nuclear free zone be established for most of Asia and the Pacific Basin, and suggested that the PRC accept a two-China policy, abandoning its claim on Taiwan. See Brzezinski, *Soviet Bloc*, p. 409.

12. Lowenthal points out that the communist movement had in fact entered a period of "polycentric autonomy," See Lowenthal, *World Communism*, pp. 193 and 198.

13. Brzezinski, *Soviet Bloc*, p. 409, and Thornton, *China*, pp. 255–56. The Soviets also lost control of communist parties in Japan, Australia, and New Zealand. See Friend, "Roots of Autonomy," pp. 35–6.

14. For the best Soviet description of the "all-people's state" from this period, see the 1961 Party Program in *Programma i Ustav Kommunisticheskoii Partii Sovetskogo Soiuza* (Moscow: Politizdat, 1964), pp. 169–85. Also see Evans, "Developed Socialism," p. 422, and Roger E. Kanet, "The All-People's State: Recent Changes in the Soviet Theory of the State," *Soviet Studies* 20 (July 1968), pp. 81–93. See also the discussion in Chapter 5, below.

15. Thornton, *China*, p. 256.

16. Quoted in Richard Lowenthal, "The Degeneration of an Ideological Dispute," in Douglas T. Stuart and William T. Tow, *China, The Soviet Union and the West: Strategic and Political Dimensions in the 1980s* (Boulder, Colorado: Westview Press, 1982), p. 65. In a letter of 14 June 1963 signed by the CCP Central Committee, the Chinese repudiated Soviet primacy in the world com-

munist movement, denounced Soviet hegemonistic economic policies and offered a "programmatic ideological manifesto" designed to justify the takeover of communist leadership by the CCP. See William E. Griffith, *The Sino-Soviet Rift* (Cambridge, Massachusetts: MIT Press, 1964), pp. 6–7 and 147–148.

17. Griffith, *Sino-Soviet Rift*, p. 169.

18. Adam Ulam points out that Hanoi had sided with Beijing in denouncing the Test Ban Treaty. See Adam B. Ulam, *Expansion and Coexistence: Soviet Foreign Policy 1917–73*, 2nd ed. (New York: Praeger Publishers, 1974), p. 699.

19. Thornton speculates that the failure to attain such a land route was one of the reasons behind Khrushchev's removal from power. See Thornton, *China*, pp. 272–3.

20. Griffith, *Sino-Soviet Rift*, p. 230.

21. Ulam makes this point in *Expansion and Coexistence*, p. 721.

22. The PRC signalled that some form of reconciliation was possible late in 1964 when it modified its previous claim that China would be the first country to establish communism. China was now said to be still "building socialism." See the report of Chou En Lai to the First Session of the Third All-China Assembly of the People's Republic, reprinted in *Pravda*, 12 January 1965.

23. *Pravda*, 12 and 16 February 1965.

24. Thornton, *China*, p. 275.

25. *Pravda*, 13 and 16 April 1965.

26. *Pravda*, 30 April and 13 June 1965.

27. Thornton, *China*, pp. 275–7.

28. *Pravda*, 12 May, 20 August, and 5 September 1965.

29. *Pravda*, 14 February 1966.

30. See, for example, *Pravda*, 30 October 1966.

31. For the speeches of Todor Zhivkov and Janos Kadar at the Ninth Congress of the Bulgarian Communist Party and the Ninth Hungarian Communist Party Congress, respectively, see *Pravda*, 15 November and 29 November 1966. For a fuller description of the East European development and use of the developed socialism, see the excellent article, "Theories of Socialist Development in Soviet-East European Relations," by Sarah Meiklejohn Terry in *Soviet Policy in Eastern Europe*, ed. Sarah Meiklejohn Terry (New Haven: Yale University Press, 1984), especially pp. 224–227.

32. Sarah Terry suggests that the Soviets in fact encouraged the East European reforms in the 1960s, in part because of Khrushchev's de-Stalinization program. See Terry, "Theories of Socialist Development," pp. 231–2.

33. Fedor Burlatskii, "O Stroitel'stve Razvitogo Sotsialisticheskogo Obshchestva," *Pravda*, 21 December 1966, p. 4.

34. *Pravda*, 25 November 1967.

35. *Pravda*, 20 February 1967, pp. 2–3. D. I. Chesnokov, "Sovetskoe Gosudarstvo, Ego Vospitatel'naia Rol'," *Pravda*, 27 February 1967, pp. 2–3.

36. V. Zh. Kelle, "Sovershenstvovanie Obshchestvennykh Otnoshenii Pri Sotsializme," *Pravda*, 5 April 1967, pp. 2–3.

37. *Pravda*, 16 March 1968, pp. 2–3.

38. See Burlatskii's report on the meeting, in *Pravda,* 17 May 1967. A Moscow conference the same year also stressed the themes of "unity" and "internationalism," See *Pravda,* 13 April 1967.

39. A *Pravda* statement in November 1967, for example, asserted that "it is well-known that the correlation of forces in the world arena depends both on the military-economic might of the Soviet Union and other socialist countries, and on the unity of all revolutionary movements and their activities in the anti-imperialist struggle." *Pravda,* 28 November 1967. The Soviets, of course, enforced the unity they sought with the 1968 invasion of Czechoslovakia. This may have been a factor in the delay of the conference.

40. This journal is also published in an English-language edition, *World Marxist Review* (Toronto).

41. This is the spelling of his name provided by the *Bol'shaia Sovetskaia Ehntsiklopediia,* 3rd ed., volume 28, p. 69. In print, however, including in his capacity as Chief Editor of *Problemy Mira i Sotsializma,* he often used the alternate spelling "Frantsev." I am indebted to Professor Jerry Hough for pointing this out to me.

42. This interpretation is in contrast to that of James Scanlan, who argues that new ideological doctrines are developed at the top of the party hierarchy and only then are debated by specialists. See Scanlan, *Marxism in the USSR,* pp. 224–225. My argument is presented in the following pages.

43. See the discussion in Evans, "Developed Socialism," pp. 410–12.

44. My use of the term "normalcy" is broader than that of Jerry Hough, who uses it in his discussion of the Brezhnev period alone. I am referring to the overall effort, common to both Khrushchev and Brezhnev, of reversing the arbitrary nature of Stalinism and injecting a measure of democracy into the Soviet political system. For Hough's views, see Jerry F. Hough and Merle Fainsod, *How the Soviet Union is Governed* (Cambridge: Harvard University Press, 1979), pp. 237–274.

45. This debate took place in the context of what Michel Tatu has described as the broader struggle among political leaders who were polarized between advocating extensive reforms and returning to the rigid centralization of the Stalin period. See Michel Tatu, *Power in the Kremlin: From Khrushchev to Kosygin* (New York: The Viking Press, 1969), especially the section "From Objectivity to Restalinization", pp. 479–493.

46. In early 1967, Walter Ulbricht proclaimed to the Seventh Congress of the Socialist Unity Party that a developed socialist society had already been established in East Germany. Developed socialism was widely used in East German writings from 1967 on, and one of the stated goals of the 1968 East German constitution was the construction of a completely developed socialist state. See *Pravda,* 15 April 1967, and 2 and 14 February 1968. For a broader discussion of Soviet-East German ideological disputes, see Hartmut Zimmerman, "The GDR in the 1970s," *Problems of Communism* 27 (March-April 1978), pp. 7-9, and Walter Voekel, "Das Problem der Ideologischen Integration," *Deutschland Archiv,* October 1973 (Special Volume), pp. 61-75. For an overview of Soviet-East European ideological relations, see Hutchings, *Soviet-East European Relations,* pp. 206–228.

47. *XXIII S"ezd Kommunisticheskoi Partii Sovetskogo Soiuza: Stenograficheskii Otchet* (Moscow: Politizdat, 1966). See especially the speeches by Sh. Rashidov, P. Masherov, A. Pel'she, and M. Solomentsev.

48. M. T. Iovchuk, "Ob Istoricheskikh Ehtapakh Stanovleniia i Razvitiia Sotsialisticheskogo Soznaniia v SSSR," *Voprosy Filosofii*, 2/1965, pp. 3–14.

49. R. Kosolapov, "Vklad XXIV, XXV, i XXVI S"ezdov KPSS v Razrabotku Teoreticheskikh i Politicheskikh Problem Razvitogo Sotsializma i Perekhoda k Kommunizmu," *Kommunist*, 5/1982, pp. 54–67.

50. See the round-table discussion, "Istoricheskoe Mesto Sotsializma, Ehtapy i Kriterii Ego Razvitiia," *Problemy Mira i Sotsializma*, 12/1970, pp. 37–59. Glezerman did eventually support developed socialism. See G. E. Glezerman and O. Reingol'd, eds., *Razvitoe Sotsialisticheskoe Obshchestvo: Sushchnost', Kriterii Zrelosti, Kritika Revizionistskikh Kontseptsii* (Moscow: Mysl', 1979).

51. P. Fedoseev, "Marksizm i Stroitel'stvo Kommunisticheskogo Obshchestva," *Kommunist*, 6/1968, p. 74.

52. Iovchuk, "Ob Istoricheskikh Ehtapakh," p. 9.

53. F. Konstantinov, "Oktiabr'skaia Sotsialisticheskaia Revoliutsiia i Marksistko-Leninskaia Filosofiia," *Voprosy Filosofii*, 10/1967, pp. 18–19.

54. It is possible that Konstantinov's doubts and second thoughts about Stalin cost him his job; he was replaced as Director of the Institute of Philosophy by P. V. Kopnin in 1967.

55. See, for example, the articles by Mitko Grigorov, *Problemy Mira i Sotsializma*, 4/1966, pp. 12–20; Stanko Todorov, ibid., 4/1967, pp. 20–29; Elena Berg, ibid., 6/1967, pp. 88–92; German Materi, ibid., 8/1967, pp. 48–54; Eric Honekker, ibid., 9/1967, pp. 67–73; Gunther Mittag, ibid., 1/1968, pp. 14–20. See also the editorial in ibid., 12/1968, pp. 2–9, in which the Soviet Union is said to be in the new stage of "building the material-technical base of communism" while "a group of European socialist countries" are "creating a developed socialist society."

56. Iu. Frantsov, "Shagi Istorii," *Pravda*, 3 November 1967, p. 6.

57. For Brezhnev's initial use of developed socialism, see L. I. Brezhnev, *Leninskim Kursom*, 8 vols. (Moscow: Politicheskaia Literatura, 1970–1981), vol. 2, pp. 92–93.

58. According to his biographical sketch in the Soviet encyclopedia, Kosolapov worked "in the Central Committee apparatus" between 1966–74.

59. Brezhnev, *Leninskim Kursom*, vol. 2, p. 100. For a similar statement, see the article on the 150th anniversary of Karl Marx's birth by Kh. Momdzhian in *Pravda*, 16 March 1968, pp. 2–3.

60. The institute's responsibilities had been increased and its authorized personnel strength raised after Fedoseev became chief in 1967. A Central Committee resolution that year concerning the improvement of social sciences in general stated that IML was "the center for the study of the ideological heritage of Marx, Engels, and Lenin." A second resolution of June 1968 further elaborated IML's duties to include publication of the classics of Marxism-Leninism and works on the current trends in party activity. See *Kommunist*, 13/1967, pp. 3–13, and 12/1968, pp. 20–3.

61. P. N. Fedoseev, "Idei Lenina i Metodologiia Sovremennoi Nauki," *Problemy Mira i Sotsializma,* 4/1967, p. 12. This article was possibly a direct response to Burlatskii's article on developed socialism, published in *Pravda* four months earlier.

62. *Pravda,* 7 April 1968.

63. P. N. Fedoseev, "Leninizm—Marksizm XX Veka," *Pravda,* 22 April 1968, pp. 2–3.

64. Suslov, *Na Putiakh,* vol. 2, pp. 155–7.

65. M. T. Iovchuk, "Marksistko-Leninskaia Filosofiia i Sovremennaia Marksologiia," *Voprosy Filosofii,* 8/1968, pp. 3–11.

66. I. Pomelov, "Obshchie Printsipy i Natsional'nye Osobennosti v Razvitii Sotsializma," *Pravda,* 14 August 1968, pp. 2–3. Pomelov had earlier supported developed socialism in his "Kommunisticheskaia Partiia v Sotsialisticheskom Obshchestve," *Pravda,* 20 February 1967, pp. 2–3.

67. S. Kovalev, "O 'Mirnoi' i Nemirnoi Kontrrevoliutsii," *Pravda,* 11 September 1968, pp. 3–4, and "Suverenitet i Internatsional'nye Obiazannosti Sotsialisticheskikh Stran," *Pravda,* 26 September 1968, p. 4. For his 1966 reference to developed socialism, see S. Kovalev, "Trebovaniia Zhizni i Obshchestvennye Nauki," *Pravda,* 6 May 1966, pp. 2–3.

68. Iu. Frantsov, "O Nekotorykh Osobennostiakh Sovremennoi Ideologicheskoi Bor'by," *Pravda,* 22 September 1968, pp. 3–4.

69. The end of the debate on a new stage of socialism was signalled by Fedoseev's capitulation in early 1969 on the major question of whether Marxism-Leninism could be used "creatively" to reflect current realities. Apparently fully convinced, he wrote: "It would be foolish to regard Marxism as a locked trunk filled with treasure and to acknowledge that one was only supposed to sit on the trunk and protect it, drawing from its ideological riches only when necessary." More important, he implicitly acknowledged that a new stage of socialist evolution was needed when he agreed that "communism could only be built on the basis of developed socialism," reiterating Brezhnev's 1967 statement. P. Fedoseev, "V. I. Lenin—Velikii Teoretik Kommunizma," *Kommunist,* 1/1969, pp. 15–16, 22.

70. For an analysis that supports this conclusion in the area of Soviet-East European relations, see Hutchings, *Soviet-East European Relations,* pp. 59–62 and 233–235.

71. For a discussion of CMEA integration, see *Pravda,* 24 January and 27 April 1969, and Paul Marer and John Michael Montias, "CMEA Integration: Theory and Practice," in US Congress, Joint Economic Committee, *East European Economic Assessment* (Washington, D.C.: Government Printing Office, 1981), p. 162. For Soviet interpretations of the results of these sessions, see O. Bogomolov, "Leninizm i Nekotorye Problemy Sotrudnichestva Stran Sotsializma," *Kommunist,* 8/1968, pp. 14–25; Grigor Podpisakov, "Novye Gorizonty," *Pravda,* 4 August 1969; and M. Lesechko, "Sotrudnichestvo Stran SEV na Sovremennom Ehtape," *Kommunist,* 4/1971, pp. 82–93. For discussions of the 1971 Comprehensive Program, see Marer and Montias, "CMEA Integration," and John Hannigan and Carl McMillan, "Joint Investment in Resource Development," US Congress, Joint Economic Committee, *East European Economic Assessment,* pp. 148–95. See also

Hutchings, *Soviet-East European Relations*, pp. 76–90. For Soviet descriptions of the Comprehensive Program, see *Pravda*, 29 January and 3 August 1971, and A. Alekseev, "Sotsialisticheskaia Integratsiia," *Pravda*, 13 August 1971, pp. 3–4. The text of the Comprehensive Program was published in *Pravda*, 7 August 1971, pp. 1–7.

72. For a discussion of these events from a Chinese perspective, see Thornton, *China*, pp. 341–60, and Juergen Domes, *China After the Cultural Revolution* (Berkeley, California: University of California Press, 1977), pp. 129–30.

73. Brezhnev, *Leninskim Kursom*, vol. II, pp. 366, 392–396, and 415.

74. Thornton, *China*, pp. 343–4. The explanation for inaction by East European leaders was that they were probably not willing to antagonize an important trading partner; Chinese trade with Eastern Europe doubled between 1965–70. See Robin Remington, "China's Emerging Role in Eastern Europe," in Charles Gati, ed., *The International Politics of Eastern Europe* (New York: Praeger Publishers, 1976), pp. 88–91, and Domes, *China After the Cultural Revolution*, p. 225.

75. Brezhnev, *Leninskim Kursom*, pp. 373 and 377.

76. Terry, "Theories of Socialist Development in Soviet-East European Relations," p. 247.

77. Leonid Brezhnev, "Kommunisticheskoe Dvizhenie Vstupilo v Polocu Novogo Pod"ema," *Problemy Mira i Sotsializma*, 8/1969, pp. 1–9. This article was reprinted in *Leninskim Kursom*, vol. II, pp. 427–47.

78. For the East European response, see "Za Postroenie Razvitogo Sotsialisticheskogo Obshchestva," based on a Bulgarian newspaper article by Stanko Todorov, *Pravda*, 14 April 1969, p. 4; Boris Volchev, "Razvitie Sistemy Upravleniia Obshchestvom v Sotsialisticheskoi Bolgarii," *Problemy Mira i Sotsializma*, 4/1969, pp. 19–26; W. Ulbricht, "Dvadtsat' Plodotvornykh Let Stroitel'stva Sotsializma," ibid., 10/1969, pp. 1–9; and Werner Lamberts, "Leninskie Printsipy Nauchnogo Rukovodstva Sotsialisticheskim Stroitel'stvom i ikh Primenenie v GDR," ibid., 2/1970, pp. 16–19.

79. Ulbricht placed the beginning of developed socialism in East Germany in 1963. See Ulbricht, "Dvadtsat' Plodotvornykh Let," p. 5. The strength of his conviction on the subject led him to commit a serious faux pas at the June 1969 conference when he urged the Soviet Union to complete the building of communism while fraternal bloc countries were building developed socialism. See his speech to the conference in *Pravda*, 11 June 1969.

80. *Pravda*, 13 May 1969, pp. 2–3.

81. Kh. Momdzhian, "O Revizionistkoi Kontsepstii 'Modelei' Sotsializma," *Kommunist*, 2/1970, pp. 60–72.

82. M. Iovchuk, "Leninizm: Sovremennaia Bor'ba Idei v Filosofii," *Kommunist*, 2/1970, pp. 47–59.

83. M. Suslov, "Leninizm i Sovremennaia Ehpoka," *Problemy Mira i Sotsializma*, 5/1969, pp. 1–15. This campaign also included important articles by Kosolapov, who referred to the "historic mission" of the working class to construct a developed socialist society, and Professor A. Kositsyn, who described socialist democracy and the "all-people's state" in terms of developed socialism. See R. Kosolapov, "Sotsializm i Molodezh'," *Pravda*, 17 March 1969, pp. 3-4, and A.

Kositsyn, "Lenin i Razvitie Sotsialisticheskogo Gosudarstvo," *Pravda*, 13 August 1969, pp. 3-4.

84. G. E. Glezerman and O. Reingol'd, *Razvitoe Sotsialisticheskoe Obshchestvo*, pp. 453–592. For a contemporary article on totalitarianism, see E. Chekarin, "Teoreticheskie Spekuliatsii Ideologov Antikommunizma," *Kommunist*, 10/1969, pp. 101–112. For one example of a discussion of convergence, see L. Skvortsov, "Sovremennaia Bor'ba Idei i Kontseptsiia 'Ideologicheskogo Razoruzheniia," *Pravda*, 7 February 1969, pp. 3–4.

85. See, for example, the remarks by K. Zarodov at the conclusion of the summary of the conference "Sotsialisticheskaia Gosudarstvennost' i Demokratiia," held in Prague on 19–20 May 1971. *Problemy Mira i Sotsializma*, 8/1971, pp. 3–23.

86. See the stenographic record of the congress, *XXIV S"ezd Kommunisticheskoi Partii Sovetskogo Soiuza, 30 Marta–9 Aprel'ia 1971 g.: Stenograficheskii Otchet*, 2 vols. (Moscow: Politizdat, 1971).

87. "Manifest Razvitogo Sotsializma," in *Kommunist*, 7/1976, pp. 1–35; also published in *XXV S"ezd KPSS: Edinstvo Teorii i Praktiki* (Moscow: Politicheskaia Literatura, 1977), pp. 9-35.

88. Lowenthal, "Moscow and the 'Eurocommunists'," p. 38. See the excellent discussions on the Communist Party of Spain (PCE) in Eusebio Mujal-Leon, "The PCE in Spanish Politics," and "Cataluna, Carrillo, and Eurocommunism," *Problems of Communism* 27 (July-August 1978), pp. 15–37, and ibid., 30 (March-April 1981), pp. 25–47. On the Italian Communist Party, see Jiri Valenta, "Eurocommunism and Eastern Europe," *Problems of Communism* 27 (March-April) 1978, pp. 41–44, Lowenthal, "Moscow and the 'Eurocommunists'," p. 45, and Friend, "Roots of Autonomy," pp. 29–34. Hutchings points out that Eurocommunist parties also began to move toward normalization of relations with the PRC, further emphasizing the threat to Soviet authority. See Hutchings, *Soviet-East European Relations*, pp. 208 and 213.

89. Valenta, "Eurocommunism," p. 49.

90. Robin Alison Remington, "Politics of Accommodation: Redefining Soviet-East European Relations," in Roger E. Kanet, ed., *Soviet Foreign Policy in the 1980s* (New York: Praeger, 1982), p. 112.

91. See the discussion in Hutchings, *Soviet-East European Relations*, pp. 218–227, and Terry, "Theories of Socialist Development in Soviet-East European Relations," pp. 247–253.

92. Joan Barth Urban, "The West European Communist Challenge to Soviet Foreign Policy," in Roger E. Kanet, ed., *Soviet Foreign Policy in the 1980s*, p. 187.

93. Kelley, *Politics of Developed Socialism*, p. 13. Recent work by Alfred Evans suggests the utility of developed socialism as a politically useful formula was diminished significantly as a result of the economic slowdown in the late 1970s and early 1980s. This had a serious impact on the regime's ability to satisfy consumer expectations that had been nurtured by Brezhnev and others beginning at the 24th CPSU Congress in 1971. See Alfred E. Evans, Jr., "The Decline of Developed Socialism? Some Trends in Recent Soviet Ideology" *Soviet Studies* 34 (January 1986), pp. 1–23.

94. In the 1986 Party Program, developed socialism is said to be the result of the plan for Soviet development outlined in the Third Party Program, adopted at the Twenty-second CPSU Congress in 1961. This neatly links the Khrushchev and Brezhnev eras and lays the groundwork for a new stage of socialist development under Gorbachev. See *Programma Kommunisticheskoi Partii Sovetskogo Soiuza* (Moscow: Politizdat, 1986), p. 4.

3

Motivating the New Soviet Man: Wage Incentives Policy

The creation of a "new man" has been an important aspect of official ideology since the 1961 Party Program. As described in Soviet writings, the new man has been developed through Soviet educational, cultural, and political policies. He is the product of a Marxist-Leninist upbringing that has altered his formerly nationalist impulses and created in him a deep concern for the international community. The new man's personality has been influenced by contact with other members of socialist society, especially in mass social organizations and local organs of government, as well as through his general participation in the ongoing construction of communism.[1]

As suggested by this ideological description, policies associated with the new man have been concentrated in educational, cultural, and social activities. Another important policy area, one with a highly sensitive ideological dimension, has been the use of material incentives to reward the new man for his labor and demonstrated commitment to regime economic goals.[2] Material incentives have been an important dimension of Soviet labor policy since Lenin. Salary increases, cash bonuses, one-time awards and other direct and indirect incentives have been used singly or in combination to increase production, improve quality, or fulfill other urgent economic requirements. In addition, negative material incentives, such as salary reductions or the withholding of bonuses, have also been used to combat worker complacency and stimulate increased efforts.

Overt reliance on such rewards presents an ideological dilemma in Marxist-Leninist political systems that are theoretically dedicated to the equal distribution of wealth. This has been most eloquently described by Richard Lowenthal:

> For the sake of the final goal, the communist regime ought to aim at creating a "new man," a man free from the egotistic ambition and avarice

characteristic of class society; yet for the sake of rapid development it must aim at educating and manipulating "economic man," the type that has created the modern industrial society precisely by pursuing his own self-interest.[3]

Soviet leaders have dealt with this problem by alternately emphasizing and then deemphasizing material rewards, at times promoting instead the use of non-material or "moral" incentives. No leader, however, has completely abandoned the concept of material reward. Ideological justification has changed along with policy, and ideological specialists frequently have had to scramble to provide a theoretical basis for rapidly changing policy preferences. The tension created by the use of material reward in a socialist society was evident throughout the Brezhnev period. Incentives policy changed several times before being firmly established in accordance with Brezhnev's policy preferences and ideological values.

Background

Soviet ideologists and economic specialists have found little guidance in classical writings on the use of economic incentives. Marx would probably have thought the question superfluous, since he believed that workers' attitudes towards labor would inevitably change during the evolution of communist society in which man would fulfill himself through labor. This change would be the direct result of the increased freedom and creativity enjoyed by workers under communism and would not depend at all on material rewards.

Lenin took a more pragmatic approach, advocating the temporary use of additional pay for scientists and other specialists to foster the rapid construction of the new society. As he wrote in "Will the Bolsheviks Retain State Power?" in late 1917:

A proletarian government will say: we need more and more engineers, agronomists, technicians, (and) scientifically educated specialists of every type. We will give all such workers responsible work to which they are accustomed. We will probably only gradually introduce equal pay for them, giving higher pay to such specialists during the transitional period. . . .[4]

On coming to power, Lenin indeed endorsed extra pay for specialists and took steps to prevent anti-Bolshevik specialists from being jailed or executed. As he told Lunacharsky: "One must spare a great scientist or major specialist in whatever sphere, even if he is reactionary to the nth degree."[5]

Lenin's policy of special treatment for certain categories of workers provided a measure of ideological justification for the further use of material incentives, although this constituted a departure from the emphasis on equality that characterized most of his writings. One of the many accommodations Lenin made in the process of gaining and retaining power, his endorsement of material incentives had long-lasting and perhaps unintended results. It simultaneously set the precedent of paying material bonuses as an element of Soviet labor policy and laid the groundwork for the establishment of systemic inequality in Leninist political systems.[6]

Stalin capitalized on Lenin's pragmatism by greatly expanding the use of material rewards, which he used as a key element in both his industrialization program in the 1930s and his postwar rebuilding efforts. Denouncing wage equalization in 1931, Stalin endorsed material incentives as a motivational factor to encourage workers to acquire needed skills—clearly a policy of a temporary nature. Going well beyond Lenin, however, Stalin's advocacy of the widespread use of material incentives made it seem as if "the call for sacrifice was now being replaced by a frank appeal to material interest."[7] And, despite the campaign of general terror directed at representatives of the former technical elite, Stalin continued to reward ideologically reliable "red specialists" he needed to achieve his development goals. After the war, Stalin directed incentives towards managers and other members of the newly emerged middleclass whose efforts were crucial to the Soviet rebuilding program.[8]

Stalin, like Lenin before him, did not address the inequality inherent in his bonus system. Nor did he justify the policy of material appeal to a particular segment of the classless society. Such a stark contrast between ideology and policy under both Lenin and Stalin is perhaps explained by the fact that, as leaders of regimes of questionable legitimacy, they could find no adequate substitute for material incentives to ensure the continued growth and development of Soviet society.[9] Faced with conflicting policy needs, they chose expediency over ideology.

Khrushchev, in a burst of what Lowenthal has called "applied utopianism" early in his regime, steered away from material incentives.[10] He advocated instead a system of "collective" rewards, including improved housing, education, and medical service in place of the former individual bonuses. He also directed revisions of the wage system with the goal of increasing wages for lower-paid workers, bringing their pay closer to that of managers. He coupled this approach with an increased appeal to ideology in numerous exhortations to the workforce. After economic stagnation led to price increases in 1962, however, it became clear that collective incentives were inadequate. Khrushchev therefore began to support a limited return to individual rewards. As was the case with his collective rewards, he coupled the renewed emphasis on individual incentives with strong ideological appeals.[11]

Material incentives were greatly expanded by the Brezhnev regime as part of the 1965 economic reforms. Incentives for agricultural workers were presented at the March 1965 plenum of the Central Committee, while monetary bonuses for industrial workers were introduced in connection with the industrial reforms announced at the September 1965 plenum. In his speeches on both occasions, Brezhnev emphasized the importance of material incentives in strengthening the economy.

However, Brezhnev's support for the new incentives was less than total. Although he did back the idea of material incentives in general, he cautioned as early as September 1965 that material incentives must be used in "correct combination" with moral incentives.[12] This was to become a characteristic phrase for Brezhnev, who began to advocate moral incentives more vigorously as part of the leadership struggle with Kosygin only to speak out in favor of material rewards again after he had gained dominance in the leadership. His preference for a balanced approach to moral and material incentives was fully reflected in Soviet incentives policy in the 1970s and in the doctrinal formulations of developed socialism. Material rewards continued to be used, but they were offset by a strong dose of moral rewards. Moreover, negative material incentives and collective rewards, both of which were also favored by Brezhnev, were expanded. By 1977, the basic structure of the material incentives system had been altered so extensively that it again resembled the pre-1965 system. The combination of restrictions in material incentives and the continuing emphasis on non-material rewards meant that the new man would continue to receive material rewards under developed socialism, but these would not be distributed as freely or as generously as they had been previously.

Ideology and Incentives Policy Prior to Developed Socialism

In connection with the overall reform effort designed to overcome the economic stagnation of the Khrushchev period and to reverse declining economic growth rates, material incentives in the form of wage bonuses introduced in 1965–1967 had two distinct purposes. In industry, bonuses were directed toward the goal of mobilizing labor force reserves and stimulating concern for quality. Bonuses had been paid for similar reasons previously in Soviet industry, but had been abolished during the overhaul of the wage structure initiated by Khrushchev in 1960.[13] Agricultural bonuses, on the other hand, were based solely on quantitative indicators. To ensure specialists and managers grasped the structure of the new bonuses, the entire spectrum of wage and bonus questions was studied at numerous conferences addressing all the economic reform measures introduced by the new regime.[14]

Throughout these discussions, and in more detailed expositions in specialist journals, there was no real debate on the subject of material incentives as there had been on developed socialism. In contrast, many specialists who disagreed on the significance of developed socialism were in complete agreement about the need for material incentives.[15] This apparent paradox is explained in part by the general consensus that the Soviet economy was in severe trouble and required new approaches to stimulate productivity. But the most important common ground for ideological agreement was the Leninist position that material incentives were only a temporary measure that would be discarded after a higher level of well-being had been attained. By placing the new policy in this context, it became acceptable in terms of both official ideology and established Soviet practice. Another important basis for ideological agreement was that the new policy reversed the practice of the Khrushchev years and thus became part of the anti-Khrushchev posture of the new regime. As stated in *Pravda*, in an obvious reference to Khrushchev: "As is well-known, until recently the principle of material interest was often ignored or violated. It has been fully rehabilitated with the decisions of the October (1964) and subsequent plenums."[16]

Since there was no real debate, most of the ideological discussion about incentives focused on the differences between socialist and capitalist societies. As described in dozens of *Pravda* editorials and journal essays, incentives in capitalist society were simply another manifestation of the overall exploitation of workers. Because such exploitation could never occur under socialism, incentives were to be understood as a means for mobilizing the potential and superiority of the socialist economy. This was acknowledged to be a contradiction under socialism, where workers were assumed to have non-materialistic motivations. The preferred approach to such contradictions was to eliminate their unwanted and destructive aspects without necessarily eliminating the contradictions (in this case, the material incentives) themselves. Since workers were well aware that their individual material interests coincided with the goal of increasing the welfare of society as a whole and understood as well the importance of non-material incentives, material incentives posed no real threat either to the integrity of the present stage of development or to the future of socialism. In other words, the temporary use of material incentives could be accommodated without damaging the underlying ideology.[17]

The last point was elaborated best by Vladislav Kelle. He pointed out that material incentives, like other economic levers, were remnants of the capitalist stage of development, and should be considered only as the "birth marks" of the new society. Echoing Brezhnev's and ultimately Lenin's views, he stated that such birth marks were only temporary and were destined to die out in the higher phases of spiritual and economic development. Moreover, since these mechanisms would undergo qualitative changes when used in socialist society, there was nothing to fear in terms of a "restoration of capitalism" or of a detrimental change in the productive relationship among workers. Under communism, when workers would give their labor willingly because of their desire to improve society, there would be no need to appeal to individual interest. Material incentives would therefore be abolished. But, since workers had not yet reached this stage, material incentives should be considered an objective necessity under socialism, particularly in the "lower phase" of communist development.[18]

A more practical justification for material incentives, and one that simultaneously distanced the new regime from the policies of Khrushchev and provided a basis for the claim of a "return to Leninist norms," was made by several specialists who compared the 1965 reforms to Lenin's New Economic Policy (foreshadowing the same comparison used 20 years later to justify Gorbachev's economic reforms). An important economics specialist and member of the Academy of Sciences, Lev Leont'ev, made this point soon after the reforms were implemented. Leont'ev considered the use of cost-accounting (*khozraschet*) to determine the effectiveness of an enterprise on the basis of its profits and the use of material incentives during NEP to be the most direct precedent of the economic mechanisms introduced under Brezhnev.[19]

Ideological discussion about incentives in the early years of the Brezhnev regime thus concentrated on distancing the new regime from that of Khrushchev and on explaining material incentives in a way that was consistent with Lenin's ideas. At the same time, the use of material incentives in general was explained in terms of basic differences between socialism and capitalism. But if there was agreement on the ideological justification for material rewards, there was disagreement about the proper application of such rewards. Not evident in 1965–1966, this became clear several years later, as discussed below. In the first years of the new regime, most attention was focused instead on practical questions such as determining the effectiveness of the material incentives in stimulating productivity. In a period of rapid change, more attention was directed to policy than ideology.

Between 1965–1970, there were no system-wide rules governing the awarding of material incentives from enterprise profits. This policy vacuum allowed a great diversity in the approaches adopted by individual enterprises. Under guidelines established with the 1965 economic reforms, enterprise profits could be used to pay bonuses directly to technical and administrative personnel and other white-collar workers. They could also be allocated for indirect incentives such as the "social fund," used by enterprises to build housing, clubs, daycare centers, and related facilities. However, there were no specific rules regarding percentages to be alloted to each area; this decision was left up to the individual enterprise. The many approaches to distributing material awards were exasperating even for the Soviets. Looking back at this period in 1971, one specialist complained that there were "as many different bonus systems as branches of industry."[20]

In general, three basic types of incentives were paid: those for meeting established norms regarding production quantity and quality; one-time, lump-sum payments to, for example, winners of socialist competition; and those factored in as part of regular wages for special assistance to needy workers. The establishment of funds for any of these bonuses required no special authorization and was accomplished by individual enterprises based solely on their profits. In addition, certain types of wage-fund bonuses that had existed prior to 1965, such as those paid for achieving economies in raw materials and fuel, were still used.[21]

Despite the new authority extended to enterprises, there were some restrictions placed on the new bonus system based on profits. Most important was the stipulation that all bonuses, with the exception of those awarded to winners of socialist competition, were authorized only for workers in designated professions within a given enterprise, or for all workers engaged in the production of certain urgently needed items. This limitation greatly narrowed the pool of employees who could receive bonuses and led to continued efforts on the part of enterprise managers to increase the number of eligible skills and professions.[22] Another aspect of the new bonus system was the introduction of negative bonuses. Negative rewards, such as the withholding of a percentage of a worker's pay for producing low-quality or damaged goods, were widely endorsed as part of the campaign to improve productivity.[23]

Despite these limitations, the new emphasis on material rewards was very popular. Enterprises in many industrial sectors responded enthusiastically to their sudden independence. One Moscow factory, for example, reported in early 1966 that it had allocated 30,000 rubles to its incentive fund as a result of the high profits it earned the year before. The highly specialized Red October Metal Processing Plant similarly reported high profits after one year under the reform program, and deposited 600,000 rubles to be used for material incentives.[24]

The renewed emphasis on consumer goods in the economic reform program was evident in the number of light and food industry enterprises in the initial increment of enterprises authorized to begin developing their own incentives funds. The highly publicized incentives for these branches of the economy, especially those for increased quality and new or improved products, were certainly meant to support statements of political leaders regarding increased emphasis on the consumer sector: if the incentives system were to be successful, there must be goods to buy with the money workers gained through their extra efforts.[25]

By 1966, success with the new incentives program was widely proclaimed in all sectors of the economy. The Krasnodarsk Meat Complex, for example, earned profits that generated 92,000 rubles for the incentive fund in only one quarter. This had led to an overall wage increase for workers of almost 80 percent. Average income had increased by a smaller amount at the Kiev Meat Processing Complex, but bonuses there had increased for every category of worker. One of the few heavy industry enterprises that had shifted to the new system had earned such high profits in the first half of 1966 that it was able to allocate 63 percent more to its year-end bonus fund than originally planned.[26]

Because of this success, Soviet economists believed the incentives system was proving very effective. They often pointed out that material incentive funds for all enterprises operating under the new conditions had increased by 80 percent, and that social funds for indirect material rewards had risen by 60 percent. Statistics on the results of the first year of the reform also showed that workers had received an average of from ten days to one month's extra pay from the various bonuses they had been awarded.[27] If the statistics were to be believed, the new man was doing quite well under the 1965 reforms.

Year-end bonuses were given special emphasis in the new system, not so much for their impact on creating a new man as for the anticipated effect they would have on the labor force. Because it stressed seniority and labor discipline, the year-end bonus was looked to as a key element in the effort to stem labor turnover and develop cadres of highly skilled workers. Rules governing the year-end bonuses were as varied as those concerning bonuses based on quantity and quality. In all cases a minimum amount of unbroken service (usually one year) at the same enterprise was required to become eligible, but then a graduated scale was used to determine how much an eligible worker would receive. The Red October Metal Processing Plant, for example, awarded workers having one and one-half to three years service 70 percent of ten days pay, while those having more than three years seniority received at least twelve days full pay, and many received more. An oil refinery in Baku, in contrast, awarded 60 percent of an average month's pay to workers having five to ten years service and 100 percent (the "thirteenth month") to workers who had remained on the job for over twenty years.[28] Negative year-end bonuses were also "awarded" and various scales were established to determine the amounts to be deducted for days lost due to unauthorized absence and other violations of labor discipline. Drunks and those who had been punished for acts of "hooliganism" were deprived of their year-end bonuses altogether.[29]

Despite the broad enthusiasm for the new incentives, however, problems soon began to emerge. One problem was the lack of sufficient funds necessary to pay all allowable bonuses and still perform other essential functions (such as replacing production equipment or building new housing) that were also to be funded from an enterprise's profit. A second concern was that the unreasonable requirements for determining eligibility for white-collar bonuses—such as having to fulfill the monthly plan within the first ten days—effectively killed the initiative of those eligible for bonuses. Complaints were also directed at the designation of certain types of enterprise as being eligible for bonuses while others were not. There were also problems due to vestiges of wage equalization (*uravnilovka*) in certain areas.[30] But by far the most disturbing problem from both an ideological and practical point of view concerned the lack of sufficient incentive money for production workers.

Under the new incentives system, worker bonuses continued to be derived from the centrally controlled wage fund and not, with few exceptions, from enterprise profits. This departure from the rules governing other bonuses created several problems for enterprise directors and minimized their effective use of the profit principle. Since the wage fund was based in part on wages paid during the previous year, any attempt to economize on labor costs to increase profits—such as through direct labor reductions or by the highly desirable introduction of new technology—meant a consequent reduction in the wage fund for the next year and, therefore, in the bonus fund for workers. Thus, if cutting labor costs to achieve higher profits meant an increase in incentive funds available for white-collar workers, it resulted paradoxically in a reduction in future bonus funds available to the majority of workers.[31]

A typical example of this dilemma was provided by the Red October Blooming Mill in Volgograd where, despite record profits in 1965–1966, there were insufficient monies in the wage fund to provide bonuses for all categories of eligible workers in 1967. This evidently was a common problem. Some enterprise directors, such as I. Kiselev, director of the Gorkii Automobile Factory, hoped to remedy the situation by allocating a greater percentage of the profit-based material incentive fund to worker bonuses.[32] This suggestion was apparently received favorably by economists concerned about the potentially explosive issue of awarding bonuses to white-collar employees and engineers and not to production workers. Although some specialists justified paying a disproportionately higher share of bonuses to white-collar workers whose contributions had been insufficiently acknowledged under previous incentive systems, most responded positively to the idea of providing funds for worker bonuses out of enterprise profits.[33]

But despite various ideas on possible improvements to the incentives system, the general thinking on material incentives had shifted by the late 1960s. Although many suggestions were eventually incorporated into the revised incentives system that went into effect in 1971–1972, in 1967–1968 the general concept of awarding monetary bonuses was suddenly being questioned. Emphasis instead was placed on non-monetary or moral incentives, such as badges of honor and establishing honor rolls for each enterprise. Broadly supported by party spokesmen, the renewed emphasis was certainly part of the overall backlash against the 1965 reforms. More than that, however, it was in large measure a reflection of the increasing power of Leonid Brezhnev.

Ideology and Incentives Policy in Developed Socialism

The economy of developed socialism, as described by Soviet theoreticians, had several distinct goals. These included a shift to more intensive forms of development to ensure the fullest use of productive resources, new levels of complexity and interdependence among all sectors, focus on proportional growth, concentration of production into ever larger economic units such as "agroindustries" and industrial associations, increased emphasis on high-tech industries, emergence of the information sciences and of the science of management, and commitment to higher levels of consumer consumption. Designed to overcome the failed 1965 reforms, the developed socialist economy reflected the increasing centralization of economic planning and a return to more administrative methods of management.[34] The trend away from reliance on economic mechanisms was particularly evident in incentives policy.

Beginning in 1968, official emphasis shifted to moral incentives as the proper form of reward for socialist labor. This was largely the result of problems created by the many types of material incentives systems that had proliferated after 1965. But there was also an ideological problem. Warnings against excessive reliance on material incentives had been sounded by key ideologists early in the regime. P. N. Fedoseev, for example, cautioned in mid-1965 that although problems stemming from "idealism and subjectivism" (i.e. Khrushchev) were highly dangerous, excessive reliance on economic mechanisms would be equally dangerous.[35] *Pravda* emphasized the need for moral incentives by urging party organizations and economic managers to improve methods for presenting non-material awards, such as organizing meaningful ceremonies and publicizing the names of winners of socialist competition.[36] Such advice went largely unheeded, however, and by late 1966, when the use of material incentives had become firmly established as the primary motivator to increase productivity, moral incentives were virtually ignored. They gained prominence again only during the redefinition of economic policy that began in 1968.

Brezhnev took the lead in this campaign. His differences with Kosygin about industrial policy, which had formed an important undercurrent in their individual speeches in 1966–1967, became explicit in 1968. Brezhnev criticized Kosygin for his inflated opinion of foreign technology and his continued support of independence for economic managers. But he concentrated his most vicious attack on Kosygin's unbending advocacy of material incentives.[37] Despite his rhetoric, Brezhnev was not advocating a total retreat from material reward. This would have been unrealistic in the modern Soviet economy and would have called into question the promise of more consumer goods that was central to the new regime's policies. Worse, it would have been interpreted as a repetition of Khrushchev's exclusive reliance on moral incentives. What Brezhnev wanted was a balanced approach. As he told the Leningrad Obkom in February 1968, the party supported material incentives. But he quickly added that, "It is important that the ruble not become the only incentive."[38]

Brezhnev was responding to both political and ideological imperatives in his strong statements on incentives. Politically, by advocating a combination of material reward that was much higher than was available under Khrushchev together with appropriate non-material rewards, he hoped to demonstrate that it was possible to maintain a steady upward course in economic development without bowing completely to economic mechanisms. In George Breslauer's terms, by casting himself as a moderate whose policy was in sharp contrast to the extreme reliance on material rewards endorsed by Kosygin, Brezhnev was able to remain within the "consensus of the post-Khrushchev era" among the Soviet leadership.[39] Ideologically, through his advocacy of non-material rewards Brezhnev provided a forceful reminder about the nature of the socialist economic system, a connection he frequently mentioned in his speeches. Addressing the Moscow City Party Committee in March 1968, for example, Brezhnev echoed Marx by referring to labor as a "spiritual need" of the Soviet people. He added, "It would not be correct to reduce everything only to material interest. This would impoverish the life of Soviet man."[40]

Brezhnev's advocacy of a balanced combination of moral and material incentives gained support of key ideologists over the next several years, leading in 1971 to a substantial revision of incentives policy.[41] The main outlines of the new policy were revealed in discussions preceding the Twenty-fourth Party Congress and adoption of the Ninth Five-Year Plan

(1971–1976), and included both a broad application of moral incentives and a general reform of the wage structure that incorporated many of the features of the former bonus system. Wage bonuses were included in the new policy. But these were to be applied more judiciously than in the past in accordance with Brezhnev's appeal for the "skillful" application of economic levers.[42] Implementation of the new policy, however, did not progress as smoothly as the ideological evolution suggests. Probably because official attention had been focused on problems caused by excessive material reward, incentives policy in 1971–1974 began to tilt too far in the opposite direction, towards an overreliance on moral incentives.

The most visible indicator that the focus had shifted to moral incentives was the increased publicity accorded socialist competition. A Central Committee resolution of September 1971, for example, called for improvements in the organization of socialist competition to "strengthen responsibility" at all levels. Winners of socialist competition were to be awarded red banners and letters of honor and would have their names inscribed on honor rolls prominently displayed at each enterprise. To support this campaign, *Pravda* published pictures of winners of socialist competition holding their red banners and other prizes. Although it is doubtful that such measures had any impact at all on most workers, Soviet economists and political specialists dutifully presented this policy in a positive way, stressing that these incentives were crucial in enlivening co-workers and stimulating productivity.[43] The campaign for moral incentives was expanded greatly after the Twenty-fourth Party Congress. Brezhnev contributed to this by continuing to emphasize the virtues of socialist competition and by downplaying the need for material reward. New non-material rewards were introduced, including a new honorary order, "For the Glory of Labor" (with three degrees of recognition), a medal, to "Veterans of Labor," and a new all-union badge, "Shockworker of the Ninth Five-Year Plan."[44]

Throughout this period material incentives received little notice. The revised wage structure introduced as part of the new five-year plan was meant to provide ample material reward. It also reflected the regime's policy of equalizing the standard of living for workers in all occupations. The new structure incorporated many of the features of the previous material incentives systems into wage and salary scales that were applied consistently throughout the country. Besides raising the minimum wage, it required consideration of a worker's qualifications and working conditions to determine his wage rate. Another new feature was the use of geographically based coefficients, or wage supplements, for workers in remote parts of the country that had not previously been eligible for bonuses. (This supported one of Brezhnev's key economic policy goals—

the development of Siberia.) Moreover, income taxes were eliminated for workers earning less than the minimum wage of 70 rubles per month, and the tax rate for other categories of workers was lowered. Other measures included increasing the differential paid for nightwork, providing a childcare allowance for families whose per capita income averaged less than 50 rubles per month, improving maternity benefits, and revising pension rules, especially for invalids. The combined effect of these changes was projected to be an overall increase in the national income from 106 percent of the 1965 level in 1971 to 138.6 percent by 1975.[45]

The problem with relying on the wage reform to complement the renewed emphasis on moral incentives was that, except for the new minimum wage, it was not put into practice immediately. It was instead phased in over the entire five-year plan. The delay in implementation had the effect of reducing significantly the funds available for material incentives, and managers and workers who had become accustomed to the many options for material rewards between 1965–1970 now had to make a difficult adjustment. This prompted expressions of concern on the part of economic managers and some party cadres. Beginning in 1972, suggestions for improvements began to appear in the Soviet press with increasing regularity. While these suggestions were within the Brezhnevian framework for material rewards—stressing bonuses to improve quality and using negative rewards to improve worker discipline—the message was nevertheless clear that more material rewards were needed.[46]

Brezhnev's initial reaction to this discussion was decidedly defensive. In December 1972, for example, he proclaimed that the material incentives problem in agriculture had been resolved through the use of increased prices for farm products, suggesting that farm workers had the opportunity to earn more profits. By 1974, however, he was more supportive of the idea of direct material rewards, suggesting the "improvement of economic levers" to increase production. This represented a much stronger position in favor of material incentives than any he had taken previously, prompting Breslauer to speak of Brezhnev's "redefinition" of incentives policy. Breslauer suggests that Brezhnev did this simply to keep the notion of material incentives on the political agenda. Such an action would have been consistent with his background and political style as a "consensus-builder." By "co-opting issues and redefining their thrust," in Breslauer's view, Brezhnev would have been able to "maintain his image" as an "innovative problem solver."[47]

In terms of the relationship between ideology and policy, however, another explanation is that Brezhnev realized that the desired balance between moral and material incentives had been lost because of the heavy emphasis on non-material rewards since the Twenty-fourth Party

Congress. Rather than acting to preserve his "image," he may have simply decided to speak out in favor of material rewards in order to restore the balance that he supported consistently throughout his tenure as General Secretary and which had already been incorporated into the official ideology of developed socialism. From this perspective, Brezhnev did not so much "re-define" incentives policy as he did repeat his own definition that he had stated several years earlier. He was thus advocating a policy that was based on his ideological values that had been frequently expressed in his speeches and writings.

Brezhnev's renewed emphasis on material incentives led to a much more candid discussion of the issues. Ideologists who had vacillated between providing theoretical support for material incentives after the introduction of the 1965 reforms only to have to rail against such rewards several years later could now support material rewards while simultaneously demanding increased discipline as the key to economic growth.[48] Similarly, those who had been essentially muzzled between 1968–1971 in their support of material incentives could now describe problems created by the lack of sufficient material incentives to achieve production goals. The support of industrial obkom secretaries was especially significant in this regard since they used the same arguments in favor of material incentives that had been presented earlier by economic specialists, indicating the broad dimensions of the consensus on this issue.[49]

By the Twenty-fifth Party Congress, a third revision to incentives policy under Brezhnev had occurred. Consistent with the precepts of developed socialism, it stressed a more balanced approach to moral and material incentives. Brezhnev once again called for the "more skillful use". of economic stimuli and levers of all descriptions, positive and negative. At the same time, he supported the effective use of material and moral rewards to intensify plan fulfillment and improve execution of contractual arrangements between enterprises. He also supported a full study of how to best combine moral and material incentives.[50] The Party Congress brought incentives policy back into focus on the new man, calling for the fullest development of particularly indirect material incentives such as improved working conditions, health services, education, and cultural opportunities essential to his development.[51]

Moral incentives under the revised system were quite different from those used several years earlier. More meaningful than red banners and factory honor rolls, moral incentives now included authorization for workers to release products without inspection, the examination by the workers themselves of labor norms pertaining to their jobs, the assignment of mentors to assist in the development of junior employees, and others.[52] These changes suggested that there was real substance underlying policy rhetoric and that discussions about ways to make non-material incentives more meaningful had occurred at high levels within the party and government.

Material rewards had also been modified. Although individual bonuses were still paid for certain types of achievement, collective rewards were promoted as the primary type of incentive. Collective awards were highly desirable politically and ideologically because they combined the spirit of socialist competition with material reward, encouraging a "communist attitude towards labor." Connected with these incentives was the planned increase in the importance of production collectives in the construction of communism. Individual material interests were to become dependent on the overall results of the collective and material rewards received by an individual therefore reflected the sum total of societal, collective, and individual interests. The continued use of collective material incentives would thus increase the consciousness of workers and lead eventually to their more active participation in the administration of their production collectives—an important goal of a developed socialist society.[53]

The material incentives system underwent a further modification in 1977 when requirements for monetary bonuses were tightened once more. This change brought into focus earlier proposals for using negative incentives as punitive measures against those who failed to meet production requirements. Directed especially against enterprise directors and other managers, the 1977 rules called for the partial or complete deprivation of bonuses for non-fulfillment of production norms in terms of either quantity, deadlines, or type of product. Quarterly bonuses were to be paid only when the production deadlines were met for each month; otherwise, these bonuses would be decreased by 50 percent. Regulations were introduced to reward managers who increased output through the introduction of new equipment and techniques. Economic organizations at the ministerial and highest government levels were required to establish firm control over the bonus system and to deal severely with any attempts at violating the newly established norms. Finally, the need for moral stimuli was reemphasized as part of the overall effort to increase production in honor of the sixtieth anniversary of the October Revolution.[54]

As Jan Adam has pointed out, the 1977 changes signalled a shift to increased centralization over the material incentives program. By effectively eliminating the innovations of the 1965 reforms, these changes reflected the almost complete return to an administrative approach to economic management that characterized the last years of the Brezhnev regime.[55] For purposes of this study, however, the main point is that the Brezhnevian formula for incentives policy was adopted into the doctrines of developed socialism and these doctrines then provided the backdrop for significant policy clarifications and corrections. Despite the many vacillations in the rules governing material rewards, Brezhnev's policy preference for a balanced combination of moral and material rewards for socialist labor became a central ideological theme and a guide for action in discussions of labor policy—and of the development of the new man—under developed socialism. As stated in Article 14 of the 1977 Soviet Constitution:

> Socially useful labor and its results determine the place of man in society. The state, combining material and moral stimuli, encouraging innovation and a creative attitude toward work, promotes the transformation of labor into life's primary want for every Soviet person.

Although Brezhnev's ideological values and policy preferences were incorporated into the official ideology, the economic decline that began in the mid-1970s made this a rather hollow victory for the General Secretary. From 1977 until Brezhnev's death in 1982 there was little attempt at innovation in any sphere of the economy. (The Food Program, begun in 1982, is the most notable exception, but this was almost certainly authored by Gorbachev, not Brezhnev.) Because of his declining health Brezhnev was unable to exert the leadership he had demonstrated earlier to bring the incentives program or other aspects of economic policy back into balance. As a result of these factors, the incentives program collapsed of its own weight.

The last years of the Brezhnev regime saw the return of wage-levelling and a more egalitarian wage structure accompanied by a downturn in the production of consumer goods, which further devalued the incentives that remained. As a result, workers began to turn to alternative sources of income, including those which were at best only quasi-legal. Such activity was countenaced by the regime in what James Millar has termed the "Little Deal"—a decision to allow increased freedom and cooperation at the lowest levels of the economy, including private enterprise and marketeering, while maintaining the status quo and lack of reform at the macrolevel.[56]

The economic stagnation of the late Brezhnev period thus set the stage for a new leadership consensus on economic reform and a new formula for incentives policy. Reversing Brezhnev's balanced approach, the emphasis shifted to a broader application of material incentives based on a demanding set of productivity and quality indicators. First articulated by Andropov, the new policy found its fullest expression under Gorbachev, as discussed in Chapter 8.

Notes

1. See, for example: *KPSS o Formirovanii Novogo Cheloveka: Sbornik Dokumentov i Materialov* (Moscow: Politicheskaia Literatura, 1976); V. Semenov, "Sotsial'naia Struktura Sovetskogo Obshchestva," *Kommunist*, 11/1965, pp. 39–48; and G. Smirnov, "Lichnost' v Sovetskom Obshchestve," *Kommunist*, 11/1967, pp. 38–50. For a statistical view of the new man's development, see V. S. Semenov, "Novye Iavleniia v Sotsial'noi Strukture Sovetskogo Obshchestva," *Voprosy Filosofii*, 7/1972, pp. 20–32.

2. Because of its ideological sensitivity, the effect of material incentives on the new man's development has not been widely publicized in the USSR. For a rare Soviet discussion of this topic, see G. Kh. Shakhnazarov et al., eds., *Social Science*, 8th ed., trans. and ed. Charles Baroch and Catherine Baroch (Lexington, Massachusetts: D. C. Heath and Company, 1973), p. 211.

3. Richard Lowenthal, "Development vs. Utopia in Communist Policy," in *Change in Communist Systems*, ed. Chalmers Johnson (Stanford, Stanford University Press, 1970), pp. 50–51.

4. V. I. Lenin, *Polnoe Sobranie Sochinenii*, vol. 34, p. 312, quoted in Kendall E. Bailes, *Technology and Society Under Lenin and Stalin* (Princeton: Princeton University Press, 1978), p. 48.

5. Quoted in Bailes, *Technology and Society Under Lenin and Stalin*, p. 48.

6. For a comprehensive discussion of inequality in socialist societies, see Walter D. Conner, *Socialism, Politics, and Equality* (New York: Columbia University Press, 1979).

7. Lowenthal, "Development vs. Utopia," pp. 76–77.

8. For a detailed discussion of Stalin's incentive system, see Mervyn Matthews, *Privilege in the Soviet Union* (London: George Allen & Unwin, 1978), p. 93. Stalin's postwar incentives efforts have been vividly described by Vera S. Dunham, *In Stalin's Time: Middleclass Values in Soviet Fiction* (Cambridge, England: Cambridge University Press, 1976), pp. 11–18.

9. Connor, *Socialism*, p. 305. The same point has been made in stronger terms by John Bushnell, who argues that the legitimacy of the Soviet regime rests heavily on the promise of material rewards. See John Bushnell, "The 'New Soviet Man' Turns Pessimist," in Stephen F. Cohen, Alexander Rabinowitch, and Robert Sharlet, eds., *The Soviet Union Since Stalin* (Bloomington: Indiana University Press, 1980.), pp. 194–195.

10. Lowenthal, "Development vs. Utopia," pp. 59–60.

11. For a description of Khrushchev's incentives system, see George W. Breslauer, *Khrushchev and Brezhnev as Leaders: Building Authority in Soviet Politics* (London: George Allen & Unwin, 1982), pp. 71–74 and 93–94. Also see Gertrude Schroeder, "Industrial Wage Differentials in the USSR," *Soviet Studies* 17 (January 1966), pp. 303–317. For a comprehensive Soviet discussion of wage incentives under Khrushchev and in the late Stalin period, see S. S. Karinskii, *Pooshchreniia za Doblestnii Trud po Sovetskomu Zakonodatel'stvu* (Moscow: Znanie, 1956).

12. L. I. Brezhnev, *Leninskim Kursom* (Moscow: Politicheskaia Literatura, 1970–1981), vol. 1, p. 217.

13. Schroeder, "Industrial Wage Differentials in the USSR," pp. 304–305.

14. See, for example, the description of a four-day conference at Moscow State University in *Pravda*, 23 June 1965, p. 2.

15. Compare, for example, Fedoseev (a strong opponent of developed socialism) with Kelle (an important advocate). Both agreed on the usefulness of material incentives. See P. Fedoseev, "Dialektika Razvitiia Sotsializma," *Kommunist*, 14/1965, pp. 17–29, and V. Zh. Kelle, "Nekotorye Osobennosti Razvitiia Sotsializma," *Voprosy Filosofii*, 3/1966, pp. 14–24.

16. *Pravda*, 21 June 1965. This point was also brought out by Fedoseev, who in an interesting piece of self-criticism acknowledged the guilt of "us philosophical workers" for supporting Khrushchev's subjectivism both theoretically and in practice. In terms of economic policy, this led to stifling workers' initiative and limiting their spontaneity. Worse yet, it caused negative manifestations such as "idle talk, time-serving, opportunism, and eyewash" in the attitude of workers at all levels. See Fedoseev, "Dialektika," p. 29.

17. For representative examples of such discussions, see E. Borisov, "Edinstvo Ehkonomicheskikh Interesov Obshchestva, Predpriiatiia, i Trudiashchikhsia," *Kommunist*, 11/1965, pp. 49–59; P. Kopnin, "K Voprosu v Protivorechiiakh Obshchestvennogo Razvitiia," *Pravda*, 10 February 1966; and D. I. Chesnokov, "Obshchestvennyi Interes i Mehkanizm Deistviia Sotsial'nykh Zakonov," *Voprosy Filosofii*, 9/1966, pp. 10–11.

18. Kelle, "Nekotorye Osobennosti," pp. 14–24. For a similar argument, see I. Kuz'minov, "Lenin i Problemy Ehkonomicheskoi Teorii Sotsializma," *Pravda*, 16 April 1969, p. 2.

19. L. Leont'ev, "Leninskie Printsipy Khoziastvennogo Stroitel'stva," *Kommunist*, 6/1966, pp. 36–38. See also I. Berkhin, "Novaia Ehkonomicheskaia Politika i Ee Rol' v Perekhodnoi Period ot Kapitalizma k Sotsializmu," *Kommunist*, 4/1967, pp. 26–35.

20. Sergei S. Karinskii, *Oplata Truda v Promyshlennosti* (Moscow: Iuridicheskaia Literatura, 1971), pp. 94–95.

21. Karinskii, *Oplata*, pp. 84–88 and 124–128. For a discussion of material incentives during their first year of operation, see *Ehkonomicheskaia Gazeta*, 8/1966, pp. 21–22.

22. Karinskii, *Oplata*, pp. 103–104. Also see A. P. Volkov, "Trud, Zarplata, Blagosostoianie," *Pravda*, 18 March 1966, p. 3.

23. See, for example, V. Tsingalenok, "Bystro, No Dolgovechno Li?," *Pravda*, 9 June 1965. For descriptions of negative incentives in the housing industry, various industries in the Leningrad area, and the transport industry, see *Pravda*, 9 February 1966 and 6 January 1967.

24. *Pravda*, 1 and 11 February 1966, respectively.

25. Many scholars have commented on the connection between incentives and the availability of consumer goods. For an excellent discussion, see Breslauer, *Khrushchev and Brezhnev as Leaders*, p. 210. Also see Erik P. Hoffman and Robbin F. Laird, *The Politics of Economic Modernization in the Soviet Union* (Ithaca: Cornell University Press, 1982), p. 77, and Cal Clark and John M. Echols III, "Developed Socialism and Consumption Policies in the Soviet Bloc: An Empirical Evaluation,"

in Jim Seroka and Maurice D. Simon, eds., *Developed Socialism in the Soviet Bloc: Political Theory and Political Reality* (Boulder: Westview Press, 1982), pp. 164–166.

26. See *Pravda*, 5 May 1966, 28 August 1966, and 2 October 1966, respectively.

27. B. Sukharevskii, "Reforma: Opyt i Problemy," *Pravda*, 12 April 1967, pp. 2–3.

28. *Pravda*, 11 February 1966, p. 2, and *Bakchinskii Rabochii*, 21 March 1965, p. 2.

29. *Pravda*, 1 November 1966, p. 2.

30. For a discussion of these problems, see *Pravda*, 25 May 1966, 30 March 1969, and 5 May and 2 September 1970. Also see I. Mishchenko, "Kollektiv, Stimuly, Reservy," *Kommunist*, 4/1968, pp. 45–52.

31. See the article by M. Korolev in *Pravda*, 8 August 1966, p. 2, and Mishchenko, "Kollektiv," pp. 46–49.

32. See *Pravda*, 8 May 1967 and 25 May 1966, respectively.

33. For the former view, see Galina Danilovna Soboleva, "The New Soviet Incentives System: A Study of Its Operation in Kiev," *International Labour Review* 101 (1970), pp. 15–33. For the latter view, see V. Rzheshevskii, "Pribyl' i Pooshchrenie," *Pravda*, 8 June 1967, p. 2, and his "Reforma i Proizvoditel'nost' Truda," *Kommunist*, 12/1969, pp. 65–76. See also Iu. E. Volkov, "Sotsializm i Proizvodstvennaia Demokratiia," *Voprosy Filosofii*, 1/1968, pp. 3–13.

34. Donald R. Kelley, *The Politics of Developed Socialism: The Soviet Union as a Post-Industrial State* (New York: Greenwood Press, 1986), pp. 59–106.

35. Fedoseev, "Dialektika," p. 24. See also V. Stepakov, "Aktivno Formirovat' Marksistko-Leninskoe Mirovozzrenie i Kommunisticheskuiu Moral' Sovetskikh Liudei," *Kommunist*, 17/1966, pp. 14–28.

36. See, for example, *Pravda*, 19 May and 21 October 1966.

37. Breslauer, *Khrushchev and Brezhnev as Leaders*, pp. 165–167.

38. Brezhnev, *Leninskim Kursom*, vol. 2, p. 176.

39. Breslauer, *Khrushchev and Brezhnev as Leaders*, p. 188.

40. Brezhnev, *Leninskim Kursom*, vol. 2, p. 210.

41. Most important in this regard was the support of Mikhail Suslov, the regime's chief ideologist and unofficial "second secretary" in the CPSU Central Committee. In October 1970, in his first major statement on incentive policy since Khrushchev's removal from power, Suslov said: "The necessity to combine skillfully the system of economic incentives with moral incentives for collectives and individual workers comes from the socialist essence of our societal structure and the ongoing reforms. Forgetting the moral factors can cause no less economic and political loss than ignoring the principles of material interest." See Mikhail Suslov, *Na Putiakh Stroitel'stvo Kommunizma* (Moscow: Politizdat, 1977), vol. 2, p. 237.

42. Brezhnev, *Leninskim Kursom*, vol. 2, pp. 238 and 271.

43. See, for example, *Pravda*, 5, 6, and 20 September 1971, and A. Chistov, "Trud i Ego Stimuly pri Sotsializme," *Pravda*, 16 February 1971, p. 3.

44. See *Pravda*, 19 January and 3 March 1974, respectively.

45. *Pravda*, 27 November 1971. See also the article by the Chief of GOSPLAN, N. Baibakov, "Plan i Razvitie Ehkonomiki," *Pravda*, 22 February 1971, pp. 2–

3. For Western discussions of this and other Soviet wage reforms, see: Jan Prybyla, "Soviet Man in the Ninth Five-Year Plan," *Current History* 61 (1971), pp. 227–234; A. J. Katsenelinboigen, "Disguised Inflation in the USSR," in *Economic Aspects of Life in the USSR* (Brussels: NATO Directorate of Economic Affairs, [1975]), pp. 101–112; Schroeder, "Industrial Wage Differentials in the USSR;" and Janet Chapman, "Are Earnings More Equal Under Socialism?," in John Moroney, ed., *Income Inequality* (Lexington, Massachusetts: Lexington Books, 1979), pp. 43–64.

46. See, for example, the article by V. Voliakov in *Pravda*, 7 November 1972, p. 2.

47. Breslauer, *Khrushchev and Brezhnev as Leaders*, pp. 208–212.

48. See, for example, P. Fedoseev, "Narodnye Massy i Sotsialnyi Progress," *Pravda*, 30 May 1975, pp. 3–4.

49. Obkom first secretaries Taratuta (Vinnitsa) and Voropaev (Cheliabinsk) were two of the strongest advocates of reintroducing incentives based on increased labor productivity and higher quality. See their articles in *Pravda* 14 December 1974 and 11 August 1976, respectively.

50. Brezhnev, *Leninskim Kursom*, vol. 5, pp. 516–517 and 531.

51. *XXV S"ezd Kommunisticheskoi Partii Sovetskogo Soiuza: Edinstvo Teorii i Praktiki* (Moscow: Politicheskaia Literatura, 1977) p. 15.

52. V. N. Cherkovets, ed., *Problemy Razvitogo Sotsializma v Politicheskoi Ehkonomiki* (Moscow: Nauka, 1977), p. 221. The more significant involvement of workers in the decision-making process of their enterprises discussed here can be seen as the precursor to many of the ideas expressed by Gorbachev in his efforts to democratize the workplace. See the discussion in Chapter 8.

53. Cherkovets, *Problemy*, pp. 219–20 and 276. The new collective awards differed from those offered under Khrushchev in that they included monetary awards. Those provided by Khrushchev were indirect material incentives such as better housing and better education. See Breslauer, *Khrushchev and Brezhnev as Leaders*, pp. 73–74.

54. *Pravda*, 18 August 1977.

55. Adam, "The Present Soviet Incentive System," p. 362. Adam notes that the new regulations put a cap on bonuses for top managers, engineer-technical personnel, and administrative staff of between 50–60 percent of their salaries. This was apparently in reaction to complaints from production workers upset by the disparity between their bonuses and those paid to their bosses. A similar trend towards wage equalization was evident in the rules for year-end bonuses.

56. James R. Millar, "The Little Deal: Brezhnev's Contribution to Acquisitive Socialism," in Terry L. Thompson and Richard Sheldon, eds., *Soviet Society and Culture: Essays in Honor of Vera S. Dunham* (Boulder: Westview Press, 1988), pp. 3–19. An earlier version of this essay was published in *Slavic Review* 44 (Winter 1985).

4

Soviet Nation
or Russian Nation?

The Soviet nation (*sovetskii narod*) is a central element in the doctrines of developed socialism. Reflecting the official view of the cultural and economic unity of more than one hundred nationalities comprising the USSR, the Soviet nation has been a component of Soviet ideology since Khrushchev. It is said to be the product of the efforts of millions of new Soviet men and women devoted to the ideals of communism and motivated by socialist patriotism. Intolerant of ethnic exploitation, oppression, and racial prejudice, people in the Soviet nation work to demonstrate class solidarity with each other and the workers of all countries. The Soviet nation is thus a new type of nationality, "never before seen in history," in which people of many ethnic backgrounds have subordinated their nationality to their common identity as members of Soviet socialist society.[1]

In contrast to its idealistic official description, the Soviet nation has had quite different meanings for Khrushchev, Brezhnev, and probably for Gorbachev as well. For these leaders, the "Soviet nation" has been a codeword signifying strongly assimilationist policies towards the nationalities, although these policies have typically be well concealed by the lofty rhetoric of official pronouncements. Evident in political, cultural, and economic policy, the trend toward subordinating the interests of Soviet nationalities to the needs of Moscow and the Russian-dominated leadership has been a consistent feature of Soviet policy since Lenin. And, although individual leaders have supported a greater or lesser degree of assimilation depending on their own political situation, none has retreated from an overall approach towards eliminating the cultural, political, and economic boundaries between nationalities to create a single, unified nation. While the Soviet nation remains more goal than reality, it is thus not the same goal it appears to be from its ideological description.

Background

The Marxist legacy on the nationality question is for the most part ambiguous. Focusing on class differences rather than ethnicity, Marx and Engels emphasized the commonality of interests within the working class and stressed their belief that these ties were stronger than those based on nationality. Neither man provided much in the way of guidance for ruling a large, multinational empire. In the eyes of both, nationalism was a by-product of capitalism and would disappear when the capitalist order was overturned. When Marx did have something specific to say about nationalism, such as his advice to the Russian Socialists on their approach to the Polish separatist movement of the 1870s, he addressed the meaning of national independence in the context of the international proletariat instead of the quite different question of national liberation itself.

The clearest expression of a classical Marxist position on the nationality issue is the guidance contained in the Communist Manifesto, in which the responsibilities of communists are spelled out in a way that has become part of the fundamental philosophical background of all Communist Party members:

> The communists are distinguished from the other working-class parties by this only: (1) In the national struggles of the proletarians of the different countries, they point out and bring to the front the common interests of the entire proletariat, independently of all nationality. (2) In the various stages of development which the struggle of the working class against the bourgeoisie has to press through, they always and everywhere represent the movement as a whole.[2]

Lenin's views on nationalities coincided with the spirit of Marx's writings, but were modified by the specific situation in Russia and the fundamental need to gain and retain power. Because of the historical background of tsarist Russia, Lenin certainly could not ignore the nationalities situation. To attract support he had to develop a policy that addressed the oppressive situation of the many national groups that had been incorporated into the Russian Empire through almost four centuries of territorial expansion. Although the worst excesses had been curtailed after 1905 with the establishment of a constitutional monarchy, continued tsarist support for Russification and other forms of minority repression combined to place nationalities policy high on the agenda for change.

As was true in other areas, Lenin's approach to the nationalities problem was connected to Marxist theory by the thinnest of threads.

Not content to wait until Marx's predictions were realized, Lenin adapted Marx's ideas to the Russian situation in a way that provided maximum tactical flexibility with no long-term commitments. Initially, for example, he supported the rights of all nationalities to determine their own destiny and to secede from Russia. He also advocated the continued use of native languages. But these were to be temporary expedients. Lenin fully expected that the center, through the Communist Party, would be able to maintain control over the periphery and preclude dissolution of the multinational Russian state. Moreover—and this is the theoretical thread linking his policies with Marx—he felt that even if nationality groups seceded, they would eventually rejoin the center once their economic interests became predominant. He also believed that, despite an initial period in which nationalities would revert to their own language, they would in due course adopt Russian because of the superiority of Russian culture.

These themes virtually disappeared from Lenin's thought after 1917, when the Russian revolution failed to trigger the worldwide communist revolution he had expected. Faced with the enormous task of governing a multinational state, Lenin soon abandoned his utopian policies and authorized the consolidation of the national republics by force. This policy, carried out between 1920–1922, was based on both economic and political necessity: Russia needed access to the oil in Azerbaidjan and had to establish political control over areas (such as the Baltic region, the Ukraine, and Central Asia) acquired as a result of the settlement of World War I and the subsequent defeat of White forces in the Civil War.

Having consolidated this expansive territory, Lenin supported in theory a federal state system to protect the rights of the national minorities. This again he viewed as a temporary measure that would not be necessary when the economic development of Soviet nationalities brought them closer together. To hasten the process of national unity, he established firm economic and political control from Moscow using both overt and subtle means. The most visible means of control were the Communist Party and the People's Commissariat for Nationalities headed by Stalin. More subtle measures included the process of "indigenization" (placement of national leaders into party and government posts) and emphasis on the use of national languages to convey party propaganda and for use in regional educational institutions. The thrust of Lenin's nationality policy was thus to grant national minorities rights in theory, but to endorse policies severely limiting these rights in practice.[3]

Stalin's nationality policy increased the gap between theory and reality. In the 1930s, he sought to strengthen central control by purging many of the nationalist elites that had coalesced through indigenization. The extent of this policy became evident in the 1936 Constitution. By acknowledging the continuity of the present Soviet state with the Russian Empire, the Constitution reflected the *de facto* subordination of the nationalities to the Russian leadership. Russian values were given precedence over those of any other national group. Cultural measures of special importance included the universal imposition of the Cyrillic alphabet and the revision of Russian history to reflect the traditional inequality of nations in the tsarist empire. Economically, the increasing centralization of planning ensured that policies favorable to the Russians would be followed. This in effect cancelled out the significance of Lenin's federal system.[4]

The full measure of Stalin's nationality policy was revealed during World War II through the well-documented deportation of seven nationalities from their homelands in southern Russia to Siberia and Central Asia. Officially justified by the threat to national security posed by these "unreliable" groups (evident, in Stalin's view, from the speed with which the Germans advanced through the southern part of the USSR), the deportation indicated that the harsh treatment of national minorities had not ended with the purges.[5] After the war, overt Russification became the central aspect of Stalin's nationality policy. The virtues of Russian history, culture, and language were not only extolled but were actively substituted for those of the national minorities.

One well-known aspect of Stalin's Russification program was his personal involvement with linguistics. Disputing the theories of Nikolas Marr, a linguist and charlatan who had gained prominence by asserting that the advent of socialism would result in the use of a single language throughout the world, Stalin declared that language was based not on economics but on history. He did agree with Marr that the victory of socialism would result in the elevation of one language to primary position. It was clear to Stalin that this language would be Russian, and he enforced this view by making the study of Russian compulsory in all Soviet schools. Stalin also provided his interpretation of Lenin's ideas about federalism. Declaring that Lenin had "substantial reservations" about federation, Stalin began to limit the autonomy of the national republics. By the 1950s, Stalin's policies had far exceeded the Russification policies of any tsar, creating a "federation of unequals" in which the nationalities were subjugated in all respects to their Russian "elder brother."[6]

The framework of Soviet nationality policy established by Lenin and Stalin provided the basis for policies of subsequent regimes. Lenin's policy of granting rights to the nationalities in theory but ensuring control from the center and Stalin's policies of Russification and tight political control over the national republics have been evident in theory

as well as in policy since Stalin's death. Although the theoretical justification for these policies has frequently been couched in more subtle
terms and the pace of policy implementation has varied, the assimilationist
trend of Soviet nationality policy was evident under both Khrushchev
and Brezhnev. Gorbachev appears to have reversed this trend somewhat,
although it is still too early to assess fully his nationality policies.

Ideology and Policy Prior to
Developed Socialism

Nationality policy evolved under Khrushchev and Brezhnev in re-
markably similar ways. Both men initially rejected the assimilationist
approach of their predecessors only to adopt a similar approach themselves
in later years as they gained political power and prestige. Like Lenin,
they maintained flexibility during the early years of their regimes, but
never lost sight of the ultimate goal of national unification. Like Stalin,
they promoted Russian values and the use of the Russian language as
the key to resolving the nationality problem.

As part of his overall rejection of Stalin, Khrushchev denounced both
the full-scale Russification practiced since the end of World War II and
the policy of eliminating nationalist elites in republican party organizations. At the Twentieth CPSU Congress, Khrushchev launched a series
of policy measures designed to reverse much of the damage inflicted
on nationality relations by Stalin. Five of the seven deported national
minorities were allowed to return to their homelands; only the Crimean
Tatars and Volga Germans remained in exile. The nationalities were
allowed to rehabilitate their history, much of which had been rewritten
at Stalin's direction. The economic position of the national republics was
temporarily improved through the Sovnarkhoz reforms of 1956–1957,
which decentralized economic planning and decision-making. Politically,
the nationalities regained some of their former independence. The indigenization policy of the 1920s was applied for a second time under
Khrushchev, providing nationality cadres the opportunity to attain important policy-making posts. These considerable gains were buttressed
in 1957 by the enactment of three federal laws delegating broadened
judicial powers to the national republics.[7]

Despite the reformist nature of these initiatives, however, Khrushchev
reversed his approach to the nationalities soon after he had defeated
the anti-party group and consolidated his political position.[8] The new
direction of his nationality policy was clarified in the 1961 Party Program,
which identified the trend of nationality relations in the current stage
of communism as leading to the "further rapprochement of nations and
the attainment of their complete unity." More telling was the comment

that the "great Russian people" had assisted in the development of nationality cultural and economic development. The Russian language was attributed "positive significance" as "the common language of inter-nationality communication and cooperation," providing as well a link to other socialist countries. But the most ominous statement in terms of nationality autonomy was that boundaries between the national republics were "losing their former significance."[9]

Khrushchev softened somewhat the assimilationist tone of the Party Program in his speech to the Party Congress. On the subject of rap-prochement, for instance, he noted that this was occurring "on the basis of free will and democracy" of all Soviet nationalities. On the sensitive subject of language, he said that the party would tolerate no forced use of any language and that Soviet citizens would continue to have the "complete freedom" to raise their children in their language of choice. He added, however, that he expected the "ongoing process of the voluntary study of Russian" would play an increasingly significant role in the development of nationality relations.[10]

Despite these assurances, the assimilationist direction of Khrushchev's nationality policy was clearly expressed in the concept of "Soviet nation." Used sparingly in the Party Program, the concept was more fully expanded by Khrushchev in his speech on the new document:

> In the USSR, a new historic community of people of various nationalities having common characteristic traits has been formed–the Soviet nation. Soviet people have: a common motherland–the USSR; a common economic base–the socialist economy; a common socio-class structure; a common worldview–Marxism-Leninism; a common goal–construction of commu-nism; and many common spiritual and psychological traits.[11]

Taken together with the other points of Khrushchev's nationality policy evident in the Party Program, especially those supporting greater Rus-sification, the idea of a Soviet nation was widely perceived as an assimilationist concept. His actions after the congress, such as establishing CPSU Central Committee Bureaus on Central Asia and the Transcaucasus in 1962–1963, lent further support to the notion that he had in mind something far more radical. Some specialists in fact thought Khrushchev intended to dissolve the federal system. Although he was removed before this threat to the nationalities materialized, the possibility that Khrushchev planned to merge all national and autonomous republics into a unitary state continued to be a strong undercurrent in nationality policies. It caused conflict again under Brezhnev, when the intense feelings roused by the threat of terminating the federal system delayed acceptance of the 1977 Constitution.

Khrushchev's statements and the assimilationist language in the Party Program touched off a debate that began in the early 1960s and continued through the Brezhnev years. Focusing on the key issues of assimilation vs. diversification and central control vs. national autonomy, the debate matched pro-assimilationists (many of whom were not specialists on nationalties) against several prominent academic experts. The assimilationists, including Petr M. Rogachev, Matvei A. Sverdlin, Pavel G. Semenov, and Suren T. Kaltakchian, followed the Marxist line that considered nations to be the direct products of capitalism. Since the common economic interests of workers were greater than national differences, economic interests would overcome ethnic interests. As nations became economically more equal under socialism, they would experience an initial period of individual growth. Gradually, however, they would become more like other nations in the socialist system until they eventually merged into a single nation. This process would occur in stages known as "flourishing" (*rastsvet*), "rapprochement" (*sblizhenie*), and "merging" (*sliianie*). In contrast, the moderates acknowledged the economic aspects of nationality development, but were not willing to dismiss ethnic and cultural factors. Specialists supporting this view included Maskhud S. Dzhunusov, Mkrtych Mnatsakanian, Tatiana Burmistrova, and Nikolai Tavakalian. They emphasized the racial, social, and psychological continuity of nations, attributing special importance to linguistic differences between nationalities. Rejecting the possibility of the merging of nationalities, at least in the near term, the moderates stressed the flourishing and rapprochement stages. They were presumably content to leave "merging" until the final victory of communism.[12]

This debate continued well into the Brezhnev years. Moderates continued to emphasize the cultural aspects of nationality development. Dzhunusov, for example, continued to insist on the importance of cultural and psychological aspects of national identity, seeing in these characteristics the main sources of cultural enrichment and mutual influence.[13] This viewpoint was supported by an important newcomer to the debate, Eduard Bagramov, Deputy Chief of the Scientific Council on Nationality Problems of the Presidium of the USSR Academy of Sciences. Bagramov joined the debate in 1968 with a *Pravda* article challenging the basic assimilationist positions. Implicitly refuting the notion that the nationality problem had been resolved, Bagramov offered the alternative notion that socialism "creates a firm basis" for a correct solution to the nationalities problem. Focusing on the political aspects of nationality relations, he emphasized that CPSU nationality policy is characterized by the "most profound attention to the interests of nations and by unending efforts to achieve their complete flourishing and rapprochement."[14]

In contrast, the assimilationists maintained their emphasis on the primacy of economics. They attacked the moderate notion that nationalities were only at the stage of flourishing, claiming instead that the subsequent stage of rapprochement had already been attained. This was the summation of Soviet nationality development policies, they argued, and could not be treated separately without destroying the essential concept of national unity.[15]

This was not simply a debate between scholars about fine points of ideology. The discussions among these specialists reflected deep concerns over the course of nationality policy and clarified the various policy approaches available to the Soviet leadership. During the early years of his collective leadership with Kosygin, Brezhnev took a neutral position. He dropped "Soviet nation" from his ideological vocabulary and adopted a cautious tone in his speeches. In a 1967 speech in the Ukraine, for example, he said:

> The flourishing of socialist nations and their success in the building of communism will inevitably lead to their eventual rapprochement. Of course, the rapprochement of nations is a complex historical process; thoughtless haste, artificial delay, or aimless drift cannot be allowed to interfere. The interests of the individual socialist nation, the country's general interest, and the building of communism as a whole must be considered.[16]

For the most part, Brezhnev avoided the sensitive issue of rapprochement. In numerous speeches he focused instead on non-controversial historic and economic themes and called for unity to achieve common goals. In his report to the Twenty-third CPSU Congress, for example, he called for the further strengthening and expansion of relations among the nationalities, emphasizing the equality of all Soviet people:

> In solving any problem regarding the political, economic, and cultural development of our country, the party will continue to be concerned about the interests and national differences of each nation, and to foster in all Soviet people the spirit of inviolable faith in the brotherhood and friendship of the peoples of the USSR. This is the only correct nationality policy.[17]

Like his rhetoric, Brezhnev's policies were also moderate during this period. He abolished the Central Committee bureaus for Central Asia and the Transcaucasus republics and reestablished all-union and union-republic ministries. He explained the latter action at the Twenty-third Party Congress in terms of the problems created by Khrushchev's territorial system of industrial management. He asserted that this organization was inefficient and had led to the fragmentation of management generally and to the disruption of unified research and development work. As a result, new technology was introduced too slowly, overall production declined, and capital development funds were improperly utilized.[18] For the nationalities, the reestablishment of the ministries meant increased emphasis was to be placed on inter-republic economic ties and on the economic specialization of each republic. As noted by other prominent officials, these policies were designed to overcome the localism that arose under Khrushchev and to facilitate the exchange of cadres among republics to increase the rate of scientific development.[19] The emphasis on greater economic interaction among national republics tempered by increased control from Moscow remained consistent throughout the Brezhnev years. While initially it may have been designed to improve the overall Soviet economy, this policy also increased central control over the economies of the national republics. This laid the groundwork for the assimilationist direction of Brezhnev's policy in the period of developed socialism.

In cultural policy the situation was somewhat different. If Brezhnev and the new regime were ready to correct Khrushchev's economic policy, they were not as anxious to change policy in the areas of art, literature, and language. Rather than denouncing Khrushchev's statements on assimilation and Russification, the new regime chose to ignore them. In his speech to the Twenty-third Party Congress, Brezhnev avoided all but the most general statements on culture and omitted any reference to language or the role of the Russians in nationality development. As became clear several years later, Brezhnev had strong views on both subjects. But in 1966, while jockeying for the top leadership position, Brezhnev concealed his real views. This was the expedient and non-controversial course to take at a time when the leadership struggle was still intense.

Reflecting Brezhnev's caution, cultural policy during this period was moderate in nature. To stress the notion of the unity of nations, much publicity was given to a broad program of cultural exchanges between two or more nationalities. These exchanges took many forms including music, film, and drama festivals, joint theoretical seminars on scientific and artistic topics, lectures on culture and art, graphic art exhibits, and an exchange of translations of national literatures into Russian and the nationality languages. The most common form of cultural exchange was the *dekada*, a ten-day exhibit of one nationality in the republic of another. Week-long and one-day exhibits were also held. Such exchanges were perceived as useful not only for educating the Soviet citizenry on the achievements of other nationalities, but also in helping to overcome harmful "local tendencies" in cultural development. These exchanges also involved other socialist countries. Hungarian art, for example, was exhibited in the Ukraine, Mongolian art was displayed in Belorussia, and an exhibit on Czech culture was held in Armenia. Such techniques were designed to develop a spirit of internationalism while simultaneously emphasizing the historical distinctiveness of national cultures both within and outside the USSR.[20]

In keeping with the general trend of avoiding controversy, Brezhnev made no policy statements on language between 1965–1968, supporting neither the favoritism shown to Russian in the 1961 Party Program nor the free development of nationality languages alluded to by Khrushchev. But if Brezhnev was reluctant to speak out, others were not. The definition of Russian as "the common language of inter-nationality communication" provided in the Party Program was the target for many specialists who wanted to prevent Russian from becoming the official "state language" (*gosudarstvennyi iazyk*). Typical was the statement of Lithuanian newspaper editor G. O. Zimanas who supported the use of Russian as a common language to facilitate the mutual enrichment of the non-Russian nationalities, but warned that this did not mean that Russian occupied a "privileged position." Moreover, it did not free Russians from the obligation of learning nationality languages, especially if they lived and worked in non-Russian republics.[21] A. Snechkus, First Secretary of the Lithuanian Communist Party Central Committee, made essentially the same point, although he couched his argument in more subtle terms by pointing out the importance of national languages in the mutual enrichment of national minorities.[22]

Leaders in other national republics also expressed concern over the potential abuse of Russian. Kazakhstan First Secretary Kunaev pointed out that the importance of Russian did not diminish the significance of the nationality languages. In a strong statement in 1967, noteworthy for its lack of any reference to Russian, Kunaev asserted: "In the period of all-out communist construction, questions of language development have important meaning in inter-nationality education. All our nationality languages enjoy equal rights, and each has unlimited possibilities for independent development."[23] M. Georgadze, Secretary of the Presidium of the USSR Supreme Soviet, expressed similar views. He stongly rejected the notion that "any language" occupied a privileged position in the USSR. He also reminded *Pravda* readers of the statement in the 1961 Party Program allowing Soviet citizens to raise their children in their language of choice.[24]

After the acceptance of developed socialism into Soviet ideology, such anti-assimilationist views were no longer published. With Brezhnev's consolidation of power, language policy and other aspects of cultural policy underwent significant modifications.

Ideology and Nationality Policy in
Developed Socialism

The adoption of developed socialism into Soviet ideology signalled
a much more assimilationist nationality policy. Centralized direction of
the economies of the national republics was expanded as was the policy
of greater specialization among republics to enhance what was now
called a "unified economic complex." Culturally, the earlier emphasis
on Russification intensified, especially in terms of language policy.
Brezhnev's policy preferences were evident in both areas and his views
were widely publicized and incorporated into policy decisions. In 1972,
Brezhnev strengthened his hold over two of the most important national
republics—the Ukraine and Georgia—by replacing the first secretaries
of the party organization in each republic.[25] But despite this show of
strength, Brezhnev went too far. His assimilationist policies eventually
brought him into conflict with the consensus thinking among not only
republican leaders but also the leadership in Moscow, forcing him to
retreat from his policy positions to gain acceptance of a new Constitution,
as will be discussed below.

In terms of ideology, official acknowledgement that Soviet society had
entered the stage of developed socialism ended the ideological discussions
about the merging of nationalities. Nationality development was now
characterized by "flourishing" and "rapprochement," but not by "merging." The latter term virtually disappeared from Soviet writings after
1969, when even the most ardent assimilationists spoke only of "rapprochement." This change in terminology did not signify philosophical
agreement between the assimilationists and moderates, but seemed rather
to reflect a tacit agreement to avoid using the inflammatory concept. A
conscious effort to avoid "merging" can be seen in a *Kommunist* editorial
in late 1969, for example, where "flourishing" and "rapprochement" are
described as the only two stages of nationality development attainable
in the near future. The editorial continues with the statement: "But the
rapprochement of nations and their international unity cannot be considered merging. The elimination of all national differences is a lengthy
process, and is possible only after the complete victory and establishment
of communism throughout the world."[26]

A second feature of ideological writings was the coordinated effort
to contrast Soviet nationality policy with that practiced by the Chinese.
Consistent with the anti-Chinese undertone of developed socialism in
general, statements criticizing Chinese nationality policy began to appear
with increasing frequency at the end of the 1960s. Editorials pointed to
the "nationalism" and "chauvinism" of Mao's nationality policy and his
discrimination against minorities. Viewed as a gross violation of the

principles of international proletarianism, Chinese nationality policy was said to destroy all previous socialist achievements of the PRC and to have nothing in common with Marxism-Leninism.[27] This theme was repeated by moderates and assimilationists alike, indicating broad agreement on this aspect of nationality theory.[28]

But these developments could not conceal the fact that nationality policy had taken a new direction. The most significant indicator that this direction was towards assimilation was the reappearance of the "Soviet nation" beginning in 1968.[29] The rejuvenation of this concept was justified, according to Soviet ideologists, by the higher levels of economic interdependence and national unification inherent in a developed socialist society. However, it soon became clear that the concept "Soviet nation" was synonymous with the earlier term "merging" since it reflected the homogenization of society through economic and cultural means. It was also clear that the concept reflected the assimilationist policy preferences of Brezhnev himself.

Breaking his earlier silence on nationalities policy, Brezhnev in 1969 began to express views that were increasingly assimilationist. Significantly, he began to advocate faster rapprochement and pointed to the growing significance of the Russian language in nationality relations. In his June 1969 speech to the World Communist Conference, for example, he described the strengthening of the bond among Soviet nationalities as "our most important task." He added that the present stage of communist development required the "closer rapprochement" of all nationalities. In 1970, he defined flourishing and rapprochement as "the two tendencies in the development of nations under socialism." And, in his April 1970 speech on Lenin's birthday, he asserted that communist development "in our multinational country presupposes the consistent pursuit of a policy directed toward the complete rapprochement of nations."[30]

By the Twenty-fourth Party Congress in 1971, Brezhnev was articulating a position that was clearly assimilationist. In sharp contrast to the neutral statements he made at the Twenty-third Congress, Brezhnev in 1971 extolled the virtues of the "great Russian people," whose "religious energy, selflessness, and industriousness . . . have earned the sincere respect of all nations of our socialist motherland." Brezhnev reported that "new steps" were being taken by the party to encourage rapprochement.[31]

Brezhnev also discussed the Soviet nation at the Twenty-fourth Congress. Although he abbreviated the definition of Soviet nation—from "a new historic community of people of various nationalities having common characteristic traits" to "a new historic community of people"—the concept was otherwise identical to that introduced by Khrushchev at the Twenty-second CPSU Congress ten years earlier. Brezhnev asserted that the Soviet nation had been united by a common ideology and the common goal of communist construction. More significantly, he indirectly acknowledged Stalin's contribution to the creation of the Soviet nation by placing its origin "in the years of socialist construction," that is, prior to 1936.[32] By referring (though implicitly) to both Stalin and Khrushchev in his initial statement on the Soviet nation, Brezhnev strongly identified his views on the nationality issue with the assimilationist preferences of his predecessors.

Brezhnev's reference to the Soviet nation rekindled the debate among ideological specialists. The 1968 conference apparently concluded with general agreement to use Soviet nation in terms of historical developments, but not as a goal for current policy. Since Brezhnev appeared to be using the concept as a goal, specialists favoring a moderate approach to nationality policy perceived a worrisome change to official policy and began to speak out in the press. Their concerns were addressed by less-moderate specialists, resulting in a new round of debates on the subject. The chief protagonists this time were Eduard Bagramov and P. N. Fedoseev, who had been key figures in the debates over developed socialism and incentives policy. The debate on nationalities policy essentially repeated the lines of the arguments developed previously, but instead of focusing on merging and rapprochement the discussion now turned on the issues of economic centralization and the role of the Russian language. The key exchange took place in *Pravda* articles published by Bagramov in June 1972 and Fedoseev in October of that year. While both used the term Soviet nation, each employed a slightly different definition. Bagramov discussed at length the economic development of the USSR, describing it as a joint effort of all Soviet people. Elaborating on the economic interdependence of the national republics, he emphasized that progress was possible only through the mutual efforts of all republics. Bagramov asserted that in developed socialism no single republic could use its geographic or other advantages to make unilateral economic decisions. By implication, this included the Russian republic. On the sensitive question of the Russian language, Bagramov spoke of the "voluntary association" with the language on the part of Soviet nationalities. He pointed out, however, that this process was taking place along with the "free development and complete equality of rights" of the nationality languages, precluding any "rivalry" among languages.[33]

Fedoseev couched his rebuttal in terms of Marxist theory. Avoiding the question of economic centralization (since Bagramov's position was not far from official policy), he argued instead that there was no basis for separating the nationality issue from the whole complex of social issues facing Soviet society. Restating the assimilationist position that class relations are more important than ethnic ties, he asserted that the equalization of urban and rural living standards and the narrowing of the difference between physical and mental labor that were inherent features of developed socialism would soon eliminate class differences and allow for the unification of all nationalities. He included among the positive developments in this direction the "strengthening of the role of the Russian language." Fedoseev made no mention at all of other languages. Summarizing his views, Fedoseev said: "In Soviet society the social causes of nationalistic prejudices and nationalistic frictions have been uprooted and there can be no justification for their manifestation. They are in contradiction to the attitudes of friendship and cooperation established among peoples of all nations in our country."[34] In this view, which is either naively idealistic or serves to camouflage deeper assimilationist yearnings, the nationalities problem does not exist because of the social guarantees provided by the Soviet system.

The debate focusing on the role of Russian was picked up by other specialists who argued as intensely on this issue as they had earlier on the questions of merging and rapprochement. Predictably, those who had taken the assimilationist position in the earlier debate now strongly favored an enhanced role for Russian. Kaltakhchian, for example, pointed out that increasing the use of Russian was a fundamental element in the rapprochement of nationalities.[35] The moderates, in contrast, emphasized the equal importance of nationality languages. M. B. Mitin, an important specialist who was the former Chief Editor of *Voprosy Filosofii* and was in 1972 Chairman of the USSR Academy of Sciences Scientific Council on Problems of Foreign Ideological Trends, pointed out that growth of Russian did not present any obstacles to the development of nationality languages. Both could occur simultaneously. Addressing the broader issue of nationality autonomy, Mitin argued that the development of nationality cultures "in the native language" was the most obvious of several indicators that Soviet national republics were in fact autonomous.[36] Another moderate, Arnold Arnol'dov, leader of a Cultural Theory Group in the USSR Academy of Sciences Institute of Philosophy, used the example of the dual language situation in most Soviet republics to demonstrate that nationality cultures were flourishing in developed socialism.[37]

In his December 1972 speech on the fiftieth anniversary of the formation of the USSR, Brezhnev expressed strong preferences on both points covered in the debates. In terms of economic policy, he stressed the importance of the "unified economic organism" consisting of all Soviet republics. Not simply the sum of its parts, the Soviet national economy was in fact a single economy formed on the basis of common goals. In the area of cultural policy, Brezhnev weighed in heavily on the side of the assimilationists by highlighting the special role of Russian:

> The rapid growth of internationality ties and cooperation has led to a heightened significance of the Russian language, which has become the language of mutual communication of all nations and nationalities of the Soviet Union. And, comrades, the fact that Russian has become one of the generally recognized world languages has pleased us all.[38]

In speaking of the "heightened significance" of Russian, Brezhnev went well beyond the description in the 1961 Party Program of the "positive meaning" of the language. In another departure, he failed to even mention the nationality languages. By implicitly modifying the Party Program with such strong, pro-Russian statements, Brezhnev was advocating a Russification policy that exceeded that of Khrushchev, placing him out of the parameters of the post-Stalin consensus on nationality policy. In 1972, while Brezhnev was at the peak of his power and prestige, this did not prove costly. In later years, however, he was forced to retreat from his assimilationist stance to gain commitment to one of his most sought-after goals, as will be discussed below.

Policies towards the nationalities under developed socialism were consistent with the preferences outlined in Brezhnev's December 1972 speech. The basic thrust of cultural policy was toward linguistic Russification. Continuing a trend that had its origins in Khrushchev's regime, nationalities were brought under increasing pressure to learn Russian. After 1970, Russian became the predominant language of publication in most national republics and was especially widespread in technical literature.[39] One of the most important uses of Russian was in the training of army recruits, many of whom were forced to learn Russian in order to cope with sophisticated weapons and training manuals. The Soviet Army, in fact, became the "preferred instrument of national integration" in the words of one analyst. Brezhnev himself called the army the "school of internationalism"—a codeword for assimilation.[40]

Russian also played an increasing role in nationality education outside the army. For example, a series of annual conferences beginning in 1969 addressed methods of studying and teaching Russian to non-natives. The conference held in Tashkent in 1975 produced a detailed program designed to achieve overall linguistic Russification. This conference proposed changes to the teaching of Russian that included the establishment of preparatory classes for six-year olds, extending Russian to the elementary school systems where it was not already used, standardizing the number of hours devoted to the study of Russian, and others.[41]

The reports of some national republic first secretaries suggested that the response to this concerted emphasis on linguistic Russification was favorable, and many expressed strong pro-Russian language sentiments in the months leading up to the December 1972 anniversary celebrations. Kirghiz First Secretary Usubaliev described the knowledge of Russian as a "powerful weapon" of communications and a source of unity. He asserted that learning Russian was an "objective requirement" for all Soviet people. Similarly, Moldavian First Secretary Bodiul addressed the importance of Russian and especially the Russian alphabet for the development of the Moldavian language. A. Rasulov reported that Tadzhiks were "eagerly" studying Russian, while Uzbek First Secretary Rashidov stated that without the use of Russian as a common language Soviet nationalities would not be able to realize the "full-blooded cooperation" necessary for rapid socioeconomic development. Rashidov added that Russian served as the common language better than any other since it was the language of the "overwhelming majority" of Soviet people and most of all because it facilitated transmittal of new scientific and technical developments.[42] However, most of these comments were probably attempts to please Brezhnev by echoing his assimilationist goals. At least two republican secretaries—Kunaev of Kazakhstan and Snechkus of Lithuania—evidently disagreed with Brezhnev. Both men had previously cautioned against ignoring nationality languages. In 1972, both were silent on the language issue.[43] In failing to support Brezhnev's view of Russian, they signalled the existence of problems with Brezhnev's overall nationality policy. These problems were to surface more explicitly several years later when Brezhnev pushed for adoption of a new Constitution.

In economic policy, Brezhnev's preference for greater centralization was evident in three areas. These included increased centralization of economic planning and management, increased territorial specialization, and a preferential treatment of the RSFSR over the nationality republics. Policies were designed to strengthen control over the economies of the national republics, reversing the trend towards greater economic independence established by Khrushchev. The shift to centralized planning was signalled in a Central Committee resolution of February 1972. Supported by the Leninist concept of "democratic centralism," the main thrust of this policy was to reduce problems created by ministerial and territorial parochialism. Centralized planning gave Moscow greater flexibility in important decisions regarding the location of various types of enterprises and resource allocation. It also allowed for more intervention in planning at the republic level, where planning organs had been increasing their independence since 1966. The new emphasis on centralized planning was reflected especially in the plan for the location

of production facilities for 1971–1980. This measure was officially publicized as the key building block for greater cooperation and interaction
between the nationalities.[44]

The goal of increasing territorial specialization was implicit in Brezhnev's statement about a "unified economic organism." In principle, the
idea was to increase the specialization of each republic in the production
of both agricultural and industrial goods. Uzbekistan would produce
cotton for the entire country, the Ukraine would produce wheat, and
so forth. Economies of scale would thus be realized and greater cost
effectiveness achieved. More important from Moscow's perspective was
that no republic would be able to become economically independent.

In practice, however, this policy was not implemented very effectively.
In Kazakhstan, for instance, production enterprises had been built far
away from any natural resources and with insufficient regard for regional
needs. According to S. Baishev, a member of the Academy of Sciences
of the Kazakh SSR, this resulted in a number of "Potemkin enterprises"
throughout the republic. The larger problem was the mismatch between
Kazakhstan's economic potential and the output required by the central
authorities. Baishev pointed out that the Ninth Five-Year Plan tasked
Kazakhstan with producing coal, rolled steel, cement, grain, and meat.
What the republic really wanted, he said, was to become involved in
ferrous metallurgy, chemical production, and hydroelectric power. These
would require more intensive development of the republic's economy,
and were more in line with the natural resources Kazakhstan possessed
in abundance.[45]

Implicit in Baishev's description of the problems associated with
territorial specialization was the problem of unequal resource allocation
among national republics. "Resource allocation" in this context is distinct
from wage and income levels. These had become relatively equalized
under Brezhnev, partly because of income transfers to the economically
depressed national republics.[46] The main problem was rather one of
investment priorities. Although some shift away from the national republics in this regard may have been inevitable because of the dispro-
portionate share of investment money they had received in the past,
this does not explain the magnitude of the shift that occurred under
Brezhnev. Brezhnev's preference for the Russian republic derived from
his goal of developing Siberia to fuel expansion of the Soviet economy
and to serve the export market. This policy had several manifestations,
including expansion of the Baikal-Amur Mainline Railroad and the creation
of Territorial Production Complexes, almost all of which were in the
RSFSR. Both led to an upsurge in resource reallocation that provided
economic advantage for the RSFSR over the national republics. While
regional investment priorities themselves were not necessarily the result

of his overall assimilationist position, when combined with similiar policies of unequal distribution in other socioeconomic categories such as the development of medical facilities and schools, a pattern of investment preference for the Russian republic over those of the nationalities stands out.[47]

Taken together, Brezhnev's statements and actions on the nationalities provide striking evidence of his Russifying, assimilationist views. Like Khrushchev before him, Brezhnev ignored the ideological precepts calling for equality among all Soviet nationalities and advocated instead a policy of greater central control. Although his views may have found resonance of the predominantly Russian and Slavic leadership of the Politburo and Central Committee, Brezhnev did begin to encounter resistance among the national republics and important academic specialists, which soon led to a tactical retreat from some of his stronger pro-Russian positions.

Brezhnev's retreat can be seen in his public statements after 1972. Whereas between 1967–1972 he frequently mentioned the Russian people or Russian language in his remarks on the nationality question, by 1973 he had begun to focus more on the accomplishments of the nationalities in Soviet historical and economic development, echoing his neutral statements in the years immediately following his assumption of power. In August 1973, for example, Brezhnev took pains to clarify that he did not favor the "merging" of nationalities, but rather sought the further development of nationality culture:

Speaking of the new historical community of people, we don't at all believe that nationality differences are disappearing in the Soviet Union, much less that the merging of nations has occurred. All nations and nationalities populating the Soviet Union retain their individuality, the traits of their national character, their language, and their best traditions. They have at their disposal all possibilities to attain even more flourishing of their national cultures.[48]

In his speech to the Twenty-fifth Party Congress, Brezhnev hardly mentioned the nationalities at all, referring instead to the "rapprochement of socialist countries."[49] Moreover, Brezhnev dropped all reference to the Russian language and Russian people. Having not mentioned these subjects in any speech in 1974–1975, he addressed neither the special role of the Russian people nor the significance of the Russian language in his speech to the party congress. This contrasted dramatically with his statements at the Twenty-fourth Party Congress five years earlier. He also maintained a neutral position on the role of Russian at the October 1976 plenum of the Central Committee, where he restricted his remarks on the nationalities to a description of the benefits to be derived by the national republics from the 1976–1980 five-year plan.[50]

Why this retreat? Did Brezhnev have a change of heart? Did he actually adopt the idealistic concept of the Soviet nation? Did he change speechwriters? Any of these are plausible, but cannot be documented. A reason that can be reasonably documented was the issue of federalism. Available evidence suggests that from the mid-1960s to the mid-1970s, federalism was the topic of intense discussion among political leaders and academic specialists. Taken together with the other problems created by Brezhnev's assimilationist views, problems over the question of federalism prolonged acceptance of a new Soviet Constitution, one that would codify the socioeconomic changes of developed socialism and secure Brezhnev's place in history.

Nationality Policy and the 1977 Constitution

A new Constitution was begun under Khrushchev in 1962. The motivation for this revision was to codify changes that had taken place in Soviet society since the 1936 Stalin Constitution. However, the new document was left unfinished when Khrushchev was removed from power. The new regime did not resume work on the project immediately, in part because of efforts to distance itself from Khrushchev, but also because an appropriate ideological formula had not yet been developed. Clearly this could not be the "Constitution of the all-out building of communism" since this would have emphasized the continuity between the two regimes. Thus, because Soviet constitutions have traditionally signalled attainment of a new stage of development, there was little chance a new Constitution could have been adopted until developed socialism became an official part of Soviet ideology.[51]

Brezhnev first called for a new Constitution in his December 1972 speech on the fiftieth anniversary of the USSR. Stressing the need for a Constitution of developed socialism, he emphasized that the Soviet Union had been the first country to attain socialism and the first to take practical steps towards the attainment of communism.[52] Although Brezhnev implied the document would be ready for approval by the 1976 Party Congress, the new Constitution was in fact not published until 1977. The gap of almost five years between Brezhnev's speech and final acceptance of the Constitution is a curiosity of his regime. Since he was at the height of his power during these years and since most of the work on the new document had presumably been completed, it seems reasonable that Brezhnev could have simply forced the issue to have the new Constitution adopted before 1977, at least by the Twenty-fifth CPSU Congress. It is possible, as Robert Sharlet has suggested, that the delay was the result of the lower overall priority placed on this project by Brezhnev himself, although Sharlet also points out that the drafting process was well underway already in the late 1960s.[53] Available evidence, however, suggests that a more likely cause for the delay was the lack of consensus on the nationalities issue.

Evidence for this can be seen in the debate over linguistic Russification. This debate clearly indicated that Brezhnev's assimilationist tendencies raised hackles. Such opposition was also evident among republican party secretaries (who no longer mentioned the role of Russian after their 1972 anniversary speeches), and in nationality demonstrations against the trend towards Russification in language policy.[54] Perhaps most significant was the lack of support from party ideology chief Suslov.[55] But the main problem was evidently lack of agreement on the fundamental question of federalism, for many specialists and officials interpreted Brezhnev's statements on nationality policy as containing an implicit threat to the federal structure of the USSR.

One high-level Soviet official implied the existence of such disagreement in 1967 when he included the issue of "the national sovereignty of the Soviet state" among the key "constitutional problems" addressed the previous year by the USSR Academy of Sciences.[56] But this issue languished until Brezhnev's 1972 speech, which sparked a renewal of the debate over federalism that had occurred under Khrushchev. In the earlier debate, those who supported abolishing the federal structure argued that there was no real need for constitutional guarantees on the role of the national republics and that elimination of republic boundaries was a prerequisite for the "withering of the state" predicted by Lenin. Those supporting Soviet federalism, in contrast, emphasized the political desirability of maintaining the federal structure which had proved to be a reliable and convenient way of administering the broad expanse of Soviet territory.[57]

The discussions over federalism in the 1970s were not as visible as the earlier debate. This may have been due to the fact that Brezhnev himself did not mention federalism in any speech prior to 1977. But enough evidence exists to confirm that federalism was indeed a vital issue. In November 1972, for example, just prior to Brezhnev's fiftieth anniversary speech, Professor A. I. Lepeshkin published an article in which he advocated the continued autonomy of the national republics in decisions regarding purely nationality or regional matters.[58] In 1973, V. S. Shevtsov described the concept of national sovereignty as being inseparable from that of national equality. He pointed out that the sovereignty of each nation is essential in determining the socioeconomic, political, and state structure of society.[59] While not directly attacking Brezhnev, who did not publicly endorse the elimination of the federal structure even in his strongest assimilationist statements of 1971–1972, these specialists did imply their disagreement with the assimilationist tone of Brezhnev's speeches. Other specialists were more open about their feelings. Robert Sharlet has described discussions with several Soviets who told of efforts to abolish the federal structure entirely during early deliberations on the new Constitution.[60]

In 1975, when the internal debate over federalism had probably reached its peak, Professor Lepeshkin published another article in which he provided several reasons for preserving the federal structure. He pointed to the further economic integration of national republics, the control of nationality "feelings" (i.e. hostility), and the continued development of nationality languages. He also cited the main trends of Soviet federalism under developed socialism. These included continued economic integration, the improvement of national unity, improvement in the administration between state and republican governments, and further democratization. Lepeshkin thus advocated both increased autonomy and increased centralization in nationality policy. His "dialectical" formulation may have in fact been the essence of a Leninist compromise on the question of federalism: the federal structure would be maintained but not at the expense of central control over all major policy areas.[61]

Brezhnev finally addressed federalism in his May 1977 speech announcing completion of the draft Constitution. Attempting to calm any fears that he favored eliminating national boundaries, he assured the Central Committee that "the basic characteristics of the federal structure have completely justified themselves," adding that there was no need to modify the existing federal system.[62] The fact that he made this statement at the same time the draft of the Constitution was submitted for nationwide referendum (and against the background of the earlier specialist discussions on federalism) suggest that Brezhnev had to compromise on this issue or risk the humiliating possibility that a new Constitution would not be adopted.

In his October 1977 Constitution speech, Brezhnev criticized "some comrades" for their suggestions about limiting the sovereignty of the national republics:

> In the USSR, as is known, a new historical community of people has been formed—the Soviet nation. Some comrades—very few, to be sure—came to incorrect conclusions about this. They have suggested including in the Constitution the concept of a unified Soviet nation (*natsiia*), to liquidate the union and autonomous republics or to sharply limit the sovereignty of the union republics by rescinding their right to secede from the USSR or to conduct foreign relations.[63]

For Brezhnev to include so much detail about the debate over federalism is unusual, and adds support to the interpretation that federalism was the main stumbling block to acceptance of the Constitution. Clearly the nationality "rights" Brezhnev mentioned are meaningless: no Soviet republic would be allowed to secede from the USSR or to conduct significant foreign relations on its own. But the tone of the General Secretary's remarks, together with other conciliatory remarks in his speech,[64] indicate the pains he took to express his support of federalism and equal rights among the republics. A compromise had to be reached on this issue for the Constitution to be adopted.

Brezhnev may have used his Constitution speech as a form of self-criticism. The highly assimilationist nature of his remarks between 1967–1972 suggest that Brezhnev himself was one of the "comrades" favoring dissolution of the federal state structure. The resulting compromise suggests that the leadership consensus on the nationality question had to be much broader than on other questions addressed in this study. Policy could not be made by the Russians in the Politburo or the Slavs in the Central Committee. Rather it had to be worked out in academic and party institutes in Moscow and elsewhere and agreed to by nationality leaders as well as by the party leadership. Brezhnev, even at the height of his power, could not force his policy preferences on the leadership on this key question. The fact that Brezhnev recognized this and quickly recanted attests to his skill as a politician. These events tend to confirm the hypothesis that Brezhnev ruled by consensus. On many issues, such as incentives policy, he directed the consensus along a middle path between extreme policy options. In the case of the nationality issue, however, Brezhnev tested his influence over that consensus, and lost.

In the broadest sense, this suggests that a new definition of power had emerged in Soviet politics. Whereas Stalin and Khrushchev (to a lesser extent) had been able to impose their nationality preferences, Brezhnev was stopped soon after he strayed from the consensus position. This was certainly true on the issue of linguistic assimilation and probably on the question of federalism as well. It was less true on the economics aspects of the nationality issue.[65] The final formulation of nationalities policy in developed socialism, therefore, was essentially a return to the Leninist position of maintaining the fiction of national autonomy while ensuring strong central control. Thus, although Brezhnev suffered a setback on this issue, he gained ground in the end because he was able to justify the nationalities policy of developed socialism as a product of the "Leninist course" he hoped would be his legacy. Brezhnev left for his successors the more difficult problem of reconciling nationality desires for real autonomy with the regime's need for centralized control.

Notes

1. This description is a composite taken from many Soviet definitions of the Soviet nation. See, for example, M. P. Kim, et al., eds., *Sovetskii Narod—Novaia Istoricheskaia Obshchnost' Liudei* (Moscow: Nauka, 1975). The word *"narod"* presents a translation problem because it also can mean "people." In many cases this is the correct translation, e.g. "The Soviet people welcomed the treaty on intermediate and short-range missiles signed by M. S. Gorbachev and U.S. President Ronald Reagan." But in the context of nationality relations, *"narod"* is synonymous with the word *"natsiia"* (nation), and the phrase *"sovetskii narod"* in this case is properly translated "Soviet nation."

2. "Manifesto of the Communist Party," in *The Marx-Engels Reader*, second edition, ed. Robert C. Tucker (New York: W. W. Norton & Company, 1978), pp. 483–484. For a comprehensive discussion of the views of Marx and Engels, see Walker Connor, *The National Question in Marxist-Leninist Theory and Strategy* (Princeton: Princeton University Press, 1984), pp. 5–27.

3. Much has been written on Lenin's nationality policy. These paragraphs draw from the analysis in: Richard Pipes, *The Formation of the Soviet Union*, rev. ed. (New York: Athenum), pp. 34–49; Robert Conquest, *Soviet Nationalities Policy in Practice* (London: The Bodley Head, 1967), pp. 16–20, and Merle Fainsod, *How Russia is Ruled*, rev. ed. (Cambridge, Massachusetts: Harvard University Press, 1963), pp. 355–364. Also see: Connor, *The National Question*, pp. 28–66; Hélène Carrère d'Encausse, *Decline of an Empire* (New York: Harper Colophon Books, 1981), chapter 1; Hans Kohn, "Soviet Communism and Nationalism: Three States of a Historical Development," in Edward Allworth, ed., *Soviet Nationality Problems* (New York: Columbia University Press, 1971), pp. 43–71; and George Liber, "Language, Literacy, and Book Publishing in the Ukrainian SSR, 1923–28," *Slavic Review* 41 (Winter 1982), pp. 673–685.

4. Hélène Carrère d'Encausse, "Party and Federation in the USSR: The Problem of the Nationalities and Power in the USSR," *Government and Opposition* 13 (Spring 1978), pp. 139–40, and d'Encausse, *Decline of an Empire*, pp. 28–29. On the imposition of Cyrillic on the Arabic-speaking nationalities, see Wasyl Shimoniak, "Russian Linguistic Policies Toward The Uzbek People and Other Muslims of the USSR," *Ukrainian Quarterly* 24 (March 1968), pp. 361–368, and Kohn, "Soviet Communism and Nationalism," pp. 54–61.

5. On the deportation of nationalities, see Conquest, *Soviet Nationalities Policy*, pp. 102–108, Conquest, *Soviet Deportation of Nationalities* (London: Bodley Head, 1970), and d'Encausse, *Decline of an Empire*, pp. 31–34.

6. For excellent discussions of Soviet language policy, see d'Encausse, *Decline of an Empire*, pp. 29 and 33–36, and Connor, *The National Question*, pp. 254–263. For discussions of Marr, see Yaroslav Bilinsky, *The Second Soviet Republic: The Ukraine After World War II* (New Brunswick, New Jersey: Rutgers University Press, 1964), pp. 144–145, and Donald M. Treadgold, *Twentieth Century Russia*, 2nd ed. (Chicago: Rand McNally & Company, 1969), pp. 453–454. For a useful comparison of tsarist and Soviet nationality policy, see Samuel P. Oliner, "The Non-Russian Peoples in the USSR: An Unsolved Problem," *Ukrainian Quarterly* 32 (Autumn 1976), pp. 261–285.

7. d'Encausse, *Decline of an Empire*, pp. 38–40. On the Sovnarkhoz reforms, see Alec Nove, *The Soviet Economic System* (London: George Allen & Unwin), pp. 72–77 and 92–95. The three laws adopted in 1957 allowed the national republics to issue their own laws on the judicial system and judicial procedures, granted them the right to form krais and oblasts, and transferred administration of transportation within republic boundaries to the national republics. See Samuel Bloembergen, "The Union Republics: How Much Autonomy?" *Problems of Communism* 16 (September-October 1967), p. 34.

8. Khrushchev's assimilationist approach first became evident in a speech in March 1959. See the discussion in Elliot R. Goodman, "Nationalities, Nations, and the Soviet World State: Khrushchev's Ambitions and Frustrations," *Orbis* 9 (September 1965), pp. 462–463.

9. *Programma Kommunisticheskoi Partii Sovetskogo Soiuza* in *XXII S"ezd Kommunisticheskoi Partii Sovetskogo Soiuza: Stenograficheskii Otchet* (Moscow: Politicheskaia Literatura, 1961), 3 vols. Relevant passages are: rapprochement, vol. 3, pp. 312–313; Russian language, culture, people, vol. 3, pp. 239 and 314; and boundaries, vol. 3, p. 312. For a discussion of nationality policy and the 1961 Party Program, see Alfred D. Low, "Soviet Nationality Policy and the New Program of the Communist Party of the Soviet Union," *Russian Review* 22 (1963), pp. 3–29.

10. *XXII S"ezd KPSS*, vol. 1, pp. 216–217.

11. Ibid., p. 153.

12. This debate was identified by Grey Hodnett in his excellent article, "What's in a Nation," *Problems of Communism* 16 (September-October 1967), pp. 2–15.

13. M. S. Dzhunusov, "Teoriia i Praktika Razvitiia Sostialisticheskikh Natsional'nykh Otnoshenii," *Voprosy Filosofii*, 9/1967, pp. 26–28.

14. *Pravda*, 7 June 1968, pp. 2–3.

15. See, for example, P. M. Rogachev and M. A. Sverdlin, "O Preobladaiushchei Tendentsii Razvitiia Natsii v Sovetskoi Obshchnosti," *Voprosy Filosofii*, 2/1969, pp. 26–31.

16. L. I. Brezhnev, *Leninskim Kursom*, (Moscow: Politicheskaia Literatura, 1970–1981), vol. 2, pp. 163–164.

17. Ibid., vol. 1, p. 364. See also Brezhnev's remarks in his speeches on the fortieth anniversary of the Uzbek SSR (20 November 1964), on the twentieth anniversary of the defeat of the Germans (8 May 1965), and on the presentation of the Order of Lenin to the Georgian republic. All may be found in Brezhnev, *Leninskim Kursom*, vol. 1: pp. 41–45; 137; and 465–467, respectively.

18. Ibid., vol. 1, pp. 306–308.

19. See, for example, the speech of Ia. Peive, Chairman of the Soviet of Nationalities of the USSR Supreme Soviet in *Pravda*, 17 July 1965, p. 2. Also see N. Baibakov, "Novyi Ehtap Razvitiia Ehkonomiki SSSR," *Kommunist*, 7/1966, especially pp. 33–34.

20. *Literaturnaia Gazeta*, 14 January 1965. See also *Pravda*, 25 September and 7 October 1966 and 10 January 1970 for discussions of nationality exhibits. For examples of a republican newspaper devoting an issue to the culture of another nationality, see *Bakchinskii Rabochii*, 24 January and 18 February 1967.

21. G. O. Zimanas, "O Sushchnosti Protsessa Sblizheniia Sotsialisticheskikh Natsii," *Voprosy Filosofii*, 7/1966, p. 9.

22. A. Snechkus, "Vospitanie Sovetskikh Liudei v Dukhe Proletarskogo Internationalizma," *Kommunist*, 12/1967, p. 20.

23. *Pravda*, 6 September 1967, pp. 2–3. Kunaev expressed an equally strong view several years later, warning against granting Russian too great a role at the expense of nationality languages. See his article in *Pravda*, 1 April 1970, pp. 2–3.

24. *Pravda*, 21 October 1967, pp. 2–3.

25. The replacement of Shelest by Shcherbitskii in the Ukraine was part of an overall crackdown on Ukrainian nationalism. Shelest was removed for sympathizing with the nationalists. In Georgia, Eduard Shevardnadze (Gorbachev's Foreign Minister) replaced V. P. Mzhavanadze, who was charged with allowing widespread corruption. See the discussion in d'Encausse, *Decline of an Empire*, pp. 147–152.

26. *Kommunist*, 13/1969, p. 10.

27. Ibid., p. 12. Also see L. M. Gudoshnikov, "Velikoderzhavnyi Shovinizm Rukovodstva KNR v Voprosakh Natsional'no-Gosudarstvennogo Stroitel'stva," *Sovetskoe Gosudarstvo i Pravo*, 9/1973, pp. 92–100.

28. Bagramov, for example, denounced Mao's policy of assimilating diverse groups by using Han Chinese customs and traditions. In Bagramov's view, this was forcing the merging of nationalities, a process that violated the spirit of socialism. See his article in *Pravda*, 3 August 1973, pp. 2–3.

29. The first sign that Soviet nation had been accepted as an ideological concept was a conference held in October 1968 in which moderates and assimilationists agreed that the concept "reflects the essence of the new international community formed as a result of the Great October Revolution and the development of socialist society in our country." See the report on the conference by V. S. Markov in *Voprosy Filosofii*, 3/1969, pp. 156–158. Consensus on this use of the term was reflected in editorials in the central press. *Kommunist*, for example, in a 1969 editorial described the Soviet nation as a "wonderful expression of the international unity and equality of Soviet socialist nations and nationalities." See *Kommunist* 13/1969, p. 10.

30. Brezhnev, *Leninskim Kursom*, vol. 2, pp. 409, 536, and 576, respectively.

31. Brezhnev, *Leninskim Kursom*, vol. 3, p. 279. For additional examples, see Brezhnev's speech to his Bauman election district in 1971 and his 1972 speech on the fiftieth anniversary of the USSR. They are in *Leninskim Kursom*, vol. 3, p. 384, and vol. 4, p. 51.

32. Brezhnev, *Leninskim Kursom*, vol. 3, p. 279.

33. *Pravda*, 22 June 1972. For additional articles by Bagramov, see *Pravda*, 16 July 1971, 3 August 1973, and 14 February 1975. See also his article, "Leninism i Nekotorye Aspekty Natsional'nogo Voprosa v Sovremennuiu Ehpokhu," *Voprosy Filosofii*, 3/1970, pp. 17–29.

34. *Pravda*, 20 October 1972. See also ibid., 15 November 1972.

35. *Pravda*, 17 March 1972, pp. 2–3.

36. M. B. Mitin, "Leninskie Printsipy Stroitel'stva Mnogonatsional'nogo Sovetskogo Sotsialisticheskogo Gosudarstva," *Voprosy Filosofii*, 11/1972, pp. 9–10.

37. *Pravda,* 16 March 1973, pp. 2–3.

38. Brezhnev, *Leninskim Kursom,* vol. 4, p. 60. His statement on the "unified economic organism" is in ibid., p. 58.

39. For discussions of these trends, see: Bohdan Krawciw, "Progressive Russification of the Ukrainian SSR," *Ukrainian Quarterly* 29 (Summer 1973), pp. 140–145; Thomas Venclova, "Two Russian Sub-languages and Russian Ethnic Identity," in Edward Allworth, ed., *Ethnic Russia in the USSR* (New York: Pergamon Press, 1980), pp. 249–259; and Joan T. Weingard, "Language and Literature in Estonia: Kulturpolitik or Natural Evolution?," in Ralph S. Clem, ed., *The Soviet West: Interplay Between Nationality and Social Organization* (New York: Praeger Publishers, 1975), pp. 8–29.

40. d'Encausse, *Decline of an Empire,* p. 159. Brezhnev's remark is from *Leninskim Kursom,* vol. 4, p. 61. For additional studies on the integrative effect of the Soviet army, see Ann Sheehy, "Language Problems in the Soviet Armed Forces," *Radio Liberty Research Bulletin* 196/78, September 1978; Teresa Rakowska-Harmstone, "The Soviet Army as the Instrument of National Integration," in John Erickson and E. J. Feuchtwanger, eds., *Soviet Military Power and Performance* (Hamden, Connecticut: The Shoe String Press, 1979), pp. 129–154; and Leon Goure, *The Military Indoctrination of Soviet Youth* (New York: National Strategy Information Center, 1973).

41. Roman Solchanyk, "Russian Language and Soviet Politics," *Soviet Studies* 34 (January 1982), p. 25.

42. See, respectively, *Pravda,* 11 and 22 August, 23 September, and 6 October 1972.

43. See the articles by Kunaev in *Pravda,* 30 June 1972, and Snechkus in ibid., 8 September 1972.

44. For Soviet discussions of centralized planning concerning the national republics, see: Kim, et al., eds., *Sovetskii Narod* (Moscow: Nauka, 1975), pp. 279–280; and G. E. Glezerman and O. Reingol'd, eds., *Razvitoe Sotsialisticheskoe Obshchestvo,* 3rd ed., (Moscow: Mysl'), 1979, pp. 107–108.

45. S. Baishev, "S Pozitsii Ehkonomicheskoi Tselesoobraznosti," *Pravda,* 5 March 1971.

46. Martin C. Spechler, "Regional Developments in the USSR, 1958-1978," in U.S. Congress, Joint Economic Committee, *Soviet Economy in a Time of Change* (Washington: Government Printing Office, 1979), vol. 1, p. 145.

47. Sources used for this paragraph were: Vsevolod Holubnychy, "Spatial Efficiency in the Soviet Economy," in V. N. Bandera and Z. L. Melnyk, *The Soviet Economy in Regional Perspective* (New York: Praeger, 1971), p. 9; James W. Gillula, "The Economic Interdependence of the Soviet Republics," in *Soviet Economy in a Time of Change,* vol. 1, pp. 621–626; David S. Kamerling, "The Role of the Territorial Production Complexes in Soviet Economic Policy," in U.S. Congress, Joint Economic Committee, *Soviet Economy in the 1980s: Problems and Prospects* (Washington: Government Printing Office, 1982), vol. 1, pp. 242–265; Peter Zwick, "Intrasystem Inequality and the Symmetry of Socioeconomic Development in the USSR" *Comparative Politics* 8 (July 1976), p. 505; and Victor L. Mote, "Regional Planning: The BAM and the Pyramids of Power" in *Gorbachev's*

Economic Plans, U.S. Congress, Joint Economic Committee (Washington: Government Printing Office, 1987), pp. 369–370.

48. Brezhnev, *Leninskim Kursom,* vol. 4, p. 243.

49. Ibid., vol. 5, p. 453.

50. Ibid., vol. 6, p. 142.

51. On the connection between Soviet constitutions and stages of ideological and political development, see: Iu. A. Poliakov, ed., *Konstitutsiia Razvitogo Sotsializma* (Moscow: Nauka, 1981), p. 8; V. F. Kotok and N. P. Farberov, "Konstitutsiia SSSR—Razvivaiushchiisia Osnovnoi Zakon Obshchestva i Gosudarstva," *Sovetskoe Gosudarstvo i Pravo,* 6/1973, p. 3; and Robert Sharlet, *The New Soviet Constitution of 1977* (Brunswick, Ohio: King's Court Communications, Inc., 1978), p. 4.

52. Brezhnev, *Leninskim Kursom,* vol. 4, pp. 97–98. Brezhnev failed to mention that East Germany and Bulgaria had already adopted constitutions of developed socialism, in 1968 and 1971, respectively. See *Pravda,* 2 February 1968, p. 3 for a report on the East German constitution. On the Bulgarian document, see Boris Belchev, "Novaia Konstitutsiia i Razvitie Demokratii v Bolgarii," *Problemy Mira i Sotsializma,* 2/1972, pp. 38–42.

53. Sharlet, *The New Soviet Constitution of 1977,* p. 5.

54. The protests at the 1976 Georgian Writers' Congress, for example, were caused by directives from Moscow implying greater Russification of nationality education. See J. W. R. Parsons, "National Integration in Soviet Georgia," *Soviet Studies* 34 (October 1982), p. 557. Similar demonstrations continued after the new constitution was adopted following changes in the constitutional status of the native languages. See the *International Herald Tribune,* 18 April 1978 and 5 May 1978, and the *New York Times,* 25 April 1978 for a discussion of these demonstrations. They are also analyzed in Connor, *The National Question,* p. 263. Connor also makes the useful point that the pressure for linguistic assimilation varies according to the extent that nationalities have been accorded political recognition through creation of a titular republic. Five of the nationalities (the three Baltic republics, Armenia, and Georgia) with a strongly developed sense of national cohesiveness have been subjected to the least pressure to switch to Russian. See ibid., pp. 259–260.

55. Suslov did not address nationality policy in a substantive way in any speeches between 1971-1973. See M. A. Suslov, *Na Putiakh Stroitel'stva Kommunizma* (Moscow: Politicheskaia Literatura, 1977), vol. 2, pp. 164–376. Suslov did support the notion of Russian primacy, but only in an historical context. See ibid., p. 325.

56. See Ia. V. Peive's article in *Vestnik Akademii Nauk,* 3/1967, p. 152. Peive was the Chairman of the Soviet of Nationalities, USSR Supreme Soviet, and a member of the CPSU Central Committee.

57. See the comprehensive discussion in Grey Hodnett, "The Debate Over Soviet Federalism" *Soviet Studies* 18 (April 1967), pp. 458–481.

58. A. I. Lepeshkin, "Osnovnye Printsipy Sotsialisticheskoi Avtonomii i ikh Osushchestvlenie v SSSR," *Sovetskoe Gosudarstvo i Pravo,* 11/1972, pp. 18–25.

59. V. S. Shevtsov, "Natsional'nyi Suverenitet: Soderzhanie i Politiko-Pravovoe Znachenie," *Sovetskoe Gosudarstvo i Pravo,* 12/1973, p. 13.

60. Robert Sharlet, "De-Stalinization and Soviet Constitutionalism," in Stephen F. Cohen, et al., eds., *The Soviet Union Since Stalin*, p. 96. Jeremy Azrael asserts that the Brezhnev leadership had considered abolishing national republican boundaries, only to relent in the final draft of the constitution because of their growing recognition of nationality hostility on this subject. See Jeremy Azrael, "The 'Nationality Problem' in the USSR: Domestic Pressures and Foreign Policy Constraints," in Seweryn Bialer, *The Domestic Context of Soviet Foreign Policy* (Boulder, Colorado: Westview Press, 1981).

61. A. I. Lepeshkin, "Sovetskii Federalizm v Period Razvitogo Sotsializma," *Sovetskoe Gosudarstvo i Pravo*, 8/1975, pp. 3–13.

62. Brezhnev, *Leninskim Kursom*, vol. 6., pp. 382–383.

63. Brezhnev, *Leninskim Kursom*, vol. 6, p. 525.

64. On the subject of rapprochement, for instance, Brezhnev had this to say: "The friendship of the Soviet peoples is inviolable. In the process of communist development their rapprochement and the mutual enrichment of their spiritual lives are proceeding without interruption. But we would start down a dangerous path if we began to artificially force this objective process of rapprochement. V. I. Lenin warned against this persistently and we will not deviate from his guidance." Brezhnev, *Leninskim Kursom*, vol. 6, p. 525.

65. The most authoritative statements on economic relations among the nationalities in developed socialism echo the line presented in Brezhnev's December 1972 speech and call for "deepening the specialization and cooperation" among republics to form a "unified economic mechanism." See Kim, et al., eds., *Sovetskii Narod*, pp. 370–371.

5

Withering of the State:
The Role of Political Participation

The notion of mobilized political participation by ordinary citizens in the administration of state affairs has been a key component of Soviet ideology since Lenin.[1] One of the primary means for transforming bourgeois society into communism, political participation has been most often discussed in connection with its ideological cousin, the withering of the state. In theory, the apparatus of state government should lose significance as more and more citizens become involved in the administration of daily affairs. Under communism, there would thus be no need for a state apparatus, and the political system would become one of "communist self-government." Brezhnev described this process in his 1977 Constitution speech:

> Millions of Soviet citizens are more and more actively participating in the work of the organs of power, in people's control committees, in the management of production and distribution, in the making of social and cultural policy, and in the administration of justice. In a word, with the development of socialist democracy, our state system is gradually changing into one of communist, public self-government.[2]

As with other issues addressed in this book, however, the reality of political participation under Brezhnev and other leaders did not coincide with the theoretical description. The promise of Leninist political systems for increasing participation of the masses in the political process has never been realized. After gaining power, communist leaders in the Soviet Union and elsewhere have typically established highly structured forms of participation in which many ordinary citizens were involved, but had little if any impact on the making of policy. Moreover, genuine participation is unlikely in these systems because of the central role played by the Communist Party. The party decides how the citizenry participates and determines the limits of such participation. Theory, which calls for greater participation in the government of a communist state, is therefore in conflict with reality, in which the party dominates the political system. Zbigniew Brzezinski suggests that this conflict, together with the party's inability to provide meaningful participation in general, may be the Achilles' heel of communist states.[3]

Early in Brezhnev's regime, there was an attempt to mobilize an increasing number of citizens into the soviets and other organs of state government. This was both in reaction to the more autonomous forms of participation advocated by Khrushchev and an element of the 1965 economic reforms. But as the failure of the reforms became evident in the late 1960s, a new definition of participation emerged. This focused on the essential role of the CPSU in controlling the participation process. This policy—which clearly reflected Brezhnev's own views—was eventually incorporated into developed socialism. In contrast to the nationalities issue, this was one area where Brezhnev's values and policy agenda for change were fully incorporated into the official ideology.

Background

Lenin's theory on political participation was derived from the works of Marx and Engels, which described the class basis of the state apparatus that had been developed to protect the interests of the bourgeoisie. In their view, the state was destined to disappear under communism as class differences were abolished. In his early writings, Lenin agreed that the state would be unnecessary under communism. He therefore advocated increasingly greater participation of all citizens in the administration of the state after the overthrow of the bourgeoisie. Later, however, Lenin revised this formulation by stressing the need for centralized control over the political system through the "dictatorship of the proletariat." Described most thoroughly in *State and Revolution*, the replacement of the existing bourgeois state by a dictatorship of the proletariat was to be the first step in the development of socialism. In Lenin's terms, the dictatorship of the proletariat was to be a "special apparatus, a special machine for the suppression of the minority of exploiters by the majority of the wage slaves of yesterday." Although he never mentioned the Communist Party in *State and Revolution*, Lenin's definition of the dictatorship of the proletariat was synonymous with his conception of the party.

Lenin's model of an administrative apparatus for a communist state was also derived from Marx, particularly from Marx's essay "Civil War in France." The principles of worker participation and administration set forth in this essay became the foundation of Lenin's view about the nature of the state under communism. Lenin believed that Soviet citizens

would gradually become more deeply involved in performing administrative functions during the period that the dictatorship of the proletariat
provided a stable environment for the development of the socialist
economy. Initially this would be "primitive democracy," but eventually
it would evolve into the true democracy characteristic of the higher stage
of communism. The state apparatus that existed during the dictatorship
of the proletariat would thus be replaced in communist society by the
citizenry itself.

After the Bolshevik seizure of power, Lenin modified his views on
the nature of the state. Acknowledging that some form of apparatus
must remain to administer the economy and related functions, he began
in his later writings to direct greater attention to problems of government.
While he never rejected participation by the broad masses, he emphasized
the need for greater efficiency through centralized control. This was
evident in the extension of Bolshevik control over the soviets, which
had originated in and grown out of the 1905 and 1917 revolutions
independent of Bolshevik influence. Using these organizations as a symbol
of Bolshevik popularity after the October Revolution, Lenin initially
gained party dominance over the soviets by relying on Bolsheviks who
were members. He subsequently expanded this control by granting greater
authority to external forces such as the Red Army and mass social
organizations. These actions had only the thinnest theoretical connection
to the ideas in *State and Revolution*, but Lenin was unwilling to allow
the expansion of uncontrolled participation in the soviets. These actions
eventually brought the soviets under party control, thus clarifying that
the dictatorship of the proletariat was in fact the same as dictatorship
of the party. In Lenin's later view, political participation was to remain
under party control.[4]

Stalin's most important contribution to the theory of the state was
directly related to his concept of socialism in one country. By implying
that the USSR was to become an enclave of communism surrounded
by hostile capitalist states, this notion provided the theoretical justification
for maintaining a strong Soviet state for purposes of national defense.
Presented to the Eighteenth Party Congress in 1939, Stalin's vision of
a more transient state may also have been prompted by the need to
justify the coercive role of the state during the purges.[5] Theoretically,
there was a less urgent need to modify the theory of the state to
correspond to the recently proclaimed stage of socialism since the
achievement of an ostensibly classless society eliminated the need for
a dictatorship of the proletariat. But Stalin cited defense as the primary
reason for maintaining a strong Soviet state. Bolstering his argument
with the purported threat posed by Trotsky and Bukharin, Stalin an-

nounced that the state would have to exist indefinitely as long as the capitalist encirclement of the Soviet Union continued.[6]

Stalin had earlier enhanced the theoretical basis of his view by modifying the notion of the withering of the state. He presented his revision of this concept to the 16th Party Congress in 1930. Characteristically, he had little difficulty reconciling the contradictory notions of a strong state with its eventual withering away:

> We are in favor of the state dying out, and at the same time we stand for the strengthening of the dictatorship of the proletariat. . . . The highest possible development of the power of the state with the object of preparing the conditions of the dying out of the state: that is the Marxist formula. Is it 'contradictory'? Yes, it is 'contradictory.' But this contradiction is a living thing, and completely reflects Marxist dialectics.[7]

Stalin thus clarified the party's ambiguity about the state as envisioned by Lenin and established the framework for the strong, vital state that has characterized the USSR. Used to serve his own political purposes, Stalin's redefinition of the state also modified the narrow approach of the functions of the socialist state as conceived by Marx, Engels, and Lenin, allowing for the adaptation of theory to the reality of the Soviet experience.[8] In recasting the state as a positive institution of social service free of considerations of class, moreover, Stalin cleared the way for the reestablishment of a tsarist-type compulsory service state in which all social groups were dependent on the state for their existence.[9] But, paradoxically, although Soviet citizens became dependent on the state under Stalin, there was little room for participation by any segment of the population. In contrast to his successors, Stalin made no effort to actively involve Soviet citizens in the organs of state and public administration. This was particularly evident in the later years of his regime.[10]

Ideology and Political Participation Prior to Developed Socialism

Khrushchev retained the broad, positive image of the state, but rejected Stalin's ideas about participation. To support both his overall repudiation of Stalin and his economic reform program, Khrushchev advocated the revival of political participation at all levels. This ranged from expanding the powers of the union republics to rejuvenating the trade unions and the local soviets.[11] A 1957 Central Committee resolution, for example, focused on the mobilizational capabilities of the soviets.[12]

In Khrushchev's view, soviets and other participatory organs could take over the administrative, economic, and social functions traditionally performed by the state. The mass of citizens would thus be able to participate in active administration, establishing an important link between the party and the masses that had been absent under Stalin. Calling on officials to mobilize the masses, Khrushchev demanded that the state bureaucracy become more responsive to the needs of the people. This was a major part of his effort, in George Breslauer's words, to change the relationship between the state and the people from one based on terror and command to one based on inspiration and trust.[13]

Khrushchev's vision of expanded democratic participation was incorporated into official ideology in the concept of the "all-people's state" (*obshchenarodnoe gosudarstvo*) introduced at the Twenty-second Party Congress and included in the 1961 Party Program.[14] The Party Program proclaimed that the dictatorship of the proletariat had fulfilled its historic mission and had ceased to be necessary. The current state structure, which had evolved from the dictatorship of the proletariat, was to retain the leadership of the working class. But it was to include an increasing number of citizens of all classes in the administration of governmental tasks, eventually leading to the replacement of all organs of government with "organs of social self-government." The soviets were to play a key role in this transformation, which would ensure the fullest realization of democracy under communism and the final withering of the state.[15]

The main effect of Khrushchev's actions was to signify the return to political normalcy after Stalin and to relink the theoretical underpinnings of the role of the state with the early ideas of Lenin. The similarity between the participatory democracy envisaged in the all-people's state and Lenin's definition of participation in *State and Revolution* helped reinforce this linkage. Khrushchev hoped his new definition of participation would rejuvenate ideological fervor and stimulate Soviet youth to take a more active role in the building of communism.[16]

But Khrushchev's participatory vision was overly idealistic. The problem with the all-people's state was the implication that the Communist Party had effectively relinquished its role in the management of the revolution and was instead content to merely administer the transformation of society as it was carried out by the masses.[17] Although Khrushchev certainly did not envision anything this radical, taken together with his ongoing campaign against bureaucrats and his encroachments on the prerogatives of Soviet officials at all levels his advocacy of what appeared to be uncontrolled participation was understood by many Soviet officials as a direct appeal to the people. By ignoring established institutions and reducing the role of the party, Khrushchev also incurred the wrath of many specialists who accused him of counterposing the all-people's state to the dictatorship of the proletariat. This had the effect, in their view, of encouraging the legislative state organs to undermine the party. Worse, it overstated the degree of harmony in society at the expense of political considerations.[18]

Against this background, the main concern of the Brezhnev regime was to clarify the nature of the relationship between the state and party in general and, most important, to establish limits for political participation. Whereas Khrushchev had based his approach on Lenin's earlier ideas, Brezhnev focused instead on Lenin's later policies that stressed the need for political control over the participation process. Although he retained the concept of the all-people's state and continued to support in theory political participation by the broad masses, Brezhnev launched a concerted effort (especially after gaining the top leadership position in 1969–1970) to restore the primacy of the CPSU in the Soviet political system. In Brezhnev's version of the all-people's state, the party was both the major benefactor and principal director of participatory democracy.[19]

In ideological statements during the initial period of his regime, Brezhnev borrowed the concept of the all-people's state directly from Khrushchev's lexicon. In his first major speech as party leader, for example, Brezhnev spoke of "our all-people's state" as the "natural development" of the dictatorship of the proletariat, representing the will and protecting the interests of the entire Soviet people. He pointed out that more citizens were becoming involved with the administration of state and social affairs, demonstrating fulfillment of the promise of the all-people's state.[20] However, using the term in the same way it had been used by Khrushchev was no longer acceptable and Brezhnev virtually abandoned the concept for the next six years. When he reintroduced it, the all-people's state had a different connotation altogether, one that reflected an important redefinition of political participation. In the meantime, there was considerable discussion among ideological specialists over the significance of the concept and its relationship to the dictatorship of the proletariat.

The focus of the ideological debate in the first years of the Brezhnev era focused on defining the all-people's state in a way that did not establish as radical a break with the past as Khrushchev had implied. Dmitrii Chesnokov, former head of the Historical Materialism Department at Moscow State University, explained in 1965 that the changes in Soviet society brought about by the elimination of the exploiting classes and the resulting unity of class interests had raised the dictatorship of the proletariat to a "new, higher level." The all-people's state was thus "not a state in the old meaning of the word," but rather an evolutionary form of state with integral links to the dictatorship of the proletariat.

In a subsequent article, he explained that the dictatorship of the proletariat had been the proper form of the state for the first phase of communism, but that the all-people's state was the characteristic form for the stage of socialism. The final withering of the state, in turn, would occur only in the higher phase of communism.[21]

Boris Man'kovskii, a Senior Researcher at the Institute of Philosophy of the Academy of Sciences, essentially agreed with Chesnokov, placing the beginning of the all-people's state somewhere between the mid-1930s and the late 1950s. He pointed out that the complete realization of this stage of development had been delayed by the harmful consequences of Stalin's personality cult. He also supported Chesnokov's idea of an evolutionary state, arguing that there was no definite boundary between the dictatorship of the proletariat and the all-people's state.[22]

An additional argument advanced by Soviet specialists against Khrushchev's version of the all-people's state focused on the role of public organizations in the development of communism. The essence of this approach was that, contrary to Khrushchev's view, the public organizations were not rapidly assuming the functions of state organizations. The latter still had an important role to play and in any case could not be totally replaced by public organizations. The thrust of this argument was to reestablish the importance of state organizations in recognition of the inefficiency of the public organizations in important areas of administration.[23]

Thus, ideological discussions in the years immediately following Khrushchev's ouster were for the most part esoteric. They concentrated more on the development of theory rather than the practical implications. These discussions did provide the theoretical basis for continued use of the all-people's state. But, by focusing on the appropriate label to attach to the Soviet state, specialists generally ignored the broader and more important question of the nature of political participation. They concentrated on what political participation was not rather than on what it should be. With the adoption of developed socialism, this situation would change dramatically.

In terms of policy, the need to expand political participation at all levels of Soviet society was a major theme during the early years of the Brezhnev regime. Policy towards the soviets and mass public organizations emphasized their growth in terms of both size and degree of public involvement. By attracting an increasing number of ordinary citizens into policy discussions on issues of local concern and, in the case of the soviets, by requiring the periodic renewal of a large percentage of cadres, the regime sought to achieve a higher level of mobilized participation in support of its reform efforts.

Prior to 1970, the regime downplayed the link between participation and party control. This was clear both in policy statements regarding specific types of participation and in more general discussions of political participation. Brezhnev, for example, pointed to the increasing participation of workers in all areas of state and social administration. He stressed that the continuation of this process was essential to the attainment of communism. In defining the tasks of socialist democracy, he spoke in June 1966 of the need to enhance the role of the Supreme Soviet of the USSR and supreme soviets of the union republics, and called for improvement in the performance of the mass social organizations such as the trade unions and komsomol. He relegated the subject of discipline and the fight against bureaucratism—key elements in his later redefinition of political participation—to third priority and only touched on the role of the CPSU. He was also cautious in his discussion of the party's role in other speeches in 1968–1969.[24]

Similarly, policy towards the soviets and organs of mass participation was characterized by relatively straightforward guidelines stressing the importance of wider participation. The media pointed out that expanding participation was essential to overcome the "consequences of the personality cult" of Stalin.[25] But the full potential of this policy could only be realized after the removal of Khrushchev. As *Pravda* put it:

> After the October (1964) Plenum of the CPSU Central Committee, when the party implemented a series of measures directed towards the strictest observance of Leninist norms and principles of party and state leadership, activity by the workers increased significantly, and their participation in managing societal affairs grew. More and more Soviet people are participating in the discussion of the most important legislation and the fundamental problems of economic, scientific, and cultural development.[26]

In a move similar to that made by Gorbachev twenty years later, Brezhnev in 1965 directed a great deal of attention to the soviets. Promoted as the "organs of genuine democracy," expressing the "aspirations and interests of the entire nation," the soviets were to be the key to the regime's efforts at revitalizing democracy.[27] This was particularly evident at the local level; local soviets enjoyed both numerical expansion and a significant increase in responsibility and, presumably, budget. One of the first decisions of the new regime was to establish soviets at oblast and krai levels, corresponding to the reestablishment of party organizations at those echelons.

As the soviets grew in size and number, their functions became more varied. In conjunction with the 1965 economic reforms, for instance, the soviets were assigned the task of ensuring that all aspects of the reforms were implemented smoothly and without delay, and were provided additional funds to accomplish this task.[28] They were also given specific responsibility for industrial enterprises. After the September 1965 Plenum, soviet organizations gained authority for overseeing production at a total of more than two thousand enterprises in the metal working, forest and wood processing, construction materials, light, food, and other industries. Their responsibilities in agriculture and other sectors, such as trade and services, were similarly expanded, and additional funds were programmed to support these activities.[29]

Some soviets bore a greater burden than others. Local soviets in the heavily industrialized Vladimir oblast, for example, were saddled with monitoring the operations of 110 production enterprises by 1969. Soviet control of these enterprises was exercised primarily through examination of reports from enterprise directors to the chairman of the soviet executive committee, whose members would in turn visit the enterprises in their area to investigate any problems. By far the most effective form of action, however, was to elect soviet deputies from among people directly involved in the production process at an enterprise or on a kolkhoz. In Vladimir oblast, 53 percent of the 12,426 deputies elected in 1969 were actively participating in some aspect of agricultural or industrial production.[30]

Beginning in 1967, local soviets were also given responsibilities for housing that was not connected to enterprises and were provided funding for this new task as well. The additional rubles apparently enabled many local soviets for the first time to construct new housing solely on the basis of their own resources.[31] Additional responsibilities were extended to rural soviets in 1967 when a March decree of the CPSU Central Committee tasked party organizations with helping rural soviets fulfill a wide range of functions in the areas of education, health care, housing, road construction, and many others.[32] This was a significant measure since rural soviets included almost three-fourths of all soviet deputies and had a much larger absolute number of deputies than urban soviets.[33]

The primary stated goal in expanding the soviets' powers was to involve more citizens in the process of administration and to increase the opportunity for political participation in general. A secondary goal, implied in many articles and editorials, was to instill a feeling of individual responsibility for improving the quality of life in one's local community or factory. This was a practical objective, appealing to what Theodore Friedgut has observed was a growing assertion of competence among local officials and a plea to allow them to do their jobs.[34]

The same goals were key to another form of political participation, that by workers. Worker participation in decisions regarding the quantity and quality of output, adequacy of working conditions, and general administration of the workplace has long been a key component in Soviet formulations about socialist democracy. Soviet commentators frequently point out the origins of this concept in the writings of Lenin. In connection with the 1965 reforms, a renewed effort was mounted to bring workers into the decision making process to help bolster production.

Three types of worker participation were emphasized most frequently: the production conference (*proizvodstvennoe soveshchanie*), the workers' meeting (*rabochee sobranie*), and the voluntary bureau (*obshchestvennoe buro*).[35] The most significant of these was the production conference, often referred to as "one of the most effective" forms of worker participation in general. More on the order of a standing committee than a conference, production conferences consisted of elected representatives who met to discuss various aspects of the production process in a particular plant, factory, or industrial complex. According to Soviet estimates, by mid-1965 there were more than 125,000 permanent production conferences in the USSR; by 1968, over five million workers took part in them. Soviet specialists point out that this was a significant increase, and suggest that it was due to the renewed interest taken by workers in their labor because of the incentives offered by the economic reforms. They also attributed the gains to the greater authority now wielded by enterprises. Such participation was seen as the wave of the future, expediting the democratization of society as a whole.[36]

The workers' meeting is an older form of participation, stemming from similar gatherings in tsarist times. The usefulness of these meetings to air grievances and problems was reemphasized in connection with the 1965 reforms as part of the overall effort to increase industrial productivity. A wide range of subjects was covered at a typical workers' meeting. These included suggestions for improving living conditions, strengthening discipline, and developing additional production capacity to increase productivity. A forum for all workers, such meetings were said to be an excellent source of information for party members who could then take the initiative in solving potential problems before they became too serious.[37]

Voluntary bureaus, the third main arena for worker participation, came into existence under Khrushchev and were used to involve workers in the establishment of job norms and standards of production. They evidently were effective in Belorussia where in 1962 (according to a Soviet report) more than 17,000 job norms were reevaluated in one automobile plant alone. This resulted in a reduction of over 1,000 manhours and a savings of over 500,000 rubles. Voluntary bureaus were given a boost with the introduction of the 1965 reforms when worker participation in the setting of job norms became an important factor in determining the amount of production required to qualify for monetary incentives.[38]

Monetary incentives were clearly the main stimulus for the increase in worker participation. According to many reports in the Soviet press in 1965–1966, workers contributed to the reduction of energy costs and to the increased quality of manufactured goods in general. They also made suggestions for improvements in the workplace and increased their interests in all aspects of the activities of their enterprises.[39] As was the case in the expanded authority of the soviets, the increased emphasis on worker participation was designed to create a feeling of greater personal responsibility for the performance of one's enterprise. Part of the general effort to mobilize Soviet citizens that was a crucial element in the new regime's approach, worker participation was, like the soviets, more or less free from the party's direct control. Participation was still more controlled than under Khrushchev, but in the early Brezhnev years it was basically free from party interference.

The CPSU did have a role in the revitalization of political participation, but this was downplayed in policy statements. In the two areas discussed, the party had a somewhat larger role in worker participation than in the revitalization of the soviets. Party members were told to involve workers in the planning process and general administration of production lines. Party committees were tasked with developing effective techniques for promoting worker involvement and becoming more active in coordinating the efforts of various committees, bureaus, and soviets within a given enterprise. *Pravda* emphasized that the new economic conditions presented "new, more complex requirements" for party work, adding that it was the responsibility of party members to mobilize workers in the spirit of the new policy.[40]

The party's role was not as evident in the new regime's policy towards the soviets. Brezhnev, for instance—possibly as a sign of his uncertainty about his position relative to Kosygin—seemed initially to place the party in a dependent status with respect to the soviets. Speaking at the March 1965 plenum, he pointed out that the party had historically activated the soviets along with other mass political organizations whenever it initiated an important new phase of communist development. Tied directly to the announcement of the economic reforms at the same plenum, this statement suggested that the party could not attain its economic goals without the help of the soviets.[41]

But this conflicted with Brezhnev's strong desires to revitalize the party. As a result, his statements on the soviets began to change. His preference for an increase in party control over the soviets was evident as early as the Twenty-third Party Congress. In his major address to the congress, Brezhnev spoke at length about the role of the soviets in promoting democracy at all levels of society and delineated the major areas in which active involvement by especially the local soviets was critical. But in addition to identifying ways in which the soviets could improve, he also pointed out the vital mobilizational role played by the "organs of people's control," which were in turn controlled by the party.[42] In describing the importance of people's control, Brezhnev implied that the CPSU not only would not be excluded from the mobilization process, but would in fact be an active player. This affirmation of the party's role was to become a key element in Brezhnev's approach to political participation after he had attained the dominant leadership position.

The extent to which Brezhnev's early efforts to stimulate political participation were successful is difficult to gauge. The Soviet sources cited above suggest that a dramatic increase in participation rates occurred because of the new political climate. Data from the Soviet Interview Project, on the other hand, suggests that, except for the increased worker participation motivated by newly available material incentives, the regime's efforts were not especially effective. Moreover, because of similarities between Soviet participation rates and those of other industrialized nations, regime attempts to increase mobilization may have been less significant than the modernization demands common to all industrialized societies.[43]

The goal of my analysis, however, is not to demonstrate the effectiveness of Soviet policy or to validate or disprove claims in the Soviet press. The aim is rather to demonstrate the linkage between policy and the theory on which it is based and, to the extent possible, to determine how such linkage relates to the agenda for change of a given leader. The effectiveness of a given policy is thus not as important as the fact that the policy is connected to a theoretical premise supported by the leader or leaders. In this case, the leadership's emphasis on the subdued role of the party in the early Brezhnev years was clear in numerous official articles and speeches. This lasted until 1969–1970 when the focus shifted to the party as the main source of mobilizational support, as discussed below.

Ideology and Political Participation in Developed Socialism

With the adoption of developed socialism into Soviet ideology, the official definition and description of the all-people's state changed very little. Ideologists generally agreed that the all-people's state was a new stage in the development of the Soviet state and not a new type of state, settling the debate of the late 1960s, but otherwise the concept was almost identical to the 1961 Party Program. The all-people's state was interpreted differently, however, both in theory and in practice. In theory, the more advanced stage of socialist development represented by the all-people's state was now juxtaposed against the political systems of other socialist states to bolster claims of Soviet primacy in the communist movement. In practice, the new interpretation was evident in the much more controlled forms of political participation promoted by the regime after 1970, reflecting the policy preferences and increasing power of Leonid Brezhnev.

The inclusion of the all-people's state in the ideological dispute with the PRC and other communist states was evident as early as 1967, during the debates about developed socialism. The thrust of this argument was that the all-people's state was an evolutionary stage in the development of any socialist state. It represented a more advanced form of socialism than the dictatorship of the proletariat, which was still used to describe the less-advanced state structure in China and Yugoslavia. Dmitrii Chesnokov contrasted the growth of social democracy in the USSR with the authoritarian nature of Mao's regime. He argued that the USSR and other countries that had completed the transition to socialism and entered the stage of developed socialism were fully utilizing the creative skills of their citizens to build a more democratic system. The state apparatus and the Communist Party were the most important institutions for teaching citizens the values and methods of democracy and thus could not be undermined as they had been under Mao, who had attempted to turn the dictatorship of the proletariat into a personal dictatorship.[44]

Taking a slightly different tack, A. Kositsyn, Deputy Chief of the Institute of State and Law, attacked the Yugoslav version of social democracy for recognizing the state only during the first phase of socialist construction. He also criticized the Yugoslav model of the communist future, which called for local self-government without any state apparatus at all. Based on the Soviet experience Kositsyn argued that the state would continue to function at every stage of communist development. This was not to say that the dictatorship of the proletariat would last until communism was achieved, a point directed at the Chinese. Kositsyn hoped to demonstrate that the all-people's state was the correct form of the state and would perform the essential state functions pertaining to economics and defense. Because of the impossibility of predicting the timing of the attainment of communism, he added that the all-people's state would last an "entire historical epoch," echoing Mao's similar remark on the longevity of the dictatorship of the proletariat.[45]

The political significance of the all-people's state as a mechanism for control was noted by many Soviet commentators. Consistent with the general policy of the Brezhnev regime, the all-people's state was promoted as an opportunity for citizens to take a more active role in disciplinary and supervisory agencies. This included both formal organizations, such as people's control committees, and informal groups like the volunteer militia and neighborhood patrols. The same principle extended also to workers' collectives in which the responsibility of each member for the production of the entire collective increased through participation in production decisions. Use of the mechanisms of social democracy in the struggle against dissidents was also emphasized. In all these areas participation was directed towards attainment of specific goals. It was not the spontaneous participation advocated by Khrushchev. Nor was it the more controlled participation evident in the post-Khrushchev years of collective leadership when the focus was on enlisting all citizens in the economic reforms and improving the mechanisms of administration. Political participation in developed socialism was rather an instrument used by the the regime to mobilize citizens in controlled and highly structured patterns. This strategy was consistent with the theoretical explanation that the state's (i.e. the party's) role in a developed socialist society was enhanced because of the increasing complexity of the political system.[46]

The message that the all-people's state and participatory democracy were not at all synonymous with unrestrained freedom resounded throughout the ideological literature beginning in 1970. Another strong message was that participation was to be directed by the "working class," or in other words the party. This point was made by several ideological specialists. A. Luk'ianov, for example, a frequent commentator on the all-people's state, put matters into this perspective:

> One cannot agree with the opinion that the transition to the all-people's state has somehow been accomplished through the "transfer of power" by the working class to the rest of society. In reality the working class is not transferring power to anyone, but is lifting society and all its social and national groups to active participation in the implementation of power and in the accomplishments of the tasks of communist construction.

According to Luk'ianov, the increase in social democracy and the broadening of political participation in large public organizations did not imply a diminution in the role of the state. He asserted that it would be a mistake to contrast the growth of social democracy to the traditional role of the state since these should be considered separate issues.[47]

The shift towards more controlled forms of participation also was evident in Brezhnev's speeches. Whereas previously Brezhnev had confined the majority of his remarks on political participation to general definitions of democracy, he began in late 1969 to stress the importance of discipline, legality and control. Most important, he clarified the enhanced role of the CPSU. He also shifted the focus of the mobilizational process from the soviets to more enforcement-oriented organizations like people's control.

Brezhnev's redefinition of participation became evident in two major speeches in 1970. In an April speech at the Kharkov Tractor Factory, he highlighted the organs of people's control as one of the main areas requiring participation by workers and defined "participation in the administration of one's own enterprise" as primarily focusing on the discovery of errors and problems.[48] A week later in his speech on the 100th anniversary of Lenin's birth, he discussed democracy in terms of uncovering problems and inadequacies in the economy. "Our democracy in action," he said, "is the right of every citizen, every collective, and every republic to participate in the solution of the problems of society, to fight against deviations from the norms and principles of socialist communal life, to criticize inadequacies and to participate in their elimination."[49]

Under Gorbachev 15 years later, this would have been a call for more glasnost in criticizing those opposed to reform. Under Brezhnev, however, it was a call for more discipline and greater party control.

Brezhnev's emphasis on discipline and control formed a key part of the overall program for improvement he presented at the Twenty-fourth Party Congress. Criticizing "heartless bureaucrats, red-tape artists," and unresponsive leaders at all levels, Brezhnev called for the increased authority of workers through their participation in production conferences and workers' meetings. Consistent with his redefinition of participation, however, he emphasized that the CPSU would be monitoring the progress of these activities through the eyes of people's control.[50] Another indication that Brezhnev had changed the rules of political participation was his reference to the "duty" of workers to report on the situation in their workplace—a clear and unsubtle reference to control.

The revised interpretation of political participation was publicized widely in the Soviet press after the Twenty-fourth Party Congress, and became a cornerstone in the doctrines of developed socialism. Socialist democracy was now defined in terms of the "responsibility" of Soviet citizens at all levels to participate in the solution of recurring economic and social problems. Organization and self-discipline became the key words in the new definition of democracy, and citizens were urged to exercise their patriotic duty in participating in the overall improvement of Soviet life. From this point on, "democracy" was to be confined primarily to the workplace as part of a broader campaign against bureaucratism and inefficiency.[51]

The most important policy changes resulting from Brezhnev's redefinition of political participation included a limitation of the powers of the soviets and a corresponding expansion of the powers of people's control. While previously the soviets had been given expanded powers with apparently little external monitoring, they were now brought increasingly under party control. The criticism of the party for undermining the authority of local soviets that was prevalent prior to 1970 no longer appeared in the Soviet press. The press instead focused on the party's role in guiding soviet activity. The strengthened position of local party organizations with respect to local soviets was highlighted beginning in 1969, when new emphasis was placed on cooperation to resolve local problems.[52] Such cooperation was to be facilitated by party members who were also members of the local soviets, a practice justified by the party's stated need to work "in the thick of the masses" and to guide and unify citizens at all levels. According to Soviet estimates, by 1970 45 percent of all local soviet deputies were either members or candidate members of the CPSU, and the party was believed able to effectively influence all levels of soviet activity. Although this number had shrunk to 43 percent by 1979, the party compensated by sending an increasing number of soviet deputies (and members of other state organizations) to higher party schools to provide them the "special preparation" necessary to bring a party perspective to their jobs.[53]

The party's control over the soviets became a dominant theme in 1970-1971 when it was incorporated into the evolving doctrines of developed socialism.[54] Brezhnev took the lead in publicizing the party's new role in a 1970 election speech to his Bauman election district. In contrast to his earlier vague statements, Brezhnev now clarified that all aspects of the soviets' work were the direct concern of the party. He stressed this theme again the following year at the Twenty-fourth Party Congress, where he defined the party's role as that of exerting the maximum influence on the development not only of the soviets but of other mass organizations as well.[55] Important specialists such as Fedoseev also emphasized the party's role, pointing out that this was the primary means for the party to strengthen its ties with the people. Other specialists made the same point in a different way, stressing that the party's leading role required it to direct the soviets and other mass organizations or risk the chance that these organizations would stray from the correct path.[56]

CPSU control over the soviets was further strengthened by the March 1971 decree on the soviets, which clearly delineated their areas of responsibility, and the September 1972 law on the status of soviet deputies. Ostensibly designed to increase the authority of elected deputies, the real thrust of this law was to bring an additional measure of control over deputies' activities by requiring them to be more responsive to the needs of their constituents.[57] Brezhnev pointed out that the law had been promulgated to bring the activities of the soviets closer in line with the needs and priorities of the party.[58] By 1975, this law was explicitly attributed to the party's effort to direct the work of the soviets.[59] Looking back from the perspective of the Twenty-fifth CPSU Congress, Brezhnev reflected on the fact that the 1972 law had "breathed new life" into soviet organizations at the local level. He suggested that similar laws might be instituted to govern the duties of soviet deputies at other levels as well.[60]

Party control of the soviets was not a new phenomenon in Soviet political life. Roy Medvedev points out that this was evident already in Lenin's early manipulation of the soviets into "silent instruments for the fulfillment of party directives."[61] Theodore Friedgut has noted that the principle of party control over the soviets has never been in doubt; what has changed from time to time is how this control is exercised.[62] But the reassertion of the party's role in 1969–1970 was especially striking since it followed four years of what was clearly an effort to deemphasize the party's involvement in local government. This policy reversal reflected a change in the leadership consensus after the failure of the 1965 reforms, a change that was probably driven by Brezhnev since it was in line with his ideological values. From granting greater authority to non-party bodies in the development of policy, the consensus shifted to one emphasizing greater party control over the entire political system.[63]

One of the most important results of the new consensus on participation was the expanded role granted the organs of people's control, an organization that eventually came to be known as the "inspectorate of the party."[64] The functions performed by people's control (and people's control itself) had existed prior to developed socialism. However, it was granted little emphasis in the first years of the new regime. Brezhnev had mentioned people's control only once (in his speech to the Twenty-third Party Congress[65]) in speeches prior to 1970. In other contexts, people's control was discussed in terms of the "help" it could render the party in educating leading cadres and the citizenry in general on the importance of protecting the national wealth and, in particular, guarding economic resources. The party's role was to protect people's controllers, who were often hindered in their investigative efforts and sometimes placed under surveillance.[66] But CPSU control over people's control was diminished significantly by the elimination of the Party-State Control Commission in December 1965. This organization, which had been ruled jointly through CPSU and soviet chains of command, was replaced by the "organs of people's control" directed exclusively by the Supreme Soviet of the USSR and soviet organizations at lower levels. This had been a blow both to the party's influence and to

Brezhnev's prestige, since in 1962 he had strongly supported the formation of the Party-State Control Committee under Khrushchev.[67]

Brezhnev reversed this decision in 1968, however, when people's control was resubordinated to the party and the soviets jointly. While the functions of control ostensibly remained in the hands of the people, the resolution announcing the resubordination made it clear that the party's role had been greatly strengthened.[68] After Brezhnev publicly redefined political participation in 1970, the new people's control organization began to receive even more attention. In party writings, it soon gained equal prominence with the local soviets as the most important forms of worker participation. The new attention directed at people's control was especially noticeable after the Twenty-fourth Party Congress. It was called upon to expand its activities, including those in the sensitive area of evaluating managers in their ability to meet established economic goals, as well as in other areas that had formerly been the responsibility of soviet organizations.[69] In line with this new authority, increased publicity was given to the investigative successes of people's controllers throughout the country.[70]

As people's control gained attention, the party's role became more explicit. In 1971, *Pravda* pointed out that, in order to ensure realization of Lenin's ideas about control, party organizations were obligated to take charge of people's control organizations, both to strengthen the effectiveness of this form of control over economic and social activity and to better coordinate it with other forms. *Pravda* underscored the fact that in the past, party leadership had been most effective when a deputy secretary or other key party official at the local level was placed in charge of people's control.[71] In 1972, *Pravda* reported that much valuable experience had been gained, and that issues concerning people's control were now regularly discussed in party organizations at all levels.[72] By late 1973, CPSU direction of people's control had become firmly established, and party organizations were at times criticized for inattention to people's control affairs.[73] Such criticism was voiced repeatedly in subsequent years, for example at the September 1975 plenum of the Latvian Communist Party Central Committee. Pointing out that one of every seven party members in Riga was a people's controller, the plenum tasked party members with providing additional support to people's control organizations in the city and elsewhere. This message was echoed to party organizations in other republics as well, reinforcing the function of people's control as a direct extension of the party.[74] By early 1978 nine and one-half million people worked in people's control organizations, concentrating much of their efforts reviewing the work of the soviets and other organizations.[75]

The elevation of people's control to a key position in the political system was the clearest evidence of Brezhnev's redefinition of political participation. With the acceptance of the new Constitution in 1977, the principle of party direction of political participation was firmly established. The knowledge that the party had regained control of the state apparatus, setting limits and providing direction for political participation, allowed Brezhnev to state with confidence in presenting the Constitution that millions more Soviet citizens were actively involved in the administration of the state (see the quote at the beginning of this chapter). Similarly, in an article in *Problemy Mira i Sotsializma*, Brezhnev discussed the significance of the new Constitution in allowing more Soviet citizens to participate in the administration of the state. He pointed out that they now had expanded powers to protect their own interests. But he also reminded his readers that the CPSU was the guiding force behind all forms of political participation, adding that this, too, was clearly spelled out in the new Constitution.[76]

The 1977 Constitution, then, solidified and made permanent the notion of controlled political participation that had been Brezhnev's stated policy preference since 1970. The increased level of participation publicized with the acceptance of developed socialism was made possible only under the auspices of the CPSU, and the party's role in an important aspect of Soviet political life was therefore significantly enhanced. The message was that there may be more participatory opportunity under developed socialism, but there were also definite limits on the extent to which Soviet citizens were allowed to participate and specific goals to which their activity was to be directed.[77]

The evolution of participatory policies under Brezhnev demonstrates the accuracy of Friedgut's observation that "participatory frameworks organized within the Soviet political system are a product of the ideological values of the regime."[78] The need for strengthening party control over the political system emerged as a strong value of the Brezhnev leadership, and was reflected in the development of ideology and policy from the late 1960s to the end of his regime. One important aspect of the reassertion of party control was the implication that the political system was not yet mature enough to operate without the party's direct intervention. As Donald Kelley has pointed out, this had the effect of further postponing the attainment of communism and the withering of the state.[79] But it did establish the party as the most important element in the Soviet political system. The gradual but steady growth of the party's influence, culminating in the prominence afforded the CPSU in the 1977 Constitution, was both the cause and effect of Brezhnev's rise to power. Representing a direct correspondence between his ideology and policy, Brezhnev's views on political participation reflected his most important political concern—the dominance of the CPSU.

Like other areas addressed in this book, however, Brezhnev's victory in gaining acceptance of his views on political participation was short-lived. Assertion of party control over the soviets and public organizations led eventually, and inevitably, to increased party involvement in economic management and public administration. As a result, local initiative was undermined and the party became over-extended to the point that it was no longer capable of providing overall guidance and direction at the local level. This contributed a loss of party authority in the late-Brezhnev period, prompting the post-Brezhnev leadership to reconsider the party's role in the Soviet political system. The substance of their reconsideration is discussed in chapters 7 and 8.

Notes

1. Theodore Friedgut makes the useful distinction between "mobilized" and "autonomous" participation in his excellent work on political participation in the Soviet Union. He defines mobilized political participation as that in which "actors external to the community, or a select group within it, are the sole initiators of participation among the masses, and it is they who establish the legitimate frameworks of participation, determining their agenda and tone." Autonomous participation, in contrast, is that in which "the initiative to be active as well as the content and forms of organization are principally determined by the participating citizen himself." The former applies to participation in the USSR, the latter to Western democracies. See Theodore H. Friedgut, *Political Participation in the USSR* (Princeton: Princeton University Press, 1979), p. 30.

2. L. I. Brezhnev, *Leninskim Kursom* (Moscow: Politicheskaia Literatura, 1971-1980), vol. 6, pp. 533–534.

3. Zbigniew Brzezinski, "The Crisis of Communism: The Paradox of Political Participation," *Washington Quarterly* 10 (Autumn 1987), pp. 167–174.

4. This discussion of Lenin's theory and policy was derived from Friedgut, *Political Participation in the USSR*, pp. 29–41; Alfred G. Meyer, *Leninism*, (Cambridge, Massachusetts: Harvard University Press, 1957), pp. 193–202; and Carl A. Linden, *The Soviet Party-State: The Politics of Ideocratic Despotism* (New York: Praeger Publishers, 1983), pp. 40-41. The text for *State and Revolution* is from Robert C. Tucker, ed., *The Lenin Anthology* (New York: W. W. Norton and Company, Inc., 1975), pp. 311–398. While Meyer sees a more radical break in Lenin's thought between *State and Revolution* and his actions after gaining power, Friedgut treats the shift in Lenin's thought as the logical result of having to deal with the practical problems of government. I tend to agree with Friedgut; the seeds for Lenin's final position were evident already in *State and Revolution*. As Robert Daniels pointed out more than 30 years ago, Lenin's proposition that the proletarian state would monitor the transition to communism ". . . served effectively to put out of mind the real problem of the relation of the state to

society and the dangers of state becoming independent of mass control." A careful reading of Lenin could thus suggest the need for a strong state in practical matters even though in terms of ideology or political philosophy the need for the state would gradually disappear. See Robert V. Daniels, "The State and Revolution: A Case Study in the Genesis and Transformation of Communist Ideology," *American Slavic and East European Review* 12 (February 1953), p. 36.

5. Daniels, "State and Revolution," p. 39. Also see L. G. Churchward, "Contemporary Soviet Theory of the Soviet State," *Soviet Studies* 12 (April 1961), p. 405.

6. "Report to the Eighteenth Congress of the Communist Party of the Soviet Union (Bolshevik) on the Work of the Central Committee (March 10, 1939)," in Bruce Franklin, ed., *The Essential Stalin: Major Theoretical Writings 1905–1952* (Garden City, New York: Doubleday Anchor Books, 1972), pp. 334–392. Although the rehabilitation of Bukharin in 1988 undercut the basis for Stalin's assertion, the Gorbachev regime is not likely to alter Stalin's concept of a strong state for purposes of national defense. See the discussion of Gorbachev's view on the state in Chapter 8.

7. Quoted in Daniels, "State and Revolution," p. 37.

8. Daniels, "State and Revolution," p. 42.

9. Robert C. Tucker, "Stalinism as Revolution from Above," in Robert C. Tucker, ed., *Stalinism: Essays in Historical Interpretation* (New York: W. W. Norton and Company, 1977), p. 100.

10. Jerry F. Hough and Merle Fainsod, *How the Soviet Union is Governed* (Cambridge: Harvard University Press, 1979), p. 183. Friedgut points out that political participation virtually disappeared between 1937–1957, adding that Soviet writers essentially ignore this period when discussing the development of participation in the USSR. Friedgut, *Political Participation in the USSR*, p. 158.

11. Hough and Fainsod, *How the Soviet Union is Governed*, pp. 226–227. Also see George Breslauer, "Khrushchev Reconsidered," in Stephen F. Cohen, Alexander Rabinowitch, and Robert Sharlet, eds., *The Soviet Union Since Stalin* (Bloomington: Indiana University Press, 1980), p. 50, and Friedgut, *Political Participation in the USSR*, pp. 156–162.

12. Friedgut, *Political Participation in the USSR*, p. 300.

13. Breslauer, "Khrushchev Reconsidered," pp. 53–55.

14. For a detailed discussion of the all-people's state, see Roger E. Kanet, "The Rise and Fall of the All-People's State: Recent Changes in the Soviet Theory of the State," *Soviet Studies* 20 (July 1968), pp. 81–93. See also James P. Scanlan, *Marxism in the USSR* (Ithaca: Cornell University Press, 1985), pp. 240–246. The concept of all-people's state was evidently developed by Fedor Burlatsky, the ideologist who introduced developed socialism to the Soviet public in his 1966 *Pravda* article. This has been pointed out by both Archie Brown and Jerry Hough. See Brown's essay, "Political Power and the Soviet State: Western and Soviet Perspectives," in Neil Harding, ed., *The State in Socialist Society* (Albany, New York: State University of New York Press, 1984), p. 98, fn. 100, and Hough's book, *The Soviet Union and Social Science Theory* (Cambridge: Harvard University Press, 1977), p. 112, fn. 13.

15. *XXII S"ezd Kommunisticheskoi Partii Sovetskogo Soiuza: Stenograficheskii Otchet* (Moscow: Politicheskaia Literatura, 1961), vol. 3, pp. 303–310.

16. Kanet, "Rise and Fall of the All–People's State," p. 87.

17. Richard Lowenthal, "Development vs. Utopia in Communist Policy," in Chalmers Johnson, ed., *Change in Communist Systems* (Stanford: Stanford University Press, 1970), pp. 96–97.

18. Breslauer, "Khrushchev Reconsidered," p. 60. Also see Hough, *The Soviet Union and Social Science Theory*, p. 110, and Kanet, "The Rise and Fall of the All–People's State," pp. 88–92. Friedgut points out that Khrushchev's approach also led to widely divergent views on the correct form of local government. See Friedgut, *Political Participation in the USSR*, p. 299. Gorbachev's democratization effort contains many of the components that caused trouble for Khrushchev. Why should Gorbachev risk this after Khrushchev's experience? The answer seems to be that the atmosphere is different and proposals for bolstering the powers of non-party organizations may have a better chance of success. Because of the stagnation of the Brezhnev period and the crisis of authority experienced by the party, the leadership consensus has changed to allow less-controlled forms of participation. Gorbachev has pushed this consensus with some of his more radical proposals, but has evidently not yet gone beyond the limits of permissible change. See the discussion on this point in Chapter 8.

19. For a similar explanation, see Friedgut, *Political Participation in the USSR*, pp. 44 and 65–66. For a different explanation, see Breslauer, "Khrushchev Reconsidered," pp. 63–64. Breslauer asserts that the Brezhnev regime simply rejected Khrushchev's focus on societal activity as the arena to raise popular consciousness and political participation. Although Breslauer agrees that the strengthening of the state was a key goal of the new regime, he does not explain the crucial role of the party in this regard. Another alternative view is put forth by James Scanlan, who offers four reasons for Brezhnev's emphasis on the all-people's state. These include: to promote the idea of a advanced political system corresponding to the stage of developed socialism; to assuage the nationalities by including all Soviet people in the concept; to justify the continued use of political coercion against individuals who are not class enemies; and to support the extension of state power into whatever sphere the leadership deems necessary. Scanlan, *Marxism in the USSR*, pp. 244–246.

20. Brezhnev, *Leninskim Kursom*, vol. 1, p. 15.

21. D. Chesnokov, "Razvitie Sovetskoi Sotsialisticheskoi Gosudarstvennosti," *Kommunist*, 17/1965, p. 14, and "Leninskoe Uchenie o Sotsialisticheskom Gosudarstve," *Kommunist*, 13/1967, p. 43.

22. B. S. Man'kovskii, "Zakonomernosti Razvitiia Obshchenarodnogo Gosudarstva," *Voprosy Filosofii*, 2/1965, pp. 135–142.

23. See the discussion in Kanet, "Rise and Fall of the 'All–People's State'," pp. 90–92.

24. Brezhnev, *Leninskim Kursom*, vol. 1, p. 15 and 433, and vol. 2, p. 106. For his subsequent caution on this subject, see, for example, his 1968 October Revolution speech in *Leninskim Kursom*, vol. 2, p. 335, and his July 1969 speech to the World Communist Congress in ibid., p. 408. Friedgut has also commented

on the caution displayed by the new regime. See his *Political Participation in the USSR*, p. 299.

25. *Pravda*, 26 February 1966.

26. *Pravda*, 11 August 1967.

27. *Pravda*, 8 May 1966. See also the speech by Iustas Paletskis in *Pravda*, 14 April 1967. See Chapter 8 for a discussion of Gorbachev's revitalization of the soviets.

28. *Pravda*, 5 and 15 December 1965.

29. A. Luk'ianov and B. Lazarev, "Sovety: Razvitie i Ukreplenie Demokraticheskikh Osnov," *Kommunist*, 13/1967, pp. 48–59. Also see *Pravda*, 27 August 1966, and F. I. Kalinychev, et al., eds., *XXIII S"ezd KPSS i Voprosy Gosudarstvennogo Stroitel'stva* (Moscow: Mysl', 1968), especially the essays by M. P. Georgadze, pp. 8–28, and F. I. Kalinychev, pp. 61–90.

30. T. Sushkov, "Mestnye Sovety i Zhizn'," *Kommunist*, 3/1969, p. 56.

31. Ibid., p. 60.

32. *Spravochnik Partiinogo Rabotnika*, 1967, pp. 347–350.

33. *Pravda*, 14 April 1967.

34. Friedgut, *Political Participation in the USSR*, p. 317.

35. Other types of worker participation included economic councils, bureaus of economic analysis, and work brigade soviets. See E. Marav'ev, "Chuvstvo Khoziaina Predpriiatiia," *Pravda*, 15 November 1965, p. 2.

36. For a sampling of many Soviet sources on production councils in this period, see *Pravda*, 9 July 1965, and 13 June and 11 August 1967. Also see Iu. E. Volkov, "Sotsializm i Proizvodstvennaia Demokratiia," and G. Popov, "Demokratiia i Distsiplina," *Pravda*, 28 January 1966, p. 2. For a Western view of production councils, see Alec Nove, *The Soviet Economic System*, second ed., (London: George Allen & Unwin, 1977), p. 232.

37. *Pravda*, 15 November 1965.

38. N. Naumova, "Novoe Otnoshenie k Trudu," *Kommunist*, 7/1965, pp. 64–73, and N. Egorychev, "Razvivat' Kommunisticheskoe Tvorchestvo Mass," *Pravda*, 4 October 1965, pp. 2–3.

39. For related discussions, see *Pravda*, 29 August and 14 November 1965 and 29 July 1966, and the editorial in *Voprosy Filosofii*, 1/1968, pp. 3–13.

40. *Pravda*, 14 and 15 November 1965.

41. Brezhnev, *Leninskim Kursom*, vol. 1, p. 97.

42. Brezhnev, *Leninskim Kursom*, vol. 1, pp. 349–350.

43. See the essays by Brian Silver and William Zimmerman in James R. Millar, ed., *Politics, Work, and Daily Life in the USSR: A Survey of Former Soviet Citizens* (Cambridge: Cambridge University Press, 1987), pp. 100–141 and 332–353.

44. *Pravda*, 27 February 1967, pp. 2–3.

45. *Pravda*, 2 October 1968, p. 3, and 13 August 1969, pp. 2–3. For Mao's position, see Chapter 1, above.

46. For a fuller discussion of the theoretical aspects of the state in developed socialism, see Donald R. Kelley, *The Politics of Developed Socialism* (New York: Greenwood Press, 1986), pp. 162–163.

47. *Pravda,* 7 June 1970, pp. 2–3.

48. Brezhnev, *Leninskim Kursom,* vol. 2, p. 523.

49. Brezhnev, *Leninskim Kursom,* vol. 2, p. 578.

50. Brezhnev, *Leninskim Kursom,* vol. 2, pp. 273 and 281–284.

51. For examples of this ideological line, see "Vo Imia Kommunizma," *Kommunist,* 14/1971, p. 91; V. Shevtsov, "Demokratiia i Gosudarstvo Pri Sotsializme," *Pravda,* 23 October 1973, pp. 2–3; and V. Shevtsov, "Edinstvo Sovetskogo Obshchestva i Razvitie Sotsial'noi Demokratii," *Pravda,* 28 March 1975, pp. 2–3.

52. See, for example, T. Sushkov, "Mestnye Sovety i Zhizn'," pp. 64–65.

53. N. Rubtsov, "Partiinoe Rukovodstvo Massovymi Organizatsiiami Trudiashchikhsia," *Kommunist,* 10/1970, pp. 49–60, and P. A. Rodionov, et al., eds., *Vozrastanie Rukovodiashchei Roli KPSS v Stroitel'stve Sotsializma i Kommunizma* (Moscow: Politizdat, 1979), pp. 179–183.

54. See, for example, B. Morozov, "Partiia i Massovye Organizatsii Trudiashchikhsia," *Pravda,* 25 May 1973, pp. 2–3.

55. Brezhnev, *Leninskim Kursom,* vol. 3, pp. 50–51 and 282.

56. P. Fedoseev, "KPSS—Avangard Sovetskogo Naroda," *Problemy Mira i Sotsializma,* 3/1971, pp. 3–11, and Morozov, "Partiia i Massovye Organizatsii Trudiashchikhsia."

57. For the text of this law, see *Pravda,* 22 September 1972. *Pravda* also published an editorial on the subject three days later.

58. Brezhnev, *Leninskim Kursom,* vol. 3, pp. 380–381.

59. N. Demochkin, "Sovety—Voploshchenie Tvorchestva Mass," *Pravda,* 22 May 1975, p. 2.

60. Brezhnev, *Leninskim Kursom,* vol. 4, p. 542.

61. Roy A. Medvedev, *On Socialist Democracy,* (New York: W. W. Norton and Company, Inc., 1975), pp. 135–136.

62. Friedgut, *Political Participation in the USSR,* p. 52.

63. Party control over the state and social organizations after 1970 was facilitated in four ways: by directives that determined the direction of the efforts of these organizations and provide goals; by preparation of joint resolutions of the CPSU Central Committee and one or more state organizations; by the systematic review by central committees at all echelons of the party of the work of soviets, trade union organizations, the Komsomol, and others; and (most important) by active participation by primary party organizations in the state and social organizations. Education of non-party members in CPSU-sponsored institutions is another method of control that became more widely used in developed socialism. See the discussion in Rodionov, et al., eds., *Vozrastanie Roli KPSS,* pp. 176–183.

64. *Pravda,* 2 December 1976, p. 2.

65. Brezhnev, *Leninskim Kursom,* vol. 1, p. 350.

66. *Pravda,* 29 August 1965 and 23 July 1966, and P. Kovanov, "Narodnyi Kontrol' v Deistvii," *Kommunist,* 7/1967, pp. 46–59.

67. On Brezhnev's role in the Party-State Control Committee, see Paul J. Murphy, *Brezhnev: Soviet Politician* (Jefferson, N.C.: McFarland & Company, Inc.,

1981), pp. 225–227. For Soviet sources on people's control in the mid-1960s, see *Pravda*, 10 December 1965 and 23 July 1966.

68. The introduction of this resolution, for example, ended with the statement: "The party organizations direct the activity of the organs of people's control and render them all possible support and assistance." See *Spravochnik Partiinogo Rabotnika*, 1969, p. 184. A full description of the organization and functions of people's control follows the text of the resolution.

69. See, for example, *Pravda*, 15 September 1971. It was also significant that people's control was the first organization listed by Brezhnev in his speech to the Twenty-fourth Party Congress, a speech in which he also criticized the soviets. Brezhnev, *Leninskim Kursom*, vol. 3, pp. 282–284 and 380–383.

70. See, for example, *Pravda*, 4 November 1971, 11 April and 15 September 1972, 8 December 1973, and 13 April 1976.

71. *Pravda*, 15 September 1971.

72. *Pravda*, 11 April 1972.

73. *Pravda*, 8 December 1973.

74. *Pravda*, 25 September 1975, 30 August 1975, and 13 April 1976.

75. Rodionov, et al., eds., *Vozrastanie Roli KPSS*, p. 60.

76. Brezhnev, *Leninskim Kursom*, vol. 6, pp. 633–635.

77. For similar interpretations, see John Hoffman, "The Coercion/Consent Analysis of the State Under Socialism," in Neil Harding, ed., *The State Socialist Society*, p. 144, and L. Churchward, *Contemporary Soviet Government* (London, 1975), p. 304. Robert Sharlet has also discussed the restraints placed on political participation by the 1977 constitution. See Robert Sharlet, "De-Stalinization and Soviet Constitutionalism," in Cohen, et al., eds., *The Soviet Union Since Stalin*, pp. 101–106.

78. Friedgut, *Political Participation in the USSR*, p. 316.

79. Kelley, *Politics of Developed Socialism*, p. 174.

6

CPSU Policy

Brezhnev's redefinition of political participation was consistent with his advocacy of a stronger party in general. One of the most visible goals of his policy agenda was to revitalize the party to overcome what he viewed as the negative impact of Stalin and Khrushchev and deal with the increasingly complex tasks facing Soviet society. The results of his efforts are reflected in the 1977 Constitution, in which the CPSU is described as "the leading and guiding force of Soviet society, the nucleus of its political system and of its state and social organizations." The Constitution acknowledged in theory what in fact was an expanded role for the party over an increased range of issues.

The apotheosis of the party, reflecting the combined effect of Brezhnev's policy and ideology, was the major change in the Soviet political system in developed socialism. In contrast to other issue areas, in which he had to wait until he attained the dominant leadership position before he could launch policies based on his agenda for change, Brezhnev was able to implement his policy preferences in CPSU policy much sooner. His position as General Secretary was clearly a deciding factor, but he also took advantage of a strong mandate for change within the party leadership. The result was a much more consistent policy than on any other issue addressed in this book.

Rejection of Khrushchev's Party Policy

Before he could realize his goal of a strengthened party, Brezhnev had to deal with the bloated, lax party organization he inherited from Khrushchev. Khrushchev's modifications to party policy were a lucrative target. Although in many ways he had revived the party from the torpor it had fallen into under Stalin, Khrushchev undermined the positive aspects of his policy with his 1962 party reorganization and by involving the party too deeply in economic management. His establishment of a Central Committee Bureau for the Russian Republic also offended party sensitivities, particularly among non-Russians. The result of these "hare-brained" schemes in the judgment of the post-Khrushchev leadership was to reduce the party's effectiveness and demoralize its members.

The loss of party leadership was the subject of the most important criticism directed at Khrushchev after he was removed from power. Ideological spokesman Vladimir Stepakov focused on Khrushchev's "deviations from the Leninist style of party leadership." Broadly termed "subjectivism" and "voluntarism," these deviations included making decisions with no consideration of whether they were realistic and taking steps in a number of important areas without completing a serious scientific study of the issues.[1] Characteristically, Mikhail Suslov placed his criticism of Khrushchev's innovations in an ideological perspective. Suslov pointed out that Khrushchev's policy of involving party members in economic administration had led to a drastic change in the party's traditional role. "In occupying themselves with current economic matters," Suslov complained, "several party organizations and their elected organs lost the political approach to the resolution of economic problems. They forgot about the necessity for ideological influence on the masses and lost their taste for ideological work."[2]

The attack on Khrushchev's party policy focused on the specific modifications that had done the most damage: the abandonment of ideological training, changes in the party structure resulting from the 1962 reorganization, reduction of the role of primary party organizations, and a greatly relaxed admissions policy. In the eighteen months between October 1964 and the Twenty-third CPSU Congress, these issues were dealt with systematically by the new regime, with Brezhnev in the lead. The need for improved ideological training was evidently considered the most urgent problem. Corrective measures were taken on this issue at the October 1964 plenum, immediately after Khrushchev's ouster. Efforts to reunify the party by reversing Khrushchev's reorganization were first discussed at the November 1964 plenum, while the need to strengthen primary party organizations was brought out at the March 1965 plenum. The issue of cadres selection was not introduced until the September 1965 plenum. The intended effect of these revisions to Khrushchev's policy was to restore traditional forms of organization and discipline to the CPSU. This process was completed at the Twenty-third Party Congress in 1966 with the abolishment of the RSFSR Bureau and the introduction of new party rules that included more stringent admissions and retention criteria.

The main thrust of the ideological effort was to remind those who had joined the party under Khrushchev of the party's leading role in Soviet society. This had always been paramount, but the new leadership felt that Khrushchev had downplayed the concept in his effort to involve the party more actively in questions of practical administration. Brezhnev focused on the need for increased ideological work in his first speech as General Secretary. Calling for the "education of the new man" and the "formation of a scientific Marxist-Leninist worldview among the Soviet people," Brezhnev stressed the urgency of improving knowledge of ideology among party members.[3] Although not stated at the time, this was in fact the beginning of a campaign for intensified ideological training among the party rank and file. The outlines of this campaign became clear in 1965–1966 with the publication of numerous reports in *Pravda* concerning improvements in ideological education. One of the most important measures was the establishment of party ideological schools. These ranged from introductory courses taught in the evenings at local institutes to two-year "basic political schools" and four-year "schools of Marxism-Leninism." They were established in many national republics as well as in main industrial centers. Party organizations were encouraged to expand such programs and to increase the number of lectures, discussion groups, and seminars devoted to ideology. Similarly, educational institutions were urged to expand and improve political education programs. The mass media was mobilized to support this effort by publishing articles dealing with the theory and practice of Marxism-Leninism. (For planning purposes, *Pravda* published a guide to ideological articles projected for publication by various periodicals in 1966.[4]) These measures were designed not only to restore ideological competence *per se*, but were also meant to provide an ideological context for party members to discuss and explain the 1965 reforms.[5]

The effort to revitalize ideology culminated at the Twenty-third Party Congress. The contrast between Khrushchev's approach to ideological training and that of the new regime was mentioned by several important speakers. A common theme in these speeches was the "well-known underestimation" of ideological work in the past. Latvian party leader Arvid Pel'she, for example, asserted that overemphasis on the study of production and technical matters at the expense of ideology had been "undoubtedly a mistake," and called for publication of a new textbook on Marxism-Leninism. Similar points were made by Belorussian First Secretary Masherov and Moscow City Committee First Secretary Egorychev.[6]

While ideological training occupied first position in the new regime's priority list, the most vehement criticism of Khrushchev was directed as his 1962 party reorganization. Based on the "production principle," the reorganization had been designed to divide the party's managerial efforts into agricultural and industrial components. This resulted in several major changes in terms of party structure: oblast and krai party committees were bifurcated into agricultural and industrial components;

agricultural committees at regional level were replaced by territorial production committees covering several kolkhozes and sovkhozes; and separate agricultural and industrial bureaus were established in republic central committees. Similar changes were implemented in trade union organizations and the komsomol.[7]

Khrushchev's reorganization was widely unpopular with party leaders, particularly local leaders whose span of authority had been reduced. The new structure was considered too complex; Brezhnev criticized it as artificial and unjustified, implying that it had been forced on the party.[8] Viewed in broader perspective, the split of party organizations created what was in effect a two-party system. While both components shared a common ideology and approach to policy, they were forced to compete with each other in many respects.[9]

Khrushchev's reorganization was attacked almost immediately upon his removal from power. Podgorny (who, like Brezhnev, had supported Khrushchev's reorganization scheme in 1962) told the November 1964 Central Committee Plenum that the reorganization was "unjustified" and "mistaken." The plenum agreed that Khrushchev's reform had destroyed party unity, especially at the raion level, and had fragmented the purposeful decision making essential to effective party activity. Action was thus taken at the plenum to restore the original party structure according to the traditional territorial principle, to reunify party organizations at oblast and krai level, and to reaffirm the principle of unified decision-making. According to the Soviet interpretation, these changes restored the structure of the party to that defined in party rules and ended confusion among party and government leaders. Perhaps a more significant benefit, as Barbara Chotiner has pointed out, is that the new regime gained the support of local party leaders whose authority had been restored.[10]

Closely related to criticism of the party reorganization was concern about the effect of Khrushchev's policy on primary party organizations. This was the third aspect of party policy addressed by the Brezhnev regime, and was introduced for discussion at the March 1965 plenum. The plenum pointed out that the 1962 modifications to party structure had led to a basic change in the approach of party workers at the crucial local level. Instead of performing their traditional role of explaining overall policy to the masses, local party workers had been forced to specialize in either agricultural or industrial matters. They were also placed in the position of having to execute policy, or at least to ensure it was implemented, down to a fine level of detail. This change in basic patterns of interaction with the masses had severely damaged the party's image and authority. Whereas previously Soviet citizens had found in their local party representative an individual who could address all areas of policy, they now found a person who was immersed in only one area. The party's role in integrating citizen demands to help formulate overall policy had thus been seriously diminished.[11]

The new regime's approach to this problem was to remove party members, especially party secretaries, from the actual implementation of policy and restore them to their former roles as mentor and interpreter of the party line. This departure from Khrushchev's policy was outlined by Brezhnev at the March plenum when he called for support in helping local party organizations in general. Although his remarks were directed at party organizations in agricultural areas, it was evident that he was encouraging an expanded and changed role for all primary party organizations.[12] Brezhnev was not advocating that primary party organizations divorce themselves completely from the production process. His preference was rather that they temper this activity with concern about social and ideological issues.[13]

Criticism of Khrushchev's reorganization of the party was directly related to a negative assessment of his cadres policy, the fourth area of CPSU policy addressed by the new regime. At the September 1965 plenum, Brezhnev criticized Khrushchev's policy of open admissions and pointed out the problems it had caused. He attributed these problems to the "lack of attention" in the recent past to the selection, deployment, and training of new party cadres. Brezhnev was careful to point out that he was not suggesting a wholesale purge of party ranks, but rather was asking for a general tightening of entry requirements.[14] Left unsaid by Brezhnev but clearly informing his thoughts was the problem created by the too rapid expansion of CPSU membership. He would soon devote a great deal of attention to the problems created by the "Khrushchev enrollment."[15]

Brezhnev's response to the cadres policy was contained in the new party rules adopted at the Twenty-third Party Congress. The major changes—requiring that prospective members up to age 23 be accepted into the party only through the komsomol and stipulating that a member have five years seniority before being authorized to recommend a new member—represented a distinct tightening of entry requirements. Moreover, abolishing the rule that allowed for members to be reverted to candidate status for disciplinary reasons paved the way for an increased number of expulsions. The new rules also expanded the authority of primary party organizations, which could now expel members with the approval of only the raion or city committee without referring to higher authority. In answer to the problems of rapid turnover created by the 1961 requirement for transferring party secretaries every two years, the new rules affirmed the principle of periodic renewal, but allowed the party organizations themselves to decide how often such renewal should occur. *Pravda* pointed out that these rules were intended to maintain the "purity" of the party's ranks and to counter the mistaken tendencies of the past. The rules changes as a whole indicated that the new regime would adopt a much more restrictive recruitment policy, a message that was reinforced in Brezhnev's frequent reference to Lenin's aphorism about party admissions: "Better fewer, but better."[16]

With the adoption of the new rules, the Twenty-third Party Congress marked the end of the campaign against Khrushchev's party policy. Having previously pointed out the "organic connection" among the October and November 1964 and March and September 1965 plenums in dealing with the problems of the past, Brezhnev spelled out the revised party policy: the party reorganization had been overturned; recruitment policy had been tightened; primary party organizations had been revitalized; and improvements had been made in ideological training. Moreover, party democracy had been strengthened through the establishment of collective leadership at the top and by the increased importance attached to party meetings and conferences. Brezhnev called for further improvement, but emphasized that much had already been accomplished.[17]

Brezhnev's Party Policy

Despite his attacks on Khrushchev's policies, Brezhnev wanted to preserve the de-Stalinization of the party begun by Khrushchev, and he emphasized this point soon after Khrushchev's removal from power. In his October 1964 speech on the anniversary of the October Revolution, Brezhnev stressed the importance of the Twentieth Congress in the "rehabilitation *(vosstanovlenie)* of genuine Leninist norms in the life of our party."[18] His objective was to recapture the spirit of party renewal evident at the Twentieth Party Congress while simultaneously reversing the effects of Khrushchev's more radical reforms and liberalizing tendencies. Quite logically, his initial efforts focused on the need to restore party discipline.

The call for increased discipline within the CPSU was consistent with the regime's overall economic reform program. Soviet citizens were admonished to exercise self-discipline and to discipline others at work, in their neighborhoods, and in their social lives. "Discipline and labor are inseparable," *Pravda* asserted, and "any violation of labor discipline is a serious social evil incompatible with the norms and principles of our Soviet life." Besides demonstrating total commitment to their jobs and the quality of the products they produced, Soviet workers were urged to economize in their use of basic materials. This included using the latest equipment and techniques, emulating the methods of leading workers, and organizing production according to scientific principles. It also meant "picking up a screw, a part, a piece of paper, or a rod, eliminating air or steam leaks, and turning off the lights and shutting off the faucets."[19]

For their part, CPSU members were urged repeatedly to set a good example by practicing self-discipline and by increasing their responsbility for the actions of others. This was not an easy task; the lack of discipline among party members was the subject of numerous *Pravda* reports written by secretaries at all levels. The First Secretary of the Kazakh Central Committee, for example, reported that disciplinary problems among party members in his republic included lax attitudes toward workers, making excuses in written reports about plan fulfillment, "eyewash" of various types, and a practice of carrying out individual duties perfunctorily and sometimes only after considerable pressure from superiors. Passive and inactive party members were a problem in the Leningrad Oblast, too, although in this case the problem was attributed to an overall lack of direction and discipline from leading cadres.[20]

Brezhnev underscored the need for discipline in his first speech as party leader, demanding that party members develop a personal sense of responsibility. He called for the expansion of criticism and self-criticism and for intolerance of violations of party norms. To face the problems associated with the new direction of economic development, Brezhnev set as the minimal standard the acceptance by each party member as a personal goal the satisfactory accomplishment of party objectives with a high degree of exactingness.[21]

Brezhnev continued to emphasize discipline throughout 1965–1966. At the March 1965 plenum on agriculture, he called on all communists to share a sense of responsibility and exactingness in carrying out the party's agricultural plans. At the September 1965 plenum he tasked party members and primary party organizations with the responsibility of ensuring the success of the industrial reforms. He also called for improvement in the caliber of workers assigned to industrial enterprises in order to counter the parochial tendencies of the past. Brezhnev reiterated his concern for discipline most emphatically at the Twenty-third Congress. Noting that the Central Committee had recently reviewed cadres work in several party organizations, he criticized the lax approach in some areas that had resulted in the admission of unprepared and immature cadres. In more general terms, he called for the strictest observation of party democracy, for the "further strengthening of the party," and for "iron discipline" and individual responsibility on the part of members. Brezhnev's emphasis on discipline to increase the authority of the CPSU became a characteristic theme in his party policy both before and after developed socialism was adopted into official ideology.[22]

Closely related to the emphasis on discipline was the theme of leadership. Highlighted in many of Brezhnev's statements and the writings of party specialists, leadership had both personal and organizational dimensions. Party members were urged in countless editorials and speeches to "set the example" for others by fulfilling all economic and social obligations. This was essential if the masses were to be mobilized to achieve the new economic goals. Party organizations in the RSFSR, Georgia, and elsewhere hammered this message home in seminars on party leadership. Their role was to ensure that individual party members adopted the new type of leadership Brezhnev desired.[23]

At higher levels, the scientific and collective approach to party leadership was portrayed as superior to that of the previous regime. The new style of leadership, according to *Pravda*, permitted an objective evaluation of all information before a decision was reached. It also minimized the possibility of mistakes, ruled out a willful, subjective approach to problem-solving, and allowed a thorough discussion of all aspects of any situation that came to the leaders' attention. The leadership style practiced by the new regime was frequently characterized as "Leninist" and "scientific." In addition, the "business-like approach" of the new regime was mentioned in almost every article on the subject of leadership and was noted by many speakers at the Twenty-third Party Congress. In an obvious reference to Khrushchev, one speaker praised the new regime for putting an end to the "high-falutin rhetoric" and "boasting" of the past. Others noted the new atmosphere of trust in cadres and increased responsibility that had been fostered by party leaders.[24]

While such an idealized portrait of the new regime may be expected whenever a leadership change occurs, the emphasis on discipline and leadership was also important in terms of Brezhnev's concerns about cadres policy. Because of Khrushchev's expanded recruitment efforts and consequent dilution of entry requirements, CPSU membership had by 1965 increased more than 70 percent since Stalin's time. This growth was especially noticeable at the end of Khrushchev's regime; new admissions for 1964 were the highest of any year of the postwar era.[25] Such rapid expansion had both diluted the significance of party membership and called into question the party's status as the vanguard of society.[26] Although the retraining of those already in the party was important, the Brezhnev regime was still faced with a bloated organization that visibly contradicted his vision of an elite, highly efficient party apparatus.

An early indication that a shift in policy had occurred was the July 1965 Central Committee resolution on the Kharkov Obkom. Describing the serious problems in the obkom's recruitment practices, the resolution stressed that quality should be more important than quantity in the recruitment process. Quoting Lenin's statement that, "it is better for ten workers not to call themselves party members than for one loudmouth to have the right and opportunity to be a party member," the resolution blasted the Kharkov party organization for its mismanagement of the overall recruitment effort. The resolution required that recruitment practices in the obkom be brought into strict adherence with party rules. To ensure this message was clear to all party organizations, the resolution added that numerical growth was not an end in itself, but rather must be based on a program of intense efforts to educate the masses. Only by ensuring quality could party growth be tolerated. In line with the overall goal of increasing party authority, the resolution noted: "In the selection of party members, it must be kept in mind that even single instances of accepting persons into the CPSU not worthy of the title 'communist' does serious harm to the party, spoils its ranks, and lowers the authority and efficiency of the party."[27]

This resolution signalled the beginning of a crackdown on party admissions and a tightening of cadres policy generally. Although Western analysts generally agree that recruitment was restricted under Brezhnev,[28] little work has been done to determine the dimensions of this policy. In part this is due to a lack of consistent data. Figures on the annual numbers of expulsions and numbers of candidates refused admission as full members—essential to any examination of the dimensions of a cutback in party growth—were not published consistently after 1967. When they were published, figures were often lumped together into five-year totals. The larger problem, however, is that many scholars have focused on cadres policy in the party's top echelons, the Politburo and Central Committee. Extrapolating from the relative lack of movement at the top level, they have characterized the overall cadres policy of the Brezhnev era as basically "stable."[29] Many scholars have also concentrated on Brezhnev's efforts to improve the social profile of the party by recruiting more workers and peasants, continuing the trend begun by Khrushchev.[30]

While there is no question about stability at the top of the party under Brezhnev or about the party's desire to improve its social profile, devoting exclusive attention to these areas has delayed a more serious effort to examine the turbulence at the party's lowest levels—the main arena in which Brezhnev's cadres policy was carried out. Beginning well before developed socialism was adopted into official ideology, he launched

TABLE 6.1
CPSU Net Growth, 1960–1982 (thousands)

	1 CPSU Members and Candidates[a]	2 Net Growth	3 Rate of Growth (percent)	4 Full Members[a]	5 Net Growth	6 Rate of Growth (percent)
1960	8,709	567	6.5	8,017	455	5.7
1961	9,276	615	6.6	8,472	580	6.8
1962	9,891	496	5.0	9,052	529	5.8
1963	10,387	635	6.1	9,581	602	6.3
1964	11,022	736	6.7	10,183	628	6.2
1965	11,758	599	5.1	10,811	737	6.8
1966	12,357	327	2.6	11,548	587	5.1
1967	12,684	496	3.9	12,135	350	2.9
1968	13,180	460	3.5	12,485	473	3.8
1969	13,640	372	2.7	12,958	437	3.4
1970	14,012	361	2.6	13,395	351	2.6
1971	14,373	258	1.8	13,746	363	2.6
1972	14,631	190	1.3	14,109	222	1.6
1973	14,821	205	1.4	14,331	163	1.1
1974	15,026	269	1.8	14,494	225	1.6
1975	15,295	344	2.2	14,719	311	2.1
1976	15,639	355	2.3	15,030	335	2.2
1977	15,994	366	2.3	15,365	337	2.2
1978	16,360	361	2.2	15,702	341	2.2
1979	16,721	361	2.2	16,043	355	2.2
1980	17,082	348	2.0	16,398	334	2.0
1981	17,430	340	1.9	16,732	345	2.0
1982	17,770	348	2.0	17,077	328	1.9
1983	18,118	—	—	17,405	—	—

[a]As of 1 January.

Source: columns 1 and 4 are from *Partiinaia Zhizn'*, 15, 1983, pp. 14–15. Modeled after a table by Aryeh L. Unger, "Soviet Communist Party Membership Under Brezhnev: A Comment," *Soviet Studies,* April 1977, p. 307.

an intense effort to restrict party growth and to strengthen party ranks by tightening membership requirements.

The extent of Brezhnev's cadres policy can be seen most clearly by reviewing annual CPSU membership statistics. The trends toward a lower rate of growth and a more restrictive admissions policy are evident in the following tables. In Table 6.1, the net growth figures for both the total membership and the number accepted as full members each year indicate a slowdown in the rate of party growth beginning in 1965. This trend was firmly established by 1966 when the party increased by just under 327,000 members and candidates, a decrease of over 45 percent compared to the net growth for 1965. Although there was a

TABLE 6.2
CPSU Net Growth, 1960–1982 (thousands)

	1 Candidate Members[a]	2 Net Increase (decrease)	3 Rate (percent)	4 Candidate Admissions	5 Net Increase (decrease)	6 Rate (percent)
1960	691	112	16.2	673	40	5.9
1961	803	36	4.5	713	(53)	(7.4)
1962	839	(33)	(3.9)	660	111	16.9
1963	806	33	4.1	771	108	14.0
1964	839	108	12.9	879	(144)	(16.4)
1965	947	(138)	(14.6)	735	(224)	(30.5)
1966	809	(260)	(32.1)	511	158	30.9
1967	549	146	26.6	669	(22)	(3.3)
1968	695	(13)	(1.2)	647	(68)	(10.5)
1969	682	(65)	(9.5)	579	0.2	0.3
1970	617	10	1.6	581	(88)	(15.1)
1971	627	(105)	(16.8)	493	(24)	(4.9)
1972	522	(31)	(5.9)	469	38	8.1
1973	491	(41)	(8.4)	507	43	8.5
1974	532	44	8.3	550	25	4.5
1975	576	33	5.7	575	35	6.1
1976	609	20	3.3	610	—	—
1977	629	29	4.6	b	—	—
1978	658	21	3.2	b	—	—
1979	679	5.0	0.7	b	—	—
1980	684	14	2.0	b	—	—
1981	698	(5.0)	(0.7)	654	13	1.9
1982	693	20	2.8	667	—	—
1983	713	—	—	—	—	—

[a]As of January.
[b]Average for 1977–1980 = 632.
Source: Column 4 is from Partiinaia Zhizn', 10, 1965, p. 9 (1960–1964) and 21, 1977, p. (1976), and Aryeh L. Unger, "Soviet Communist Part Membership Under Brezhnev: A Comment," Soviet Studies, vol. 29, p. 307 (1965–1975).

slight upturn in 1967 (the result of an intensified recruitment effort in anticipation of the fiftieth anniversary of the October Revolution), the reduced rate of party growth continued until 1975. This trend intensified in 1971 when developed socialism became part of official ideology, signalling Brezhnev's dominance over the leadership. It began to slacken and then to reverse itself only in 1974–1975, when restrictions eased and a more liberal recruitment policy took effect.

While the restrictive growth policy affected the entire party membership, the most remarkable effect was in the recruitment and admission of new candidates, illustrated in Table 6.2. The number of new candidates and total candidates were reduced almost every year from 1964–1971.

In 1966, for example, just over 500,000 individuals were admitted to candidate status, a drop of over 300,000 compared to 1964. This reflected both a tougher admissions policy and a more stringent apprenticeship for candidates. The latter proved too difficult for many prospective members, and the rate of denial of full membership status to those who had completed their one-year candidacy reached its highest level in twenty years. The overall "failure rate" for the five-year period 1966–1970 has been calculated at 3.5–4 percent.[31]

These trends were reinforced by an increased number of members dismissed from the party. Although the annual number of expulsions was not published after 1967, the data that is available suggests that expulsions were an important part of Brezhnev's overall cadres policy. In 1966, 80,112 members and candidates were expelled. The reasons for this included behavior unbecoming a party member or "having lost contact with the party organization," a euphemism for not paying dues for three consecutive months. This represented an increase of almost 16 percent over the number expelled for the same reasons in 1964.[32]

While not of the magnitude of Gorbachev's policy in 1986–1987 (see Chapter 8), Brezhnev's cadres policy in the early stages of his regime was nonetheless significant since it reversed existing trends and sent a clear signal that old guidelines no longer applied. Moreover, in terms of the major premise of this study, Brezhnev's cadres policy demonstrates consistency with his ideological values. There was very likely a leadership consensus that action needed to be taken, but in my view the extent of the changes in cadres policy that occurred in the first years of the new regime were due to a strong push by Brezhnev himself. It was a fruitful way for him to demonstrate his ideological values and the strength of his commitment to change. It also demonstrated his ability to control the party apparatus.[33]

Party Policy in Developed Socialism

Unlike other policy areas discussed in this book, the adoption of developed socialism into official ideology in 1971 did not signal a radical departure in terms of Brezhnev's party policy. Because he was able to implement his policy preferences in this area from the outset, there was a great deal of continuity throughout his regime. Party policy in developed socialism was thus characterized by an intensification of policies implemented earlier.

In the 1970s, the Brezhnevian themes of discipline, ideological training, and leadership continued to inform discussions on the party. The main difference from similar discussions in the mid-1960s was a more intense effort to elaborate the nature of party leadership in the stage of developed socialism.[34] To these, two new themes were added: the importance of leading role of the CPSU in the communist movement, especially the superiority of the CPSU over the Chinese Communist Party (CPC); and the Leninist nature of the party under Brezhnev in contrast to both Stalin and Khrushchev. Both of these themes were consistent with the broad ideological thrust of developed socialism and with Brezhnev's ideological values. In terms of policy, the party's role was officially recognized in many areas that had previously been exempt from direct party control. This change necessitated greater organizational efficiency and measures were taken to improve party procedures accordingly. The restrictive cadres policy of the late 1960s was continued, culminating in the exchange of party cards conducted in 1973–1974. All these events reflected Brezhnev's increasing power over party policy.

The theme of the superiority of the CPSU in the communist movement was implied in Brezhnev's June 1969 speech to the Moscow Conference of the World Communist Movement. Concentrating his criticism on the Chinese for the damage they had caused to international communist unity, Brezhnev attacked the rules introduced at the Ninth CPC Congress that promoted the ideas of Mao Tse-Tung as alternative theoretical guidance for communists throughout the world. Brezhnev reminded conference delegates that Beijing had at one time or another insulted them all for refusing to launch a revolution or for committing some other "mortal sin." He concluded that the CPC's attempt to gain hegemony was the direct result of its belief in the messianic role of China. Brezhnev broadened this attack in his speech to the Twenty-fourth Party Congress to include revisionist parties of any description. He juxtaposed the efforts of the CPSU to retain the purity of Marxism-Leninism against the efforts of revisionist parties to undermine international communism.[35]

The superiority of the CPSU was the subject of several articles published after the Twenty-fourth Congress. P. N. Fedoseev was the most prominent author of these articles, and the similarity between his words and Brezhnev's speech to the Party Congress suggests that Fedoseev may have been one of Brezhnev's main speechwriters during this period. Fedoseev especially criticized the Chinese for the destructive effects of the Cultural Revolution on the CPC. He also asserted that the new rules adopted at the Ninth CPC Congress had transformed the party into a "military-bureaucratic dictatorship" established for the sole purpose of implementing Mao's ideas. The leading role of the working class had thus been destroyed and the CPC had ceased to be a Marxist-Leninist party. Like Brezhnev, Fedoseev contrasted the Chinese and other revisionist parties with the CPSU, which had become the "decisive link" in the struggle to retain ideological purity in the communist movement.[36]

The superiority of the CPSU was also featured in contrasting the party under Brezhnev in the stage of developed socialism with the Stalin and Khrushchev periods. The main line of argument here was that the CPSU had survived both the violations of party principles under Stalin and the willful, arbitrary approach of Khrushchev. Not only had it survived, the party had taken decisive steps to rid itself of the effects of Stalin and Khrushchev and had restored Leninist norms of democratic centralism and intra-party democracy.[37] It was therefore a much stronger and more capable institution than it had been in the past forty years. This contrast between the party's past and present image under developed socialism was a leitmotif in many of Brezhnev's speeches, most notably in his address to the Twenty-fifth Party Congress in 1976. Speaking of the increased authority enjoyed by party organizations throughout the country, Brezhnev characteristically attributed this change to the adoption of the Leninist style of work within the party: "The Leninist style is a creative style, devoid of subjectivism and permeated with a scientific approach to all societal processes. It makes great demands of oneself and others and rejects any manifestations of bureaucratism and formalism."[38]

The theoretical underpinning for the CPSU's expanded role emphasized the party's traditional functions of coordinating and combining distinct interests and demands to develop a single coherent policy line. According to Soviet theorists, these functions became more complicated because society itself had become more complex. These theorists attributed the need for greater party involvement to five main factors. First, the tasks associated with building communism became increasingly larger and more complex, demanding the highest levels of political and organizational leadership. Extending across economics, culture, scientific, and social policy areas, these tasks had to be analyzed in terms of the worldwide scientific revolution. Second, the "subjective factor" in building communism became more important. This referred to the need to analyze and make judgments about objective aspects of societal development, such as the elimination of differences in living standards in rural and urban areas, the reconciliation of physical and mental labor, and the growth of the intelligentsia, especially in the engineering and technical fields. The third reason for the party's enhanced role was the development of political participation as a feature of Soviet life. As socialism gradually evolved into communism, more and more citizens would become involved in the democratic administration of society. Fourth, the tasks facing Soviet society in developed socialism required the further development of Marxist-Leninist theory. This was especially urgent because of the need to define exactly what was involved in the construction of a communist society. Fifth, the party's role must be enhanced because of the increasing complexity of the international situation. According to these theorists, the party was the only institution in Soviet society that could fulfill these various needs. This is because of its historical mission in the formation and development of the Soviet Union and its effort to develop leadership and authority. To retain its authority in these areas, the party must continue its unwavering observation of Leninist norms, stimulate further activity among lower party organs, and continue to strengthen its cadres.[39]

Justification for an expanded role for CPSU was frequently described in Soviet literature in terms of a redefinition of the principle of democratic centralism. Although in the narrow sense this concept describes only the decision-making processes within the party, in which the decisions of higher bodies are binding on lower elements, the definition of democratic centralism was broadened under developed socialism to justify the party's greater involvement in other policy areas as well. As described by one Soviet specialist: "The main principle of the party's life and activity, democratic centralism, allows it to develop the general will on the basis of broad discussion and then to implement this general will. . . . By relying on party organizations and on communists in state and social organizations, the party manifests its political leadership and directs the activities of the entire political system of Soviet society."[40]

The central message in discussions of the party's enhanced role in developed socialism is that the primary of politics had been reasserted in all areas of societal development. Since Stalin's time, the CPSU has been increasingly represented as the "sole centripetal force in a society consisting of increasingly powerful centrifugal forces."[41] In Paul Cocks' terms, the party's "higher political consciousness enables it to have better vision and knowledge of the long-term needs and general interests of society."[42] The party's main role, then, is to control and direct the use of power in the actual administration of society. While this has been true to a greater or lesser extent in every stage of Soviet history, it became an explicit component of Soviet ideology and policy in developed socialism. The party's role in developed socialism was not to be the hands-on management of the Khrushchev era, The party was rather to be the leading, guiding force in all areas of social, political, and economic development in accordance with Brezhnev's Leninist vision.

Two significant aspects of CPSU policy in developed socialism were based on these theoretical formulations. First, the authority of the primary party organization was expanded as part of the effort to broaden the party's impact. This policy was accompanied by a call for greater efficiency at all levels of the party apparatus to meet the new demands. Second, the emphasis on increased selectivity of cadres was continued, culminating in the exchange of party cards in 1973–1974. In contrast to the past emphasis on entry-level members, cadres policy now affected the party leadership, too, reflecting Brezhnev's increased power. This was evident in the 1972 replacement of Ukrainian party chief Shelest and Georgian party leader Mzhavanadze.

The most striking policy was the expansion of the authority of the primary party organization. As described by Brezhnev at the Twenty-fourth Party Congress, primary party organizations had been established in key areas of railway transport and in major production organizations, greatly increasing the party's ability to influence these sectors. The same approach was to now be used in scientific research institutes and in cultural and medical establishments.[43] As one Western analyst has pointed out, these steps to ensure party control over administration exceeded even Stalin's most ambitious efforts.[44] Other instances of expanding party control, while not as dramatic, were equally significant. In March 1972, for example, the CPSU Central Committee required the Tbilisi City Party Committee to improve its leadership of mass social organizations. Party officials were urged to investigate in detail the work of the soviets, trade unions, and Komsomol, and to ensure that proper control was maintained in their efforts to improve working conditions and to increase productivity. To ensure that the general message of the resolution was understood, *Pravda* published an editorial pointing out that the actions required by the Tbilisi Party committee were relevant for all party organizations. The objective of this was "to perfect the style and methods of party leadership of the economic, ideological and political edification of Soviet citizens."[45]

The same message was promulgated by specialists, most notably F. Petrenko. In articles published in 1973 and 1974, Petrenko described the relationship between the party and the mass social organizations in terms of the functions performed by each. Whereas the soviets and trade unions provide "management" (*upravlenie*), according to Petrenko, the CPSU provides "leadership" (*rukovodstvo*). Petrenko further defined this distinction in terms of socialist democracy:

> The fact that relations between the ruling Communist Party and state and social organizations are deeply democratic provides the unarguable virtue and advantage of the political system of socialism. . . . The party does not give orders, undermine, or take the place of state and social organs, but rather proposes tasks, convinces, directs, and leads. It develops and suggests to the people its policies and scientifically based solutions to pressing societal problems and serves as the organizer to implement these policies and solutions.[46]

The distinction between leading and managing in the area of political participation was also evident in the party's involvement in economic administration. In numerous resolutions from 1973–1977, party organizations were tasked with providing greater leadership in such diverse areas as chemical production, consumer goods industries, machine building, and oil and gas production.[47] The party was in essence taking a greater role in areas that had been the exclusive domain of the economic ministries after 1965.[48]

The party's expanded involvement required it to improve and maintain both its organizational efficiency and the quality of its personnel. As described by Brezhnev, the primary areas for improvement included intra-party democracy, the exchange of information at all levels, and, most important, criticism and self-criticism. To allow for better interaction between CPSU party congresses and those held in the national republics and to give the party greater input into the development of five-year plans for economic development, Brezhnev also suggested that CPSU congresses be held every five years instead of every four. This was clearly more than a suggestion, however, since it had been five years since the last CPSU congress, indicating that the policy had already been put into effect.[49]

The need for greater effectiveness at lower levels of the party was the subject of a 1972 resolution on the Tbilisi City Party Committee. The resolution criticized the Tbilisi City Committee for its lack of ability to solve "those problems which a city committee is called upon to resolve." Among these was the requirement to effectively manage primary party organizations and to stimulate them towards greater activism.[50] The need for improved criticism and self-criticism by party members was the subject of a Central Committee resolution in 1975, immediately following the Twenty-fifth Party Congress. This resolution was directed against the Tambov Obkom, but as with other resolutions of this type was applicable to all party organizations.[51] Brezhnev mentioned the Tambov resolution at the congress. He also stressed the importance of party organizations following through on decisions that had been made, adding that this had been the subject of a special letter from the Politburo to all party organizations.[52]

Closely related to the need to improve organizational effectiveness was the continuing emphasis on the selection and training of the most qualified party cadres. The most important impact of this policy was the exchange of party cards announced in 1972 and conducted in 1973–1974. Brezhnev had hinted at the possibility of an exchange of party cards in his April 1970 speech on Lenin's birthday.[53] But it was not until the Twenty-fourth Party Congress that he spelled this out fully. He pointed out that seventeen years had elapsed since the previous exchange of party cards and the validity period of the present cards had expired. Rather than conducting a simple exchange, however, Brezh-

nev proposed using the issuance of new cards as an "important organizational measure" that would strengthen party ranks and increase
activism and discipline.[54] The same point was made in the May 1972
resolution announcing the exchange.[55] Further discussions in *Pravda*
emphasized that this was not a purge since the need for purging party
ranks had disappeared with the elimination of "hostile class elements"
within the party. *Pravda* added that the party could now maintain the
purity of its ranks "without resorting to such measures."[56]

The party card exchange was the subject of special seminars and
meetings throughout the remainder of 1972. The exchange itself was
begun on 1 March 1973. To ensure that party organizations had adequate
time, a phased approach was employed. Initially conducted in a few
city and regional party committees, the exchange was extended to all
party organizations over the next two years.[57] Progress reports were
published in *Pravda* for the information of those party organizations
that had not yet undergone the procedure. In most of these reports, the
importance of using the issuance of the new cards to conduct individual
counselling sessions was presented as the primary benefit of the phased
approach. Party secretaries in Novgorod and Chernigov, for example,
described the detailed discussions they had held with party members
in their organizations.[58] The value of the exchange to raise disciplinary
standards was also mentioned. The First Secretary of the Chernigov
Obkom, for example, reported that he had spoken with many members
who had received a party reprimand in the past. In the Tadzhik Communist
Party, issuance of a new party card was used as an added counselling
session to discuss one member's history of drunkeness.[59]

Despite Soviet assertions to the contrary, the exchange of party cards
in 1973–1974 has correctly been termed a "mini-purge" by Jerry Hough.
Party membership was reduced by about 1–1.5 percent during this
period.[60] But the exchange of party cards was only part of Brezhnev's
continuing effort to reshape the party. The data in Tables 6.1 and 6.2
suggest that a major effort was undertaken between 1971–1974, not just
in 1973–1974, to further tighten membership restrictions and reduce the
rate of party growth. As Table 6.1 indicates, the overall rate of growth
fell below two percent in 1971 and remained there until 1975. A
complementary trend, illustrated in Table 6.2, was a dramatic reduction
in the rate of candidate admissions. Although this began earlier, it was
an important factor in the slowed rate of growth for 1971–1974 since
there was a smaller pool of candidates to choose from.

The rate of expulsions is difficult to assess. Since these figures were
not published after 1967, the number of party members expelled each
year can only be estimated. By subtracting the party's net growth for
a given year (Table 6.1) from the number of candidates admitted that

year (Table 6.2), the number of those dismissed can be approximated. This number also includes those who died or retired in a given year, and there is no way to separate these numbers from the number purged. Nevertheless, assuming more members are removed from the party each year than die or retire, both an absolute number and a percentage of the membership at the beginning of the year can be derived using this methodology. My calculations for 1971–1974 suggest that the number of members expelled (or died or retired) averaged 1.7 percent per year, roughly equalling the party's net growth. The impact on party membership was much thus greater than suggested by focusing on the exchange of party cards alone. Brezhnev launched a more intense effort to restrict party growth and tighten membership requirements coinciding with his recognition as top party leader—and the adoption of developed socialism into official ideology—in 1971. This was consistent with his efforts in the mid-1960s, but the magnitude was greater. The exchange of party cards was the centerpiece of this renewed effort, but it was not the only manifestation of Brezhnev's more restrictive policies.

The exchange of party cards was also an effective part of Brezhnev's longstanding campaign to improve discipline. This was essential to enable the party to fulfill its increasingly important and expanding leadership role. As stated in a February 1975 resolution: "The principal result of the exchange of party documents is that our party has been enriched by new experience in organizational and political work. It has strengthened its ranks and secured its contact with the masses. Its role as the leading and guiding force of Soviet society in the struggle to attain communism has increased even more."[61]

But in fact the opposite had happened. The greater latitude given the party under developed socialism resulted in more party interference in administration and management, possibly even more than existed under Khrushchev. Although the dimensions of such interference are unknown, it is clear from criticism of the Brezhnev era by Gorbachev and others that the party in the late-1970s became more active in day-to-day management than in providing overall direction to all elements of society and the economy. Moreover, beginning in 1975 Brezhnev apparently modified his cadres policy. In his speech to the Twenty-fifth Party Congress, he began to speak of the "party of all the people" (*partiia vsego naroda*), reminding his listeners of Khrushchev. Brezhnev's ironic use of this phrase was followed by a more liberal admissions policy that became evident in 1975–1977, illustrated in Table 6.1. In his speech, Brezhnev implied that such an easing of restrictions was taking place, explaining it has the logical result of societal development under socialism. He added that the party was not "forcing its numerical growth" and would continue to rely on stringent requirements to ensure that only the best people joined.[62]

While it is true that the expanded admissions policy did not represent a return to the wide-open recruitment policy of Khrushchev's regime,[63] the effort to open the party's doors to a growing number of people was unexpected based on Brezhnev's previous performance. The most convincing explanation for this reversal was that Brezhnev was facing new pressures because of a series of policy failures in 1975 that called his leadership ability into question. The economic assistance he had expected from the United States and Japan did not materialize, the former because of the Jackson-Vanik amendment to a broad US-Soviet trade bill which required guarantees of larger emigration quotas for Soviet Jews and the latter because of Japanese reluctance to become more deeply involved in the economic development of Siberia. The already poor domestic situation was exacerbated by the drought and crop failure of 1975. But, as if these problems did not exist, the new five-year plan for 1976–1981 called for a continuation of past policies. The prospect of little or no change led to criticism of Brezhnev's approach and questioning of his overall leadership ability, most notably by Alexei Kosygin.[64]

Brezhnev responded to this challenge by further consolidating his position in the leadership. In early 1977, he removed Nikolai Podgorny from the Politburo and took Podgorny's position as Chairman of the Presidium of the Supreme Soviet. Brezhnev also had himself named Marshal of the Soviet Union, unprecedented for a peacetime situation. He then used his enhanced power and authority to launch a campaign for greater economic efficiency, the main thrust of which was a series of attacks on the state bureaucracies, especially the economic ministries and Gosplan.

It is likely that Brezhnev began to ease up on restrictions on party growth and admissions in response to this departure in policy. To ensure his program was carried out, he probably felt he needed more intervention in the economic process. His endorsement of broader participation by People's Control committees (discussed in Chapter 5) would help monitor the performance of local managers. His expanded recruitment program buttressed this effort and provided greater leverage over the state apparatus. It also demonstrated his continued power over the party apparatus. The reversal of his previous party policy can thus be explained in terms of expediency rather than as a change in his ideological values. At this point, Brezhnev was fighting to maintain control.

Although the economy continued to falter, the challenges to Brezhnev's leadership disappeared with the removal from power of Podgorny and the death of Kosygin in 1980. This resulted in a change in Brezhnev's rhetoric about the urgency of economic improvement and about the need for exactingness on the part of party cadres, and this new tone was evident in his speech to the Twenty-sixth Party Congress.[65] The lack of any real challenge to his leadership led to a period of complacency that lasted until Brezhnev's death. No longer demanding leadership and discipline from the party, Brezhnev spoke of the corruption that was becoming increasingly evident among party and non-party officials. But, at this point, Brezhnev had little to offer. Further demands of the party would have to await new leadership.

Notes

1. See the articles by Stepakov in *Pravda*, 17 May 1965, p. 2, and *Kommunist*, 16/1965, pp. 32–40. Condemning Khrushchev for voluntarism and subjectivism in 1965–1966 was, of course, relatively common. For one of many other examples, see the lead article in *Voprosy Filosofii*, 6/1965, pp. 2–14. Stepakov became an important member of the ideological hierarchy after he was transferred to the Central Committee from the Leningrad Obkom in September 1965. See Wolfgang Leonhard, "Politics and Ideology in the Post-Khrushchev Era," in Alexander Dallin and Thomas B. Larson, *Soviet Politics Since Khrushchev*, (Englewood Cliffs: Prentice Hall, 1968), p. 45.

2. M. A. Suslov, *Na Putiakh Stroitel'stva Kommunizma* (Moscow: Politicheskaia Literatura, 1977), vol. 2, p. 11. A similar view was expressed by the head of the Organizational and Party Work Department of the Odessa Obkom, N. Zotov. Zotov pointed out that the former regime's approach had resulted in party secretaries at, for example, regional level bypassing secretaries at lower levels to deal directly with the manager of a plant or sovkhoz. Moreover, party secretaries were so caught up in economics they often conducted business in party meetings as if they were production managers. See N. Zotov, "Vospitanie Delovitosti," *Pravda*, 20 January 1966, p. 2. Many of the criticisms of Khrushchev's party policy were incorporated into the 1976 edition of the CPSU history, which attributed the "serious anxiety" among both party and non-party Soviet citizens to Khrushchev's mistakes. See *Istoriia Kommunisticheskoi Partii Sovetskogo Soiuza* (Moscow: Politicheskaia Literatura, 1976), p. 617. (Hereafter referred to as *Istoriia KPSS*.)

3. L. I. Brezhnev, *Leninskim Kursom*, vol. 1, p. 34.

4. *Pravda*, 6 September 1965.

5. See the following *Pravda* articles for information on improvements to ideological training: V. Stepakov, "Ovladet' Velikim Ucheniem Marksizma–Leninizma," 4 August 1965; N. Ivan'kovich, "Povyshat' Deistvennost' Partiinoi Ucheby," 13 September 1965; and the editorials on 14 February, 8 September, and 16 October 1965 and 4 May 1966. See also the articles in *Kommunist*, 1/1966, pp. 24–29 and 6/1966, pp. 3–12.

6. *XXIII S"ezd Kommunisticheskoi Partii Sovetskogo Soiuza: Stenograficheskii Otchet* (Moscow: Politizdat, 1966), vol. 1, pp. 128–129, 174, and 192.

7. *Istoriia KPSS*, p. 614. Western analysts have offered two slightly different interpretations of the reasons behind Khrushchev's party reorganization. One

view holds that it was consistent with Khrushchev's overall effort to expand the party's role and allow it to take more direct intervention in economic activity. See Barbara Ann Chotiner, *Khrushchev's Party Reform* (Westport, Connecticut: Greenwood Press, 1984), pp. 78–84; and Carl A. Linden, *Khrushchev and the Soviet Leadership* (Baltimore: Johns Hopkins Press, 1966), pp. 210–211. For a more detailed discussion of Khrushchev's ideas about interventionism, see George W. Breslauer, *Khrushchev and Brezhnev as Leaders* (London: George Allen & Unwin, 1982), pp. 124–125. A second view holds that the 1962 reorganization was a characteristic Soviet response to an area experiencing difficulty by increasing party control over that area. See Michel Tatu, *Power in the Kremlin* (New York: Viking Press, 1970), p. 288; and Merle Fainsod, *How Russia is Ruled*, rev. ed. (Cambridge: Harvard University Press, 1963), pp. 203–205.

8. Brezhnev, *Leninskim Kursom*, vol. 1, p. 67 (March 1965 plenum speech), and p. 342 (Twenty-third Party Congress speech).

9. This interpretation is offered in Roy A. Medvedev and Zhores Medvedev, *Khrushchev: The Years in Power* (New York: Columbia University Press, 1976), pp. 154–155.

10. Chotiner, *Khrushchev's Party Reform*, p. 275. Similar interpretations can be found in Linden, *Khrushchev and the Soviet Leadership*, p. 208; Jerry F. Hough and Merle Fainsod, *How the Soviet Union is Governed* (Cambridge: Harvard University Press, 1979), pp. 250–253; and George W. Breslauer, "On the Adaptability of Soviet Welfare-State Authoritarianism," in Karl W. Ryavec, ed., *Soviet Society and the Communist Party* (Amherst: University of Massachusetts Press, 1978), pp. 6–7. For Soviet interpretations, see *Istoriia KPSS*, p. 619; Brezhnev, *Leninskim Kursom*, vol. 1, pp. 66–67; and the editorial in *Pravda*, 18 November 1964.

11. *Istoriia KPSS*, p. 620. Also see Chotiner, *Khrushchev's Party Reform*, pp. 86–87, and Fainsod, *How Russia is Ruled*, pp. 229–239. George Breslauer points out that the trend towards specialization was intensified under Khrushchev in 1963–1964 with the recruitment of an increasing number of agricultural and industrial specialists into the party. See Breslauer, *Khrushchev and Brezhnev as Leaders*, p. 131.

12. Brezhnev, *Leninskim Kursom*, vol. 1, pp. 96–97. Brezhnev addressed industrial primary party organizations at the September 1965 plenum. See ibid., pp. 217–218. For Soviet discussions on the expanded role of local party organs in response to Brezhnev's appeal, see I. Kehbin, "Pervichnym Organizatsiiam— Osoboe Vnimanie," *Pravda*, 29 March 1965; N. Sobol', "Glavnaia Opora," *Pravda*, 5 July 1965; and the editorial in *Pravda*, 18 November 1965. Also see A. Kravchenko, "Pervichnye Organizatsii—Osnova KPSS," *Partiinaia Zhizn'*, 9/1965, pp. 13–21.

13. Brezhnev, *Leninskim Kursom*, vol. 1, p. 97. See also Breslauer, *Khrushchev and Brezhnev as Leaders*, pp. 158–159. Brezhnev's admonitions were not successful, however, in keeping the party out of the production process. The continuation of party interference has been one of the key complaints levied by Gorbachev against the Brezhnev regime. See Chapter 8 for a discussion of Gorbachev's approach to this problem.

14. Brezhnev, *Leninskim Kursom*, vol. 1, pp. 218–219 and p. 348. For additional information on the cadres problems encountered by the new regime, see the editorials in *Pravda*, 5 and 20 August 1965.

15. For a detailed discussion of the dimensions of the expansion of party membership under Khrushchev, see T. H. Rigby, *Communist Party Membership in the USSR, 1917–1967* (Princeton: Princeton University Press, 1968), pp. 296–323. Also see Fainsod, *How Russia is Ruled*, pp. 275–282. Several examples of the problems caused by Khrushchev's cadres policy were published in the Soviet press. Iu. Ruben, Secretary of the Riga City Party Committee, described the haste with which some leading cadres had been appointed. The process was frequently accomplished "at random," according to Ruben, with insufficient consideration of an individual's qualifications. This practice resulted in a situation where the city committee in many cases simply did not know the person it appointed. The mandatory transfer of cadres after 1961 also had a negative effect. As described by Georgian party leader V. Mzhavanadze, this practice resulted in a group of party secretaries who lacked experience and had little opportunity to develop a feel for party leadership. See Iu. Ruben, "Rabote s Kadrami—Prodummanuiu Sistemu," *Kommunist*, 1/1966, p. 35, and V. Mzhavanadze, "Pervichnaia Organizatsiia i Partiinii Komitet," *Pravda*, 14 August 1965. The Riga Gorkom's answer to the problem described by Ruben was to establish cadres commissions to deal systematically with the selection of party leaders. Recommendations from the commissions were validated by the party bureau or by a plenum of the gorkom.

16. On the new rules, see Brezhnev, *Leninskim Kursom*, vol. 1, pp. 355–358; *Istoriia KPSS*, pp. 629–630; and *Kommunist*, 7/1966, pp. 3–11. The *Pravda* statement is from 13 April 1966. For further discussion of the expanded powers of the primary party organizations, see Rigby, *Communist Party Membership in the USSR*, pp. 320–322.

17. Brezhnev, *Leninskim Kursom*, vol. 1, pp. 232 and 341–349. For related discussions, see *Kommunist*, 1/1966, pp. 24–29, and the editorial in *Pravda*, 22 March 1966.

18. Brezhnev, *Leninskim Kursom*, vol. 1, p. 33.

19. *Pravda*, 7 and 27 July 1965, and 5 January 1966.

20. See D. Kunaev, "Organizovannost' i Distsiplina," *Pravda*, 14 December 1965; G. Popov, "Demokratiia i Distsiplina," *Pravda*, 28 January 1966; and V. Berezov, "Pod Znakom Vysokoi Otvetstvennosti," *Kommunist*, 1/1966, pp. 24–29.

21. Brezhnev, *Leninskim Kursom*, vol. 1, pp. 32–35.

22. Brezhnev, *Leninskim Kursom*, vol. 1, pp. 39, 216–219, and 345–347.

23. Sources used for this paragraph included "Sila Primera," *Kommunist*, 1/1966, pp. 3–11; and *Pravda*, 24 January and 4 July 1965, and 7 February 1966.

24. For discussions of the new leadership style, see F. Burlatskii, "Politika i Nauka," *Pravda*, 10 January 1965; V. Afanas'ev, "Nauchnoe Rukovodstvo Sotsial'nymi Protsessami," *Kommunist*, 12/1965, pp. 58–73; S. Shchetinin, "Ovladet' Iskusstvom Rukovodstva," *Partiinaia Zhizn'*, 12/1965, pp. 8–16; and *Pravda*, 10 and 15 April 1965. See *Pravda*, 29 April 1965, for a discussion of the Leninist

leadership principles evident in the new approach to party management. For speeches to the Twenty-third Congress, see *XXIII S"ezd KPSS*, vol. 1, p. 602, and the speeches by Rashidov, Masherov, Rasulov, Nikolaev, and Obezov.

25. Rigby, *Communist Party Membership in the USSR*, p. 300, and *Partiinaia Zhizn'*, 10/1965, p. 9.

26. This point is made most effectively by Darrell P. Hammer, "The Dilemma of Party Growth," *Problems of Communism* 20 (July-August 1970), pp. 16–21. For a different perspective, see Jerry Hough's argument on party saturation in Jerry F. Hough, *The Soviet Union and Social Science Theory* (Cambridge: Harvard University Press, 1977), pp. 125–139.

27. The text of the resolution can be found in *Spravochnik Partiinogo Rabotnika*, 1966, pp. 383–386. For representative Western discussions of the Kharkov resolution, see Rigby, *Communist Party Membership in the USSR*, pp. 256–257; and Tatu, *Power in the Kremlin*, pp. 501–503. Most analysts agree that the resolution was aimed at Podgorny, who was transferred out of the Central Committee five months later (see footnote 33).

28. A notable exception is Jerry Hough, who suggests that the reversal of Khrushchev's recruitment trends would have occurred anyway. He cites as reasons for this the decline in party admissions in the 1960s, reflecting a basic change in the age distribution of the population; the fact that the actual numbers of admissions remained quite high; and the continuing effort to improve the party's social profile. See Hough and Fainsod, *How the Soviet Union is Governed*, pp. 336–340. A successful argument against Hough's first point is provided by Aryeh L. Unger, "Soviet Communist Party Membership Under Brezhnev: A Comment," *Soviet Studies* 29 (April 1977), pp. 306–309. The second point is countered by Unger as well, and by my own analysis of the net growth rates of the party, below.

29. See, for example, Jerry F. Hough, *Soviet Leadership in Transition* (Washington: The Brookings Institution, 1980), p. 63; Hough and Fainsod, *How the Soviet Union is Governed*, pp. 261–263; Stanley Rothman and George W. Breslauer, *Soviet Politics and Society* (St. Paul: West Publishing Company, 1978), p. 175; and John S. Reshetar, Jr., *The Soviet Polity: Government and Politics in the USSR*, 2nd ed. (New York: Harper & Row, 1978), p. 111.

30. See, for example, Rigby, "Soviet Communist Party Membership Under Brezhnev," *Soviet Studies* 3 (July 1976), pp. 327–334; Unger, "Soviet Communist Party Membership Under Brezhnev: A Comment," pp. 310–314; and Hough and Fainsod, *How the Soviet Union is Governed*, pp. 323–354.

31. See Ellen Mickiewicz, "Regional Variation in Female Recruitment and Advancement in the Communist Party of the Soviet Union," *Slavic Review* 36 (September 1977), pp. 444–445, and Ronald J. Hill and Peter Frank, *The Soviet Communist Party* (London: George Allen & Unwin, 1981), p. 25.

32. Brezhnev's early cadres policy is discussed in Rigby, *Communist Party Membership in the USSR*, pp. 322–323. On the number of expulsions, Rigby excludes the number of members removed for not having paid their dues. His numbers for those expelled, then, are 30,763 for 1964 and 62,868 for 1966. Soviet sources add both categories together. See *Partiinaia Zhizn'*, 10/1965, p. 10, and 7/1967, p. 8.

33. Brezhnev exercised his control over the party in other ways as well. He made substantial changes in the ranks of obkom first secretaries in the RSFSR, and changed his title from "First Secretary" to "General Secretary." See T. H. Rigby, "The Soviet Regional Leadership: The Brezhnev Generation," *Slavic Review* 37 (March 1978), p. 9. Brezhnev's ability to implement his cadres policy was certainly helped by the transfer of Podgorny from the Central Committee to the Supreme Soviet in December 1965. The connection between the rivalry of the two men and cadres policy has been discussed by many analysts. Barbara Chotiner points out that both Brezhnev and Podgorny supported Khrushchev's 1962 reorganization. Chotiner, *Khrushchev's Party Reform*, p. 94. Carl Linden makes the same point, adding that Brezhnev and Podgorny were brought into the Central Committee at the same time in 1963 as "rival heirs." Linden, *Khrushchev and the Soviet Leadership*, pp. 205–206 and 241. Hough suggests that Podgorny probably held a post in charge of the party apparatus before he was transferred to the Supreme Soviet. Hough and Fainsod, *How the Soviet Union is Governed*, p. 256. The three most forceful arguments supporting the hypothesis that Brezhnev removed Podgorny in light of this background are in Paul J. Murphy, *Brezhnev: Soviet Politician* (Jefferson, North Carolina: McFarland & Company, 1981), pp. 250–251; Tatu, *Power in the Kremlin*, pp. 501–503; and Teresa Rakowska-Harmstone, "Toward a Theory of Soviet Leadership Maintenance," in Paul Cocks, Robert V. Daniels, and Nancy Whittier Heer, eds., *The Dynamics of Soviet Politics* (Cambridge: Harvard University Press, 1976), p. 61.

34. Donald Kelley has described four themes in Soviet literature on the nature of the party leadership in developed socialism. These include: the need for a more long-range view of development problems; the need for assimilating modern economic and social management techniques; the need for the party to increase the pace of economic and social development; and the need for greater party supervision over non-party organizations. See Donald R. Kelley, *The Politics of Developed Socialism* (New York: Greenwood Press, 1986), pp. 143–144.

35. Brezhnev, *Leninskim Kursom*, vol. 2, pp. 391–394, and vol. 3, p. 309.

36. See Fedoseev's articles "Vozrastanie Roli Partii—Zakonomernost' Stroitel'stva Sotsializma i Kommunizma," *Kommunist*, 15/1971, pp. 72–91, "KPSS—Avangard Sovetskogo Naroda," *Problemy Mira i Sotsializma*, 3/1971, pp. 3–11, and "KPSS—Partiia Nauchnogo Kommunizma," *Pravda*, 28 April 1971, pp. 2–3. For additional criticism of the Chinese after the Twenty-fourth Party Congress, see: O. Vladimirov and V. Riazanov, "K 50-leitiiu Kommpartii Kitaia," *Kommunist* 10/1971, pp. 76–90, and "Deistvennost' Leninskoi Vneshnei Politiki," ibid., 14/1971, pp. 73–81.

37. G. E. Glezerman, et al., eds. *Razvitoe Sotsialisticheskoe Obshchestvo*, pp. 291–292, and V. M. Sikorskii, *KPSS Na Ehtape Razvitogo Sotsializma* (Minsk: BGU, 1975), pp. 151–152.

38. Brezhnev, *Leninskim Kursom*, vol. 5, p. 526.

39. G. E. Glezerman, et al., eds., *Razvitoe Sotsialisticheskoe Obshchestvo*, pp. 284–289; Sikorskii, *KPSS*, pp. 72–79; and R. Kosolapov, "Politicheskii Avangard Sovetskogo Obshchestva," *Pravda*, 4 November 1971, pp. 2–3.

40. Sikorskii, *KPSS*, pp. 84–85.

41. Erik P. Hoffman, "Changing Soviet Perspectives on Leadership and Administration," in Cohen, et al., eds., *The Soviet Union Since Stalin*, p. 83.

42. Paul M. Cocks, "Administrative Rationality, Political Change, and the Role of the Party," in Ryavec, ed., *Soviet Society and the Communist Party*, p. 51.

43. Brezhnev, *Leninskim Kursom*, vol. 3, p. 303.

44. Sidney Ploss, "New Politics in Russia?," *Survey*, Autumn 1973, p. 26.

45. *Pravda*, 6 and 13 March 1972. Besides its importance for overall party policy, this resolution was almost certainly aimed at Mzhavanadze, who was replaced by Eduard Shevardnadze in September.

46. F. Petrenko, "Vozrastanie Role KPSS—Zakonomernost' Kommunisticheskogo Stroitel'stva," *Pravda*, 19 October 1973, pp. 2–3, and "Partiia i Demokratiia," *Pravda*, 9 June 1974, pp. 2–3. See also his article, "KPSS—Avangard Rabochego Klassa, Vsego Naroda," *Pravda*, 9 April 1976, pp. 2–3.

47. See the resolutions published in K. V. Kapitonov, ed., *Voprosy Organizatsionno-Partiinoi Raboty KPSS* (Moscow: Politicheskia Literatura, 1978), pp. 558–598. See also *Pravda*, 4 and 30 September 1975.

48. For additional examples of the expansion of the party's role, see Breslauer, *Khrushchev and Brezhnev as Leaders*, pp. 263–264. For a Soviet perspective, see P. A. Rodionov, et al., eds., *Vozrastanie Rukovodiashchei Roli KPSS v Stroitel'stve Sotsializma i Kommuniza*, (Moscow: Politicheskaia Literatura, 1979), pp. 40–150.

49. Brezhnev, *Leninskim Kursom*, vol. 3, pp. 299–301 and 304–305.

50. *Pravda*, 6 March 1972.

51. *Pravda*, 28 February 1975. Within two months, party organizations began reporting on the improvements in criticism and self-criticism. See, for example, *Pravda*, 28 March 1975, p. 2.

52. Brezhnev, *Leninskim Kursom*, vol. 5, pp. 526–527.

53. Ibid., vol. 2, p. 580.

54. Ibid., vol. 3, pp. 301–302.

55. *Pravda*, 20 May 1972.

56. *Pravda*, 24 June 1972.

57. *Pravda*, 19 February 1973.

58. N. Antonov, "Kogda Vozrastet Trebovatel'nost'," *Pravda*, 5 September 1975, p. 2, and N. Umanets, article in *Pravda*, 1 March 1974.

59. O. Latifi, "Vnimatel'nym Vzgliadom," *Pravda*, 13 September 1974, p. 2.

60. Hough and Fainsod, *How the Soviet Union is Governed*, p. 336. The lower figure is provided by Unger, "Soviet Communist Party Membership Under Brezhnev: A Comment," p. 308. The higher figure is from Rigby, "Soviet Communist Party Membership Under Brezhnev," p. 322.

61. *Pravda*, 7 February 1975.

62. Brezhnev, *Leninskim Kursom*, vol. 5, pp. 520–521.

63. Unger, "Soviet Communist Party Membership Under Brezhnev: A Comment," p. 308.

64. See the thorough discussion of these events in Breslauer, *Khrushchev and Brezhnev as Leaders*, chapter 13.

65. Ibid., pp. 237–244. Brezhnev continued to articulate the need for exactingess up to the end of his regime. See the discussion in Kelley, *Politics of Developed*

Socialism, pp. 150–151. But towards the end of his tenure, Brezhnev's words on this subject were no longer accompanied by any significant action. The best evidence for this is Andropov's vigorous drive to remove corrupt officials and his retreat from the "trust in cadres" formula from the very beginning of his short regime. See ibid., pp. 151–153.

7

Between Brezhnev and Gorbachev

This study has demonstrated a strong correlation between Brezhnev's ideology and policy throughout his tenure as General Secretary. Though his approach to various policy areas changed over time in recognition of the shifting limits of permissible change, Brezhnev's overall agenda remained for the most part consistent. The values he stressed in his ideological statements served as the basis for policy initiatives from the time he became General Secretary until the late 1970s. The central element in Brezhnev's program for change was the reestablishment of centralized party control over the economy and political system and Soviet primacy within the international communist movement. This was the main contrast between Khrushchev and Brezhnev: whereas Khrushchev encouraged the devolution of authority from the center to regional and local government and economic organs, Brezhnev reasserted the power of the center over the political and economic system.

Brezhnev was not alone alone in these policy preferences. Archie Brown has pointed out that there was a growing revulsion among the post-Khrushchev leadership against many of Khrushchev's policies, particularly those emphasizing de-centralization of party control.[1] This led to an evolving consensus for change. Brezhnev capitalized on this consensus, reshaped it according to his own policy preferences, and developed a new consensus for change that, while retaining the rejection of Stalinism that was initiated by Khrushchev, redefined the scope, pace, and features of the de-Stalinization process in a more conservative way. Developed socialism was the ideological expression of the Brezhnev consensus.

By the end of the Brezhnev period, however, this consensus had begun to erode for several reasons. In foreign policy, the Soviet international position had deteriorated (especially relations with the US and China). Consequently, the authority of the CPSU declined among world communists. This decline was evident in the documents of the 1976 World Communist Conference, which emphasized non-interference and cooperation instead of promoting the leading role of the CPSU. Domestically, the decline of party authority was evident in the stagnation of the economy that began in the mid-1970s and in the increasing corruption of the late Brezhnev years. The loss of authority was exacerbated by the threat to party rule implied in the Polish crisis of 1980-1981, a message not lost on Moscow. Just as the failure of Khrushchev's policies led to a new leadership consensus, these difficulties of the late Brezhnev period called the Brezhnev-inspired consensus into doubt, leading eventually to the development of a new consensus championed by Mikhail Gorbachev.

Demise of the Brezhnev Consensus

Brezhnev's speech to the Twenty-sixth Party Congress in 1981 indicated that certain aspects of his policy agenda had already been called into question.[2] The speech was a curious mixture of praise of past accomplishments and clear hints that change was necessary. This was especially noticeable in statements regarding the USSR's position in the communist movement and about foreign policy generally. While Brezhnev provided the obligatory statements about the strength of international socialism, he changed the earlier formulation of the role of the USSR in the socialist community. He now called for closer study of "the experience of fraternal countries" and for developing ways to "utilize it more broadly." He stated that "no one is imposing any stereotypes or patterns that ignore the distinctions of any country." Although he still accused the Chinese of distorting "the principles and essence of socialism" and criticized the PRC for its 1979 incursion into Vietnam, he held open the possibility of improvements in Sino-Soviet relations. He indicated similar flexibility in other statements on Soviet foreign policy. To emphasize the Soviet desire for peace, he called for a freeze on the deployment of medium range missiles, proposed the establishment of peace zones in the Far East and Europe, offered to negotiate on Afghanistan either by itself or in the context of the Persian Gulf situation, suggested establishment of an international committee of scientists to help prevent nuclear war, and called for a special session of the UN Security Council to discuss ways of improving the international situation.

These were major departures from Brezhnev's previous statements. His Party Congress speech demonstrated the cumulative negative effects of the costs of Moscow's aggressive Third World policy, the danger posed by a new trend towards economic and political reform in Eastern Europe, and the changing strategic situation due in part to the increasing rapprochement between China and the United States. Although Brezhnev did not suggest that the call for greater flexibility internationally was

related to problems in the Soviet economy, there is little doubt that the
continuing decline in Soviet economic performance had contributed to
the reformulation of Soviet goals in foreign policy. All these elements
were to remain part of the post-Brezhnev consensus, but were not given
their full expression until Gorbachev came to power in 1985. Brezhnev's
inclusion of these ideas in his 1981 speech indicates that the party
leadership was already considering new directions in foreign policy well
before Gorbachev's "new thinking" took hold.

A change in the Brezhnev consensus on economic policy was also
evident in his speech. Although Brezhnev asserted that "the seventies
may be summed up as a major step in developing the national economy
of the country," he went on to describe many disturbing problems,
particularly in agriculture. Pointing to the need to increase private
agriculture and to ensure an uninterrupted supply of food to population
centers, he announced the creation of the Food Program that was to be
introduced the following year.[3] The overall direction of economic policy,
however, was consistent with Brezhnev's program since the late 1960s;
development of heavy industry was still seen as the key to economic
progress. The other objectives of the 11th Five-Year Plan were consistent
with Brezhnev's characteristic themes of discipline, accelerated progress
in science and technology, and the need for economizing resources. He
also repeated his longstanding preference for strengthening the military.
He criticized severely economic managers who had engaged in the
practice of downward plan revision, and repeated the need for strengthened contract discipline that had been the subject of a campaign in
1979. In terms of labor policy, Brezhnev recast his preference for a
balance between moral and material incentives by asserting that only
those who worked hardest should receive incentives, while those who
did not work should receive no incentives. He called for a greater effort
to satisfy the consumer needs of the population, something he had
mentioned many times previously. Presaging the anti-alcohol programs
of Andropov and Gorbachev, Brezhnev also admitted that the "ugly
phenomenon" of Soviet drinking needed to be combatted as part of the
overall effort to improve labor discipline.

In terms of the political system, Brezhnev touched the characteristic
themes of improving the performance of the soviets and the primary
party organizations. He also stressed the continuing need for ensuring
the party's decisions were carried out, identifying this as a "major weak
spot" for many party organizations. To buttress his call for improvements
in the Soviet economy, he advised recruiting more economic specialists
into the party, and criticized party members working in the economic
ministries for their ineffective "armchair leadership."

These were not new ideas. Something that was new was Brezhnev's insistence on the need for improving party leadership, a topic that had been largely absent from his speeches since the late 1960s, although it was a key aspect of developed socialism. He addressed this theme in terms of the crisis facing the Polish Party, but it was obvious to his listeners that Brezhnev had in mind the CPSU as well. Brezhnev blamed the crisis on "the imperialists and their accomplices" who were trying to turn the Polish people against socialism. His main point was that "the pillars of the socialist state" were jeopardized by the inability of the party to end the crisis and restore order. Brezhnev pointed out that, "the events in Poland show once again how important it is for the party, for the strengthening of its leading role, to pay close heed to the voice of the masses."

Much of what Brezhnev advocated in economic and political policy represented a major departure from his previous agenda, one that had been consistent for 15 years. The fact that he was articulating different positions in 1981 does not mean he changed his policy preferences. It does, however, represent a definite change in the leadership consensus on several major issues. The revised formulation about the relative position of the USSR in the international socialist community, the need for new measures in the economy, and the importance of strengthened party leadership in light of the Polish situation were almost certainly the result of many leadership discussions leading up to the Party Congress. These were not Brezhnevian themes, but Brezhnev had to articulate them because they represented the consensus of the party leadership. The evidence that Brezhnev did not completely agree with the need for change was in the overall program he outlined. His agenda repeated the old solutions: more bureaucracy, greater discipline, dependence on heavy industry as the solution to economic problems, and a continued preference for the military. Moreover, the theoretical underpinning for these policies was unchanged. Brezhnev emphasized that developed socialism was still the theoretical framework upon which policy was created. He asserted that the party had "spelled out and specified the ways and time limits for the attainment of our program aims and defined long-term strategy and tactics" on the basis of developed socialism. He noted that mass political work had become "fossilized," and called for the restructuring of ideological work to answer the needs of the population. But there was no major redefinition of ideology. And, although Brezhnev called for a revised Party Program, he implied that its purpose was to more summarize the accomplishments of the past than to chart a new course for the future.

Brezhnev's speech was thus a curious mixture of both his own preferences and a newly evolving leadership consensus that something had to be done. He described serious economic problems, but provided no new solutions. He talked of the loss of ideological vitality, but continued to promote the shopworn formulas of developed socialism. He called for peace, but advocated the continued strengthening of the military. It seemed as if Brezhnev was reluctant to address the problems he had raised, suggesting that he, too, had become an armchair manager. Perhaps Brezhnev should not be judged too harshly; he was less than two years from his death at the time of the Party Congress and his deteriorating health was already apparent. He still wielded substantial power and authority, evident in the fact that he was allowed to insert his policy preferences in his 1981 Party Congress speech. But Brezhnev was clearly out of step with the new leadership thinking.

Beginning with Andropov and Chernenko, the new leadership consensus came into sharper focus. It contained a revised program for Soviet development and a modified ideological formulation to justify it. This consensus has found its fullest expression in Gorbachev's call for perestroika, democratization, glasnost, and new thinking. But, despite the publicity given to Gorbachev's innovations, many of the central elements of Gorbachev's program had been developed by the party leadership as much as four years before he came to power. Gorbachev, of course, was part of the leadership during this period. But in developing a new strategy of domestic political and economic reform and a more subdued foreign policy, Gorbachev was not alone.

The Emerging Consensus Under Andropov and Chernenko

Brezhnev's death in November 1982 provided the impetus for a broad reexamination of policy in all areas. During the transitional regimes of Andropov and Chernenko, it was clear that the leadership consensus had shifted. As each of Brezhnev's first two successors defined their policy preferences, however, the dimensions of this consensus remained in flux. This was not because of major disagreement between the two men. In fact, they agreed on many key points including the need for economic reform, the need to improve agriculture and the food supply, the need for reasserting the party's authority, and the continuing need for heavy expenditures for the military.[4] Moreover, they agreed that developed socialism should remain the theoretical basis for policy on all fronts. Where they differed was in terms of focus. Andropov placed the need for economic reform at the top of the priority list; Chernenko stressed instead the urgency of restoring the party's authority.

The logical explanation for the different perspectives of the two men (aside from personal preference and interest) is the positions they occupied prior to attaining the position of General Secretary. Andropov's position as head of the KGB would have given him a detailed understanding of the state of the economy and problems caused by the downturn in economic growth. Chernenko's career of assignments in party propaganda organs, as Central Committee Secretary in charge of the General Department, and Politburo member with supervision of ideology gave him a better picture of the deteriorating situation regarding the party's authority. Chernenko's views were no doubt influenced by his access to the thousands of letters that poured into the Central Committee each day, a fact he mentioned frequently.[5]

Both Andropov and Chernenko agreed on the continuing viability of developed socialism as the theoretical underpinning of the party's actions, although they modified the concept slightly. In his speech to the June 1983 plenum of the Central Committee, Andropov pointed out that developed socialism had not yet been completed as a stage in communist development. Since there were still many difficulties and problems facing the CPSU, the party's goal should be the "perfection" of developed socialism. Andropov also stated that developed socialism could no longer be claimed as the only correct path to communism, expanding on Brezhnev's call to the Twenty-sixth Party Congress to study the experience of other socialist countries. Andropov pointed out that the socialist world had become "diverse and complex" and stressed that there were different approaches to socialist development, "even if at one time it had seemed that these would be more similar." The main thing, in Andropov's view, was to make sure that existing differences did not hinder the increased levels of economic and social integration among communist states.[6] Chernenko reiterated the need for perfecting developed socialism in his speech to the June 1983 plenum and in his 1984 presentation to the Central Committee commission charged with drafting a revised Party program.[7]

A new direction in economic policy was the element of the emerging consensus representing the major departure from Brezhnev. In his speech to the November 1982 plenum, Andropov asserted that "there are many urgent problems" because of reliance on old habits and inertia. Surprisingly, he admitted that he had no solutions. Pointing to the Food Program as the main new initiative in economic policy, he outlined many other areas in which improvement was needed. Calling for mobilization of the masses and the movement of cadres if necessary to achieve near-term goals, Andropov stated that the party's "duty" to ensure economic growth and improvement in the quality of life for Soviet citizens. This was not to be done at the expense of defense, however. Andropov made it clear that the Politburo considered it "obligatory to provide everything that is necessary" to the military in light of the international situation.[8]

Andropov amplified his plan for change at the June 1983 plenum. Consistent with his overall campaign for discipline and increased productivity, he directed that the proposed revision of the Party Program contain a clear explanation of how to boost the effectiveness of labor. The Program was to include details on how material rewards would be apportioned according to an individual's labor, and on ways for improving planning and administration and socialist competition. Andropov's incentives policy was thus much more restrictive than Brezhnev's (and is probably the one Brezhnev hinted at in his Twenty-sixth Party Congress speech). Andropov underscored the severity of his policy by stating that "each of our citizens has the right to only those material goods that correspond to the quantity and quality of his socially useful labor. Only to that."[9] This was to become the central element in Gorbachev's labor policy.

Andropov followed these statements with a series of economic experiments in 1984. Close in many ways to the 1965 reforms, Andropov's experiments sought to stablize plan fulfillment, make enterprises more responsive to consumer demands, and bring manager and worker rewards much more in line with results, particularly in terms of economizing resources. He also encouraged wide-ranging debates on economic reform. The bonus system established in conjunction with Andropov's program was very strict, forcing economic managers to become much more efficient before they qualified for additional pay. In the year following Andropov's death, Konstantin Chernenko continued these programs. But, although he did not reverse the course Andropov had established and encouraged continuation of economic debates, Chernenko contributed nothing substantive to the development of economic policy in general, or incentives policy in particular.[10]

On the nationalities question, Andropov stated a position that was in line with the moderate tone of the 1977 Constitution. He called for a well-developed, scientifically based nationality policy appropriate to the stage of developed socialism. In his view, this should be a direct representation of the Leninist principle of equal rights for all nationalities.[11] Chernenko, in contrast, evidently advocated an assimilationist approach similar to Brezhnev's position in the early 1970s. Although he never fully spelled out his program for nationality relations, Chernenko gave a strong indication of the direction his policy would take by referring to the importance of the Russian language in communications and education.[12] This was the old assimilationist formula. Thus, the two men had different views on this important question. Neither, however, made nationality policy an important part of their agenda for change, probably because neither was tested on this issue.

The two men had similar views on political participation and the role of the CPSU. Andropov appeared to advocate greater autonomy for the soviets and seemed willing to risk the possibility of loosened party control over the state apparatus to stimulate local initiative. He called for a reduction in the size of both the party and state bureaucracy and pushed for strengthening socialist democracy. Most important, he described a new departure in party-state relations that would end the duplication between the two and increase the responsibility of state administrators. He also called for greater glasnost in informing the public of the leadership's activities and plans.[13] Chernenko echoed much of what his predecessor had to say, including several references to glasnost. He went beyond Andropov, however, in the critical area of party leadership. Consistent with his speeches and articles while Andropov was still alive, Chernenko continued to stress the need for revitalizing the party as the central focus of his party agenda upon assuming the General Secretary's chair.

Chernenko's concern about the party's authority was evident as early as 1980. In a *Kommunist* article in November that year, he spoke of the need for party members to deal more directly with the masses. He also addressed the importance of ensuring the unity of word and deed, pointing out that this was essential to increase the party's authority and provide effective leadership to society as a whole. Chernenko repeated these concerns a year later in a second *Kommunist* article. He also pointed out the problems caused by excessive party intervention in economic and administrative management. The main problem was that economic managers, soviet leaders, and others were not doing their jobs. They instead turned to the party to do their work for them. Chernenko complained that party committees had become so bogged down in daily tasks they were unable to provide the overall guidance that was their primary concern. Chernenko compared the party's role to the director of an orchestra, setting the tone and providing guidance, but not playing the instruments himself. Turning again and again in these articles to the need for increased ties with the masses, Chernenko strongly implied that the party faced a crisis of authority and legitimacy. He was quick to indicate that he did not advocate a return to Stalinism, when there were "coarse violations of Leninist norms of party and state activity." (In this regard, he noted the party's "unambiguous view" about the need to face its history squarely.)[14] But he was very persuasive on the dilemma faced by the party in trying to launch new initiatives at a time its overall authority was shrinking.

This discussion of the views of Andropov and Chernenko helps demonstrate the outlines of the post-Brezhnev consensus. It was clear from the degree of emphasis on the need for economic reform and the importance of ensuring the party's authority that both men thought these were the fundamental concerns facing the party leadership. They developed these two themes throughout the interregnum, closing the door on the Brezhnev period and setting the stage for Gorbachev. It was equally clear that neither man viewed the international communist movement to be the same unified entity it once had been, particularly in light of the Polish crisis; in the early 1980s the Soviets had too much to worry about within their own borders to be overly concerned with what was happening elsewhere. Both Andropov and Chernenko relied on developed socialism as the theoretical underpinning for their agendas for change, although they did modify this slightly to "perfecting developed socialism" to underscore the need for continuing change. Both men insisted that theory be used to help solve the problems of the present and point the direction to the future. Ideology could no longer be used to celebrate the achievements of the past. Nor could it become fossilized into empty phrases that had no connection with contemporary Soviet life.

The ground was thus prepared for Gorbachev by his predecessors. That men as far apart on the political spectrum as Andropov and Chernenko agreed that change was necessary indicated the broad dimensions of the consensus within the leadership. The fact that this consensus has not been thoroughly examined by Western scholars is due more to their focus on the succession struggles of the early 1980s than to lack of evidence.[15] As this survey indicates, Gorbachev came to power with a broad mandate for change to restore vitality to the economy and political system and to reshape Soviet foreign policy along less-aggressive lines. The debates and obstacles he was likely to encounter would be about the scope and pace of reform, not its necessity. And despite the fact that developed socialism had not been completely rejected as the theoretical basis for the party's activity, it was evident that the Brezhnevian agenda had been changed enough to warrant a corresponding change to official ideology that was so clearly identified with his policy preferences.

Notes

1. Archie Brown, "Leadership Succession and Policy Innovation," in Archie Brown and Michael Kaser, eds., *Soviet Policy for the 1980s* (Bloomington: Indiana University Press, 1982), pp. 229–230.

2. L. I. Brezhnev, *Report of the Central Committee of the CPSU to the XXVI Congress of the Communist Party of the Soviet Union and the Immediate Tasks of the Party in Home and Foreign Policy* (Moscow: Novosti Press Agency Publishing House, 1981).

3. Gorbachev was certainly the moving force behind the Food Program in his role as Central Committee Secretary responsible for agriculture.

4. Chernenko's support for the military was not as strong as Andropov's. He had advocated a reduced level of defense spending in the two years immediately prior to becoming General Secretary, calling instead for increased consumer goods production. Chernenko's outspokeness was likely attributable to his view that domestic unrest posed a greater threat to political stability than the military threat of hostile nations. See the analysis in Marc D. Zlotnik, "Chernenko Succeeds" *Problems of Communism* 33 (March–April 1984), pp. 26–27.

5. In 1980, Chernenko stated that 9.4 million letters had been received in party committees in the four years since the Twenty-fifth Party Congress. In 1981, he mentioned that more than 3 million letters had been received in the Central Committee alone between the Twenty-fifth and Twenty-sixth congresses. This averages out to over 1,600 letters per day, and is close to the 1,500 figure Brezhnev mentioned at the Twenty-sixth Congress. See Chernenko's articles in *Kommunist* 17/1980, p. 22, and 13/1981, p. 15, and Brezhnev, *Report of the Central Committee of the CPSU to the XXVI Congress*, p. 132.

6. *Kommunist*, 9/1983, pp. 6 and 13.

7. *Kommunist*, 9/1983, pp. 19–20, and 7/1984, pp. 4–8.

8. *Kommunist*, 17/1982, pp. 14–19. Andropov's statement could be read to mean that military spending may be reduced, since the wording "everything that is necessary" is ambiguous. Similar wording has become the basis for Gorbachev's promise of "reasonable sufficiency" for the military, which in his vocabulary means a cutback for defense to gain resources for the domestic economy.

9. *Kommunist*, 9/1983, p. 10.

10. For a comprehensive discussion of the Andropov economic experiments, see Ed A. Hewett, *Reforming the Soviet Economy* (Washington, D.C.: The Brookings Institution, 1988), pp. 257–273.

11. *Kommunist*, 9/1983, p. 11.

12. Ibid., p. 35.

13. Ibid., pp. 10–11.

14. *Kommunist*, 17/1980, pp. 10–26, and 13/1981, pp. 6–22. Chernenko repeated these themes in an article in *Kommunist*, 9/1983, pp. 17–39, and in his speech to the April 1984 plenum concerning the revised Party Program. See *Pravda*, 11 April 1984 and *Kommunist*, 7/1984, pp. 4–8.

15. See, for example, Jerry F. Hough, *Soviet Leadership in Transition* (Washington: The Brookings Institution, 1980), and his "Andropov's First Year," *Problems of Communism*, 32 (November–December 1983), pp. 49–64. For a similar analysis of the post–Andropov period, see Zlotnik, "Chernenko Succeeds."

8

Gorbachev's Ideology and Policy

Mikhail Gorbachev was the right man to articulate the post-Brezhnev consensus and push the CPSU towards new goals. While still a regional party secretary, he authored numerous articles on the key policy issues faced by the Soviet leadership in the late Twentieth Century. As early as 1967, he addressed problems of the local (and by implication, national) economy, the nationalities question, party leadership, and others. His articles were impressive for their candor, straightforward language, detailed knowledge of the problems of the day, and concrete recommendations.

Gorbachev's positions in the Central Committee Secretariat and Politburo between 1978–1985 gave him the broad perspective and knowledge of Moscow politics to round out his experiences as regional party secretary. He also gained insights into the corruption and inertia of the late Brezhnev period. He continued to articulate his ideas after Brezhnev's death, impressing both Soviet and foreign audiences with his knowledge and charisma. At a time of personal risk when, as Yegor Ligachev told the Nineteenth Party Conference, one could have easily "ended up as ambassador to a very remote country," Gorbachev gained the respect of his colleagues in the leadership by championing a truthful examination of Soviet ideology and policy.[1]

The central theme of Gorbachev's work during the past twenty years is the need for radical and immediate change. He gives credit to his predecessors for their contributions to Soviet development—Stalin for industrialization and collectivization, Khrushchev for overcoming the arbitrariness of Stalin's rule, and Brezhnev for reversing Khrushchev's improvised economic management techniques and for gaining strategic parity with the US—but points to the cumulative nature of problems that mounted up over time. He told the Twenty-seventh Party Congress that for several years problems had accumulated faster than they could be resolved. "The situation demanded change," he said, "but in the central organs and even locally a peculiar psychology came to the fore.

It was as if things could be improved without changing anything. But it does not happen this way, comrades."[2]

Although Gorbachev has pushed the bureaucracy, the party, and society itself to revise past practices, he has no intention of altering the socialist foundation of the Soviet system. He has downplayed ideology as a motive force in his reform program, but has not abandoned theory. He has in many ways redefined ideological precepts long taken for granted and has initiated policies based on his redefinitions. In *Perestroika,* Gorbachev clarified that, "We are not going to change Soviet power, of course, or abandon its fundamental principles, but we acknowledge the need for changes that will strengthen socialism and make it more dynamic and politically meaningful."[3] This statement provides insights into Gorbachev's ideological values and serves as an abbreviated theoretical justification of his policy agenda.

Gorbachev's agenda for change became evident during the interim regimes of Andropov and Chernenko. Many of his ideas were derived from the consensus that evolved during that period. A comprehensive reading of Gorbachev's speeches and articles following Brezhnev's death conveys the strong impression that Gorbachev was in fact one of the principal architects of that consensus. He was almost certainly author of the Food Program introduced in 1982 and vigorously supported the need for greater labor discipline first articulated by Andropov. He also shared Chernenko's concern that the party had lost touch with the masses. But, while remaining generally within the bounds of this consensus, Gorbachev developed a policy agenda that is clearly his own. His program stresses the independence of nations within the world socialist community, advocates greater democracy and participation by Soviet citizens in the political process, and calls for a rejuvenation of the party to enhance CPSU credibility and authority.[4] Most important, it calls for a radical reform of the Soviet economy based on several factors: a reallocation of resources from the defense to the non-defense sectors; a dramatic shift in the locus of control of economic management; profit-and-loss methods of economic accountability; and expanded private and cooperative ventures, particularly in the service sector. While many of these policies have only begun to be implemented, Gorbachev's blueprint for the future is clearly revolutionary.

Although there is general agreement within the Soviet leadership about the need for change, it is the broad scope and rapid pace of change desired by Gorbachev that has resulted in opposition to his agenda. Gorbachev is well aware of this and has demonstrated unusual adroitness in staging tactical retreats when necessary to protect his overall program. He has also manipulated the leadership to concentrate an increasing number of his supporters in the top echelons, and has used this support to reshape the leadership consensus in accordance with his own values.

A more detailed examination of Gorbachev's approach to the issue areas addressed in this book illustrates not only key elements of his reform program, but also the ways in which the new leadership consensus differs (and in some cases, does not differ) from the consensus that evolved under Brezhnev.

Ideology

Many analysts have focused on Gorbachev's pragmatism.[5] While it is true that he has not dwelt on the theoretical foundations of his policies, Gorbachev has strong ideological values and is keenly aware of the need to develop a theoretical underpinning for his policy agenda. But, as described in Chapter 1, it takes time for a leader's values to emerge in the official ideology. He must first convince the party as a whole—and especially key members of the leadership—that his values are legitimate. He must then set in motion a series of policy changes based on his ideological values. Only when the policies have been implemented can his views be incorporated into the official ideology. Like any Soviet leader, Gorbachev knows that it is essential to establish linkage between ideology and policy. But he also knows that the official ideology, flexible as it might be, cannot be changed overnight. Most of Gorbachev's pronouncements on ideology *per se* have therefore focused on the irrelevance of old ideological formulas, in particular developed socialism.

Rejection of Developed Socialism

In a speech in late 1984, soon after he took on the ideology portfolio in addition to other duties within the Politburo, Gorbachev addressed the need for improvements in ideology. Although his speech contained a modest tribute to developed socialism, the main theme was that official ideology was inadequate. Gorbachev echoed Central Committee resolutions of 1979 and 1983 in calling for ideology that was both more responsive to changes in contemporary life and more goal-oriented. "Our contemporary," he said, is a person of high cultural values. He is educated and has lived through many of the formative experiences of the Soviet Union. This person understands what is truth and what is not, knows the sources of the problems that concern him and will not accept simplified explanations. "We are obliged to speak only the truth to him, with no simplification, innuendos, or generalized or pompous phrases." He added that "Our ideology is directed at reason, at the best feelings, and to the political experiences of the masses themselves. Life has convincingly demonstrated that the candid, honorable word of the party . . . will always be understood and accepted. . . . That is how it was when we were building, strengthening, and defining socialism. That is how it stands today. And how it will be in the future."[6]

This speech (and subsequent speeches and writings) made it clear that Gorbachev's ideological values differed significantly from his predecessors. He offered no policy departures from what Andropov or Chernenko had said either before or after Brezhnev's death. But Gorbachev differed from both men in his strong rejection of the ideological formulas of the past. And he did so in a manner that was coherent, convincing, and, for his supporters, inspirational. Most important, he demonstrated a clear understanding of the direction that needed to be taken in both theory and practice. Upon assuming the General Secretary position, he intensified his urgings for more truthful ideology. He continued to stress that ideology could not stand still, that party members could not continue to rely on old formulas to motivate the population to pursue new policies. In his speech to the Twenty-seventh Party Congress, Gorbachev noted that ideological work had been out of the mainstream of Soviet life. He stated that the most important goal of ideology was to convince all Soviet citizens of "the critical nature of the present time and its pivotal role" in the development of the Soviet economy and society.[7] He also clarified that the Brezhnevian ideology of developed socialism could no longer serve as the basis for policy.

In discussing the 1986 revision of the Party Program, Gorbachev indicated that many people had suggested deleting all references to developed socialism. Others had suggested that the concept be more fully explained. Gorbachev pointed out the difficulty of simply omitting developed socialism from the party's basic document since the concept had entered the lexicon not only of Soviet ideology but of many East European countries as well. "Nevertheless," Gorbachev added, "it is appropriate to recall that *we used the thesis of developed socialism in reaction to the simplification of ideas about the paths and time periods for accomplishing the tasks of communist construction.*" Over time, he continued, this concept was used only to tout successes instead of focusing on the many problems facing society and the economy. Eventually, developed socialism *"served as a unique justification for slowing down the resolution of pressing tasks."* Such an approach, Gorbachev underscored, was no longer acceptable. In contrast, the strategy of the revised Program was to use ideology to focus on the need for change and for strengthening the dynamism of societal development. The emphasis would now be on acceleration and on resolving the problems inherited from the past.[8]

Gorbachev thus categorically rejected the theoretical underpinning of the Brezhnev period just as he rejected most of Brezhnev's policy agenda.

In his statement that developed socialism had been "used . . . in reaction to the simplification of ideas about the paths and time periods for accomplishing the tasks of communist construction," he was admitting that the concept was essentially a band-aid measure to counter Khrushchev's 1961 prediction about the imminent arrival of communism. Despite this surprising revelation, Gorbachev could not simply abolish developed socialism from the party's theoretical lexicon. But he left no doubt that he would abandon the tenets of developed socialism to guide his program for change. With Gorbachev's speech to the Party Congress, developed socialism has been consigned to the past.[9] In his rejection of the "old formulas," Gorbachev has lashed out against the "simplified and mechanical understanding of socialism" encountered in most theoretical formulations. He insists that theory be derived from real-life situations.[10]

Two important elements in Gorbachev's rejection of developed socialism have been his effort to reestablish friendly relations with the PRC and the campaign to reveal the truth about Stalin. As described in Chapter 2, developed socialism was based on the notion that the Soviet model of communism based on industrialization was inherently superior to the Chinese model based on communal agriculture. After an initial attempt at reconciliation with the Chinese in 1965–1966, the Brezhnev leadership reverted to the ideological hostilities that had characterized the Sino-Soviet split of the early 1960s, justifying this action with the new doctrines of developed socialism. Although Brezhnev again attempted to reach out to the Chinese near the end of his tenure in office,[11] he continued to use developed socialism to support his policy agenda. While Brezhnev seemed not to recognize it, there was little hope that even a post-Mao leadership would respond favorably to any Soviet overtures about reconciliation as long as official Soviet ideology contained an implicit rejection of Chinese communism.

Gorbachev, however, changed all this. In his Party Congress speech he rejected the traditional view that the USSR was the leader of the communist movement. In tune with the post-Brezhnev consensus and the revised Party Program, he reiterated that there was much to be gained for the Soviets in studying the experiences of other communist countries. He stated that the Soviets did not consider "unity to have anything in common with uniformity, with hierarchy, with interference by some parties in the affairs of others, or with the attempts of any party to have a monopoly on the truth." He added that, "the communist movement should and must be strong by its class solidarity and in the cooperation of all fraternal parties, enjoying equal rights, in the struggle for general goals." With regard to China, he said that, although differences remained in the approach to several foreign policy issues, there were signs that "there is a possibility in many areas to work together, and to cooperate on an equal and principled basis without damage to the interests of other countries." He noted that cooperation was in the best interests of both China and the USSR because of their mutual desire for socialism and peace.[12] Gorbachev continued his opening to the Chinese six months later with his highly publicized Vladivostok speech that unveiled an expansive set of Soviet goals for Asia and the Pacific Basin. Specifically, it contained a long list of policies designed to address Chinese security concerns and demonstrate Gorbachev's seriousness about improving relations.[13]

Soviet actions since Gorbachev's Vladivostok speech have been generally consistent with this policy program. Although wary of Soviet intentions at first, the Chinese have become increasingly more responsive to Soviet initiatives. Trade has increased, particularly border trade between China's northeastern provinces and the eastern part of the Russian Republic. Numerous scientific and cultural agreements have been signed, and bilateral talks have begun to address the sensitive question of the exact demarcation of the Sino-Soviet border. Related Soviet foreign policy actions such as the withdrawal of Soviet forces from Afghanistan and encouragement of the Vietnamese to withdraw from Cambodia have enhanced prospects for improved relations with Beijing. While conflicting policy interests in Southeast Asia, the Middle East, and elsewhere will prevent total reconciliation, the past four years nevertheless represent an important reversal of the trends of the Brezhnev era. Moreover, the Chinese are now listening carefully to Soviet rhetoric, which no longer contains an implicit rejection of the Chinese approach to communism. Their agreement to a summit meeting in 1989 between Deng Xiaoping and Gorbachev demonstrates China's renewed interest in dialogue with Moscow and indicates the success of Gorbachev's policy.

Gorbachev's treatment of Stalin is his second major departure from developed socialism. Although the "Stalin question" was addressed under Brezhnev, it was in the context of mostly esoteric debates about the periodization of socialism. Those who felt developed socialism should be declared a new stage in Soviet ideology believed it was important to separate the Stalin period from the post-Stalin era to signal the end of the command economy and arbitrary rule. While Brezhnev attempted to distance himself from Stalin, he never made Stalinism a major issue in his public statements. Gorbachev, in contrast, has brought the issue from the pages of theoretical journals and scholarly discussions into full public view. Giving Stalin credit for industrialization and collectivization, he has also criticized the former leader for violations of socialist principles of government and of Soviet law.

The campaign against Stalin began in early 1987 with Gorbachev's speech to a group of Soviet media officials in which he called for filling in the "blank pages" of Soviet history. This was to include both the successes and the "mistakes."[14] The first blank page was Lenin's "testament" about the unsuitability of Stalin to be top leader, published in the central press. This was followed by discussion in major newspapers about the significance of Lenin's remarks and about the nature of Stalin's regime. Many letters (and editorials based on them) described Stalin's role in World War II. The public debate was intensified with the release of a Mikhail Shatrov film on Lenin, which included sympathetic portraits of Lenin's long-ignored contemporaries like Nikolai Bukharin. The discussion of the Stalin era continued in April 1987 with the publication of Anatoly Rybakov's novel, *Children of the Arbat*, and its stories of the horror inflicted during Stalin's purges. These events were accompanied by numerous articles in the Soviet press describing the damage caused by Stalin to the authority of the party and the integrity of Soviet socialism.[15]

Gorbachev did not mention Stalin by name until his November 1987 speech on the 70th anniversary of the Bolshevik Revolution. He gave a more balanced account of Stalin than had been expected, crediting Stalin, for example, with his leadership in World War II. He also defended Stalin's non-aggression pact with Hitler. But the main thrust of Gorbachev's remarks was to provide a devastating account of the effects of Stalin's personality cult. He cited Stalin's "real crimes based on the abuse of power," including "mass repression" of "party members and others." To answer possible objections that Stalin simply was unaware of the crimes being committed in his name, Gorbachev indicated that, "documents in our possession say this is not so. The guilt of Stalin and those closest to him before the party and the people for the mass repressions and lawlessness that were permitted are immense and unpardonable. This is a lesson for all generations." Gorbachev acknowledged that some of those falsely accused had been rehabilitated after the Twentieth and Twenty-second Party Congresses. But he noted that this effort had been stopped in the "mid-1960s" and must now be completed. He promised to create a commission to investigate party archives in search of the truth. His speech touched off an explosion of letters and articles in the Soviet press about Stalin and the need to fill in additional blank pages of Soviet history. This continued through 1988, although Gorbachev himself began to urge caution in reassessing Stalin. In the February 1988 plenum of the Central Committee, for example, he warned against "hasty statements and hurried assessments" in reviewing historical questions.[16]

Gorbachev's campaign against Stalin fulfills several needs. First, like his restatement on the Soviet position on international communism, his rejection of the Stalinist economic and political model sets him apart from the policies of the past, enforcing his message that old formulas are no longer valid. Moreover, by dealing with the Stalin issue directly, he has created a clear distinction between his approach and that of Brezhnev. Second, by criticizing Stalin's "crimes against socialism," Gorbachev clears the way for reestablishing ideological links to Lenin. Since many of his own policy initiatives are based on Lenin's later writings, particularly those emphasizing creative solutions to pressing economic problems, Gorbachev must reject Stalin's distortion of Lenin's policies.[17] The third and most important objective of the anti-Stalin campaign is to assist in restoring the authority of the party. Gorbachev's unflinching discussion of Stalin and related acts such as the rehabilitation of Nikolai Bukharin demonstrate Gorbachev's willingness to cope with sensitive questions of party history. It also indicates his determination to be truthful and implies that the CPSU is capable of facing up to other sensitive issues, such as the corruption and cynicism of party officials in the late Brezhnev period.

The main lines of Gorbachev's rejection of developed socialism are thus clear: the simplistic formulas developed under Brezhnev are no longer applicable to Soviet society seeking to solve many problems; the USSR can no longer claim dominance over world communism, but must learn from the experiences of other communist countries; and the party must deal with the problems created by Stalin's arbitrary and at times criminal rule and, by extension, with the larger questions of party authority. What is less clear is the nature of the ideological formulation that will eventually replace developed socialism in official ideology.

Gorbachev's effort to focus on the Leninist nature of his policy represents a natural fallback position in the absence of a specific ideological formulation. Like Brezhnev and Khrushchev before him, Gorbachev has had to rely on Lenin to provide an irrefutable theoretical basis for his reforms. At the same time, he and his ideological spokesmen have attempted to discredit Brezhnev's use of Leninism by describing the "neglect" of Lenin in the Brezhnev era.[18] This is also not surprising, since Gorbachev could not justify departures in policy by using the same ideological justification as his discredited predecessor. Gorbachev's reliance on Lenin is thus both a return to "basics" to place his reforms in a readily understood theoretical context and a temporary measure until a new ideological formula can be devised.[19]

Ideology and Domestic Policy

In his Twenty-seventh Party Congress speech, Gorbachev suggested several goals for ideology in terms of his domestic reforms. First, it was essential to revitalize society. No plans for improvement could succeed without the active involvement of the masses. To achieve acceleration of socioeconomic development, Soviet people must participate in the solution of existing problems as well as in the creation of new approaches. Gorbachev has referred to this as activating the "human factor." Second, words must be accompanied by deeds. People will only respond to theoretical demands, according to Gorbachev, if they can feel real improvements in areas of their greatest concern: housing, food supply, the quality of consumer goods, the level of health care, and others. He pointed out that ideological work in the past had lacked realism. People's thinking can be changed and intertia overcome only if they see concrete actions resulting from the goals set forth in the ideology. Each party member must engage in individual ideological work with the masses, Gorbachev's third goal. The "wholesale" approaches of the past (lectures to large audiences, articles in newspapers, etc.) were insufficient by themselves. To bring theory closer to everyday life, party members must discuss things one-on-one with Soviet citizens. This effort had to be consistent, unflagging, and spontaneous. Gorbachev also called on the media and the arts to assist in improving ideological work, but he made it clear that the most critical ingredient was the individual effort by each communist.[20] Revitalization of society, making ideology more consistent with reality, and political rejuvenation of the party are thus the essential values underlying Gorbachev's reforms.

Consistent with his ideological values, Gorbachev has launched policy initiatives focusing on economic renewal and political rejuvenation. Abbreviated in the slogans perestroika and *"uskorenie"* (acceleration), his program of economic reform is designed to overcome the traditional problems of a centrally planned economy. To make Soviet goods competitive, he has called for improvements to the scientific and technological base and for a reallocation of defense industrial resources to the civilian economy. Aside from replacing a substantial number of economic managers with men presumably more sympathetic to his policy agenda, the state acceptance system *(gospriemka)* introduced in July 1986 and the new law on enterprises introduced at the June 1987 Central Committee Plenum are the most important policies Gorbachev has implemented so far. Most of the major elements of his economic program are scheduled to come into effect in the Thirteenth Five-Year Plan in 1991.[21]

In the political arena, Gorbachev's demands for more democratization and glasnost are designed to ensure greater involvement by Soviet workers in the decision-making process at their enterprises and local governments and to produce pressure from below on local and regional party secretaries. The major innovation is the establishment of a "presidential" system of government introduced at the Nineteenth Party Conference. This will not only broaden the base of representation of officials elected to the new Congress of People's Deputies, but will also make the "President," or the new Chairman of the Supreme Soviet, accountable to the Congress. The other major innovation at the conference was Gorbachev's suggestion that the posts of party first secretary and chairman of the soviet be held by the same person. Although this concept has created controversy at the local level, Gorbachev will surely set the example by his certain election as the first Chairman of the Supreme Soviet.

The party conference also affirmed the overall direction of Gorbachev's proposed reforms of the political system. The resolutions were much stronger than the theses published several weeks prior to the conference, indicating that extensive give-and-take occurred during the conference itself.[22] If all the reforms proposed by the conference are implemented, the "all-people's state" first announced by Khrushchev and redefined by Brezhnev will have been redefined again in a way that will transfer substantial power from the party to the government, especially at the local level.

On the other hand, the party conference demonstrated that there is disagreement within the party about the scope and pace of reform. This was underscored by the dramatic exchange between Boris Yel'tsin and Yegor Ligachev. Yel'tsin, the deposed Moscow party chief, argued that perestroika was not moving fast enough and was not making substantial changes in either the economic or political system. He criticized the hasty preparation of the conference theses and the non-democratic nature of delegate selection. He gained applause by suggesting a nationwide referendum on the proposal to combine party and soviet leadership posts. Ligachev, who himself was demoted several months after the conference from party "Second Secretary" to head of the new Agricultural Commission of the Central Committee, countered that perestroika is a "difficult and prolonged process." He added that it is important to tackle pressing problems vigorously, "yet without being impulsive, and circumspectly, while giving consideration to the consequences. Engaging in politics is not like gulping soup. . . . One has to be circumspect as well as resolute." Elsewhere in his speech, Ligachev reminded conference participants that Gorbachev had been elected in April 1985 by the slimmest of margins.[23]

This exchange illustrates the extremes of debate within the party leadership. The "liberal" view is that change is not occurring fast enough; the "conservatives" think things are happening too fast. Gorbachev has to wend his way among both positions, carefully balancing his push for greater reform against the entrenched resistance of Soviet bureaucracy.

Ideology and Foreign Policy

Gorbachev's ideological values regarding Soviet foreign policy have been dramatic and highly visible. His China policy and shift away from

Soviet dominance of world socialism are emblematic of the more fundamental shift in Soviet foreign policy that has occurred since he became General Secretary. As part of his "new political thinking," Gorbachev has advocated political rather than military solutions to international conflict. He has pointed out many times that such a change is necessary because of the dangers of nuclear or large-scale conventional war. International relations must now be based on "moral and ethical norms that are common to all mankind," according to Gorbachev. Moreover, "ideological differences should not be transferred to the sphere of interstate relations, nor should foreign policy be subordinate to them, for ideologies may be poles apart, whereas the interest of survival and prevention of war stand universal and supreme."[24]

A significant change in the ideological basis for Soviet foreign policy has been Gorbachev's redefinition of "peaceful coexistence." No longer considered a "specific form of class struggle" as it was during the Brezhnev era, peaceful coexistence now refers to the natural, but peaceful competition between differing social systems. As Gorbachev indicated in *Perestroika*, the "dialectical unity of opposites" in the world and particularly between the superpowers is today ideologically acceptable.[25]

One interpretation of this change to established doctrine is that ideology has ceased to play a role in Soviet foreign policy. This view would be supported by Gorbachev's emphasis on "human" instead of "class" interests and by many of his policy initiatives, which seem to be based more on considerations of realpolitik than ideology. This was indeed the interpretation offered by Yegor Ligachev in an August 1988 speech.[26] Ligachev proclaimed that, "We proceed from the class character of international relations. Raising the question in another way only confuses the minds of the Soviet people and our friends abroad." Ligachev was responding to an earlier speech in which Foreign Minister Shevardnadze called the previous definition of peaceful coexistence "anti-Leninist."[27]

Despite the shift in emphasis from class interests to universal human values, ideology is still important. The goal of Soviet policy under Gorbachev, in the words of party ideologist Vadim Medvedev, is "to determine forms of collaboration whereby socialism would participate even more actively in the processes of world development and the international division of labor, while maintaining its socialist primacy and strengthening its influence."[28] Shevardnadze provided a similar definition in his July 1988 speech to a Foreign Ministry Conference:

> If mankind is moving toward a unity of diversities and toward a community of equals who freely choose their own path—and it is undoubtedly is moving toward this—then our interests consist in strengthening in every

possible way our unique socialist individuality and esssence and heightening their attractiveness to the rest of the world.

He added that the Soviet Union's role is thus found in "being one of the unifying forces of the world and contributing to the development of integration forces in the spiritual and material spheres of common human life."[29]

Underlying the new thinking in Soviet foreign policy, then, is the ideological premise that socialism has major contributions to make in the resolution of global problems, but that it first must become more attractive to the world community. Gorbachev will not allow the fact that other nations have different ideologies to interfere with Soviet policy. But Soviet policy itself is based on a theoretical framework that assumes the continuing viability of the socialist model.

The changes in Soviet foreign policy are connected to Gorbachev's domestic reform program in direct and important ways. While expressing the need for domestic reform from the earliest days of his regime, Gorbachev chose foreign policy as the most visible area to demonstrate his commitment to change. This was the expedient course of action since foreign policy is the area most amenable to control by the General Secretary. In contrast to the dozens of ministries involved in the domestic economy, there is only one ministry (the Ministry of Foreign Affairs) involved in the making of foreign policy. Gorbachev moved quickly to consolidate his control over the MFA by replacing Andrey Gromyko with Eduard Shevardnadze. He then launched a series of policies in line with his ideological values. His many initiatives—the regional security proposal presented to the Twenty-seventh Party Congress, the INF Treaty with its startling authorization of US inspectors at Soviet missile bases and production facilities, the November 1986 "Delhi Declaration" on the need for a nuclear-free world, the withdrawal of Soviet forces from Afghanistan—share with the Soviet opening to China the fundamental objective of demonstrating both to the world at large and to Soviet citizens that Gorbachev is a bold and able leader. By tying his actions so closely to his words, Gorbachev hopes to demonstrate that he (and by extension, the Communist Party) is the dynamic leader the Soviets need. His success, and ultimately his political survival, depend on his being able to accomplish domestically what he has already achieved in foreign policy.

A Search for Balance

It is too early to judge the results of Gorbachev's domestic or foreign policy initiatives. While he has achieved some important successes in foreign policy, the results of his domestic agenda are more ambiguous. His policies have encountered serious resistance among both party and non-party economic managers. His ultimate success depends on many variables: the support he is able to garner among party officials and economic managers; his ability to demonstrate concrete results to the population at large; maintaining a generally benign international situation; and other factors, including luck. But for our purposes, the success of Gorbachev's policies is not critical. The most important conclusion in terms of the major premise of this book is that Gorbachev's policy agenda is consistent with his ideological values.

Assuming Gorbachev remains in power, his values will eventually be incoporated into official ideology. Evidence that this has happened will be creation of a succinct phrase or concept that encapsulates his agenda for change. As discussed in Chapter 1, such a formula is important because it provides a shorthand reference for ideologists and party members and serves as a reminder of the leader's policy preferences and the allowable dimensions of change.

While its exact phrasing is still unknown, the new formula must stress what was termed at the February 1988 plenum an "ideology of renewal." As defined in *Kommunist*:

> This is the ideology of developing Marxism-Leninism, a revolutionary critical ideology based on the dialectical method, which opposes dogmatism and scholasticism, and which negates fatalism and authoritarianism. It is an ideology alien to utopianism, and is based on a sober analysis of realities both within the country and in the world. It takes the people's social experience into account, and relies on their consciousness. It is an ideology of energetic action that seeks to accomplish practical everyday tasks and, at the same time, is oriented toward the future. It is an ideology that augments the socialist values nurtured by generations of Soviet people.[30]

Gorbachev has said that he has no "ready-made formulas."[31] However, attempts to create a new ideological slogan have already begun in the ideological establishment. The term "real socialism" *(real'nyi sotsializm)*, for example, was used several times in the revised Party Program and in *Perestroika*, but seems unlikely to take hold. When an acceptable phrase is developed, it will incorporate the ideas of revolutionary change and renewal central to Gorbachev's ideological values and will emphasize the ongoing nature of his reforms. Possibilities include, "revolutionary renewal of socialism," "ongoing socialist renewal," or simply "revolutionary socialism." Although as unwieldy in Russian as they are in English, these phrases share the virtue of combining the idea of change with the need for continuing what has been started. They also avoid the sticky question of declaring a new stage of socialist development, a debate Gorbachev would probably like to avoid.[32]

Members of Moscow's ideological bureaucracy who are wrestling with the question of a new ideological formula include Georgii Smirnov, Director of the Central Committee's Institute of Marxism-Leninism. Smirnov has acknowledged that a "new system of socialist theory" is being created at the party's ideological research institutes. The new theory will be "based on the foundations created by Marx, Engels, and Lenin, but at the same time it will be to a considerable degree a renovated theory of socialist development."[33] Oleg Bogomolov, another influential spokesman, has written that, "it would be no exaggeration to say that a collective search is being conducted for a new model of socialist society suitable for the contemporary era," adding that, "as yet there is no complete unity of opinions about this model."[34]

One of the more important opinions is that of political commentator Fedor Burlatskii. In a 1988 *Literaturnaia Gazeta* article reminiscent of his 1966 *Pravda* article on developed socialism (see Chapter 2), Burlatskii provided the outlines of what he terms a "new model of more efficient democratic and humane socialism" in Gorbachev's policies. This model, which—like developed socialism—is being derived in part from the experiences of other socialist countries, contains the essential economic and political elements of perestroika: it is based on a plan-commodity economy with economic accountability and many types of social ownership; it assumes the subordination of the state to civil society; it projects the evolution of self-management of society by Soviet citizens through elections and debate; and it presupposes overcoming the "authoritarian-patriarchal culture" of the past. Burlatskii added that it would take a long time, "running into several decades," before this model of socialism can be completely established in the USSR.[35]

One reason for the lack of unity on an appropriate ideological model may be Gorbachev himself. As sensitive as he is to the connection between theory and reality, he no doubt realizes the danger of changing the official ideology too soon. If he unveils a new ideological formula before his reform policies produce any concrete results, he risks creating a credibility gap. Soviet citizens are unlikely to be motivated by more calls to sacrifice without some evidence that improvements are being made. On the other hand, if Gorbachev does not express the theoretical basis for his policies in a way that can be readily understood by party members who must explain his reform program, he faces the more serious risk of creating confusion in party ranks and alienating his supporters in the leadership.

To Westerners who typically have little feel for the role of ideology in the Soviet system, the need for a clear, easily understood theoretical basis for action may seem inconsequential. For Gorbachev, however, it is pivotal. Those he hopes to lead within the CPSU must be convinced that Gorbachev's agenda has a sound foundation in theory before they will give him their full support.

The ideological component of Gorbachev's agenda for change thus represents a clear departure from the Brezhnev era and developed socialism. It strikes a more objective formulation in describing the USSR's position in the world communist movement and alters the basis of Soviet foreign policy. It stresses the need for decentralizing control of the economy and democratizing the political system. Most important, it demands consistency between word and actions on the part of every communist, party leadership, and the party as a whole. Like his predecessors, Gorbachev is an ideological politician. His values are different because of his age, education, and experience, and they have been modified by what he views as the permissible limits of the post-Brezhnev consensus. But despite differences with some of his more conservative peers, Gorbachev has continually presented his agenda in terms of strong ideological values. For this as much as for any other reason, he has gained respect within the Soviet political system. Without a sound theoretical basis, his policy agenda would have remained in the background of Soviet politics and we would in all likelihood be discussing the ideas and policies of a different General Secretary.

Incentives

Incentives policy is an integral part of Gorbachev's overall economic reform program designed to lead to an acceleration of economic growth in the 1990s. The stated goal of the reforms is to reverse the policy of "extensive" growth that led to economic decline under Brezhnev in favor of "intensive" growth that will maximize the use of existing resources and capital stock. While many decrees have been issued and new bureaucratic structures created, the full set of Gorbachev's reforms, to include price reform and reliance on market mechanisms, will not be implemented until the 13th Five-Year Plan in 1991.[36]

To ensure the reforms are carried out, Gorbachev is relying on the "human factor" (*chelovecheskii faktor*) to overcome the lax labor discipline that contributed to the economic stagnation of the past decade. He does not expect workers to respond to his appeals solely for the common good; in return for increased commitment he promises ample reward in the form of higher wages and material incentives. As he told the June 1987 plenum, "For a long time we tried to lead the economy on the basis of enthusiasm, and sometimes by force of decree. But we forgot Lenin's precepts—that production growth can be assured on the basis of personal interest and material commitment, with the help of enthu-siasm."[37]

On the surface, this may sound like the Brezhnevian formula that emphasized a balanced use of material and moral rewards. But in fact Gorbachev does not have much good to say about Brezhnev's incentives policy. In his address to the January 1987 plenum, Gorbachev pointed out that wage bonuses under the old system were not closely enough tied to qualitative measures. The amount of a worker's bonus depended almost exclusively on achieving high levels of output. This contributed to the extensive growth of the economy by encouraging greater production. Another problem was the restriction on enterprises using their profits for paying bonuses. Finally, the policy of combining material and moral incentives was inconsistent, leading to false accounting and payment of unjustified bonuses.

Gorbachev's most severe criticism was that the old system contributed to the broader problem of wage leveling that characterized the Brezhnev period. The erosion of wage and incentive differentials led eventually to loss of motivation among many workers. "All that hit those workers who could and wanted to work better," said Gorbachev, "while making life easier for the lazy ones." Worst of all, it created cynicism, skepticism, and even amorality, and added to a mounting list of social ills such as alcoholism and drug abuse. Although Gorbachev himself did not make the connection, he implied that rejection of the Brezhnevian incentives system was a key element in the leadership consensus on the need for radical economic reform.[38]

Gorbachev's incentives policy stresses the need to adjust what he calls the "measure of labor and the measure of consumption" *(mera truda i mera potrebleniia)*. In essence this means that incentives will be connected much more directly to an individual's labor than in the past. Discipline, productivity, and above all quality are now the determining factors in deciding whether a worker or manager is to be paid a bonus. Enterprises have greater authority to use their profits for bonuses, but it is up to the individual to decide how much effort he puts forth, and therefore how much extra pay he receives.

Gorbachev uses Lenin's approach to incentives as the ideological basis for his policy. As he wrote in *Perestroika*, "What we need is not 'pure,' doctrinaire, invented socialism, but real, Leninist socialism."[39] In other words, any approach is legitimate as long as it works towards attaining regime goals. Gorbachev also adopted Andropov's formula for material reward that itself is a modification of socialist principles: "From each according to his ability to each according to his work." This, according to Gorbachev, is the proper approach for the stage of socialism. Only in communism can the principle of "from each according to his ability to each according to his needs" be put into effect.[40]

So far, the main practical impact of Gorbachev's approach to material rewards has come in the form of the industrial wage increases that went into effect in early 1987. The new wage structure contains large differentials for workers in the same basic pay grade, providing an inherent bonus system within existing wage scales. Beginning in the middle pay grades, wage differentials of up to 24% are paid workers producing the highest quality goods. (The lowest grades are ineligible, presumably because workers at these levels are either trainees or menial laborers.) Differentials up to 12% are paid for higher productivity. In addition, wage "supplements" (i.e. true bonuses) can be paid for exceptional performance or to workers holding critical jobs. Such supplements are limited to a maximum of 50% of the basic wage. The revised wage and bonus scales mean that there will be much greater opportunity for workers to earn incentives than under the previous system. This is also true for specialists, designers, and other technically skilled employees. Moreover, individuals in the latter categories will receive wages ranging from 30–40% above those of production workers.[41]

Assuming the new guidelines are enforced, the wage leveling of the Brezhnev era will have been replaced with a system much more dependent on individual effort than on centrally controlled wage policies. At the same time, Gorbachev's crackdown on unearned incomes will help ensure that wage differentials and bonuses remain the primary means of earning extra pay.[42]

The new system thus incorporates a broader and more meaningful appeal to material interest than existed under Brezhnev. Moral incentives (Gorbachev's "enthusiasm") have receded into the background. This reemphasis on material incentives as part of an economic reform seems, on the one hand, to duplicate the situation at the beginning of the Brezhnev era when the Kosygin reforms were introduced. It also fits into the traditional Soviet cycle of alternating appeals to material interest with ideological stimuli, as discussed in Chapter 3. But Gorbachev has placed so much emphasis on material incentives—and material reward generally—that it will be difficult to revert to non-material forms of reward. His emphasis on rewards for those who produce work of high quality, and especially his ideological modification to justify such rewards ("to each according to his work"), suggests that he has stricken non-material incentives from the list of viable alternatives for Soviet labor policy.

Gorbachev's departure from Brezhnev's policy may reflect his understanding of the important role played by material incentives both economically and politically in contemporary Soviet society. Results of the Soviet Interview Project imply that a high correlation exists between material reward and support for state control, even when such support tends to erode as a result of other factors such as education. In reviewing these data, Brian Silver suggests that "subjective" material satisfaction (i.e. people's perceptions of how their wants have been satisfied) tends to act as a "cognitive filter" that mitigates potentially negative feelings about the regime.[43] I think Gorbachev has recognized this and is using it as the primary rationale for his policy. Simultaneously, however, he is demanding maximum effort from Soviet workers with dire consequences if they fail to comply.

Gorbachev's reforms of the wage and bonus systems have been aptly termed by Elizabeth Teague a "renegotiation of the social contract" between the state and the worker. Previously, Soviet workers could count on a comprehensive system of social welfare, including a low but steady income and guaranteed employment in return for minimal effort together with an implicit promise to remain quiescent. Under the new system, with its emphasis on market mechanisms, there are few guarantees.[44] To become eligibile for the highest rates of pay and bonuses, workers must put forth maximum effort and concentrate on producing goods of the highest quality. If they don't, they suffer and their enterprise suffers. If the enterprise suffers enough, the workers are not paid at all. In extreme situations, they can be fired.

For Gorbachev's wage and incentives policy to be effective, however, he cannot rely solely on threats to job security. There must also be an increase in the number and quality of consumer goods to motivate workers to strive for higher earnings. Gorbachev is well aware of this and continues to predict dramatic improvements in the consumer goods sector. One of his key economic advisers, Abel Agenbegyan, has described the "economy of the future" as one in which above all "production is subordinated to social needs. There are no shortages. The market for means of production and objects of consumption is saturated. The consumer choses whatever is advantageous for him."[45] Although his incentives system may be quite different from that of Brezhnev, it is Gorbachev's ability to deliver on Agenbegyan's promise that will determine whether the new program is sufficient to promote substantial improvement in economic growth. On this key question, the jury is still out.[46]

Nationality Policy

Unlike his incentives policy, Gorbachev's nationality policy was not an essential component of his overall reform program. It is not clear that he even had a specific program on the nationalities issue upon assuming the General Secretary position, although he had addressed the subject previously.[47] He did not mention nationalities at all in his April 1985 plenum speech in which he outlined the main points of his reform program, and he had little to say about the topic in general until the Twenty-seventh Party Congress. This was consistent with the pattern of Andropov and Chernenko, neither of whom placed nationalities policy high on their agenda for change. But Gorbachev's overall reform program, with its emphasis on glasnost and democratization, has encouraged various nationalities to express pent-up frustrations, forcing him to develop a policy to deal with this critical and potentially explosive area of Soviet domestic policy.

Gorbachev created opportunities for a broad discussion of nationalities problems in his Party Congress speech. Addressing the issue for the first time since becoming General Secretary, Gorbachev startled his audience by rejecting the thesis of the previous forty years that the nationalities question had been "resolved" in the USSR. He acknowleged the successes of the past in overcoming the nationality repression and stark inequalities that characterized the pre-revolutionary period. And he termed the Soviet nation a "qualitatively new social and international community, united by their economic interests, ideology, and political goals." "But," he added, "our achievements must not create the impression that there are no problems in nationality processes. Contradictions are inherent in any development, and they are inescapable in this sphere as well. The main thing is to see the aspects and dimensions of these contradictions as they arise, and to seek and provide timely and truthful answers to the questions life presents."[48] Gorbachev added another thought in *Perestroika*. "Regrettably," he said, "we used to stress our really considerable achievements in the solution of the nationality problem, and assess the situation in high-flown terms. But this is real life with all its diversity and all its difficulties."[49]

As this statement suggests, Gorbachev's policy has evolved in the context of the failure of Brezhnev's approach to the nationalities. This has been most visible in the replacement of former republican first secretaries, most notably in the Central Asian republics where corrupt party leaders had used the leeway they enjoyed in the late Brezhnev period to create scandal-ridden personal fiefs. These abuses and the fates of the previous party leaders have been frequently detailed in the Soviet press.[50]

Brezhnev's economic and language policies have also been criticized. Academician Iulian Bromley, a specialist on nationalities, told an *Izvestiia* correspondent that the "stagnation phenomena" of the "recent past" had led to distortions in the economies of the national republics. "We are essentially paying for the fact," said Bromley, "that for too long we considered the nationalities question solved and did not attach serious significance to the deep-seated processes which never ceased." In an earlier article, Bromley discussed the problems of uneven economic development of the national republics since 1971, thus indicting the entire period of developed socialism.[51]

Soviet commentary on language policy has indicated that efforts to upgrade nationality capabilities in Russian have failed and little attention has been devoted to improving the teaching of native languages. The lack of progress in Russian is a particular concern to the military, which has become more dependent on high-technology equipment while being forced to deal with a draft-age population that is increasingly non-Slavic and poorly trained in Russian. The need for Russian language training prior to military service has thus become critical. Military writers have complained bitterly about the poor knowledge of Russian among conscripts, and efforts to improve the situation in the military have been widely reported.[52]

In response to these problems, Gorbachev has promised to deal with "real life." In rejecting the formulas of the past, he has indicated a philosophical commitment to deal with nationalities issues on a case-by-case basis, not as part of a packaged response conveyed by tired slogans. As he told the January 1987 Central Committee Plenum, "Now that democracy and self-government are expanding, that there is rapid growth of the national awareness of all nationalities . . . it is especially important to settle promptly and fairly outstanding questions in the only possible way—in the interest of the progress of each nationality and ethnic group, in the interest of their further drawing closer together, and in the interest of society as a whole."[53]

Unlike Brezhnev, there is no evidence that Gorbachev would like to dissolve the federal structure of the Soviet Union, although he does continue to publicize the goal of a "Soviet nation." But while Gorbachev remains committed to this ideal, he is also intent on dealing with problems in a way that will ensure the integrity of the multinational state and provide a broad foundation for his overall reforms. This approach is consistent with his continuing emphasis on restoring party credibility and authority.

Like his incentives policy, Gorbachev also has a Leninist basis for his approach to nationalities. As he told the Party Congress, this emphasizes "special tact and caution in everything related to nationality policy, in everything that touches the interests of each nation and ethnic group, and the nationalistic feelings of the people. At the same time, it is a principled struggle against national narrowness and arrogance, nationalism and chauvinism, in whatever guise."[54] Gorbachev has enforced this position with far-reaching cadres changes in the national republics. In addition to the replacement of republican first secretaries, he has also orchestrated the replacement of cadres at lower levels of the party and state apparatus. This large-scale turnover is intended to place leaders sympathetic to Gorbachev's program in positions where their support will be most helpful.[55]

As Gorbachev's policy toward the nationalities has evolved, it is evident that changes have occurred in the leadership consensus in the key areas of economic and language policy. These changes, expressed both by Gorbachev and academic specialists, represent a series of compromises between the assimilationist and moderate approaches that became polarized under Brezhnev. Gorbachev has also called for intensive study of the nationalities situation. Criticizing social scientists for writing "treatises reminiscent at times of complimentary toasts rather than serious scientific studies," he has demanded objective studies of the "very involved and contradictory" phenomena in nationality relations.[56]

In economic policy, there is a renewed commitment to provide significant incentives to the national republics. Gorbachev mentioned to the Party Congress that, in line with the overall economic reforms, national republics would be able to retain for local use or sale products that exceeded state delivery quotas. He also promised strengthening the "territorial" approach to planning so as to prevent further "disproportions."[57] However, there is an equivalent demand that the republics support the national economy. In his Party Congress speech, Gorbachev asserted that, "In developing the basic direction of nationality policy for the future, it is especially important to be concerned that the contribution of all republics to the development of a unified economic complex correspond to their growing economic and cultural potential." The development of cooperation and effective interaction among republics, he added, "is in the highest interests of our multinational state and each republic."[58] He has thus established a *quid pro quo* approach that provides the republics significant incentives to excel in return for continued loyalty to Moscow. This approach was reaffirmed by the June 1988 Party Conference, although conference resolutions concentrated more on extending new rights to the national republics than on their obligations to the center.

Gorbachev considers language policy a two-way street as well. In *Perestroika*, for example, he acknowledges the need for literature in nationality languages, pointing to his former region in the North Caucasus as an example of how such literature helps to promote good relations among diverse ethnic groups. Lack of attention to people's lawful rights in this regard, he said, was the result of bureaucratic mistakes. "There is sometimes heated debate on the development of ethnic languages in this country," he added. "What can be said on this score? Even the smallest ethnicity cannot be denied the right to its own mother tongue."[59]

Gorbachev's call for equal treatment of nationality languages is a clear departure from the policy of the Brezhnev era, when the emphasis was on minorities learning Russian. His encouragement of nationality aspirations has resulted in an upsurge in nationality language instruction and status.[60] But, consistent with the Brezhnev consensus, Gorbachev has also insisted that Russian be the common language of all Soviet citizens. As he stated in *Perestroika*, "Everybody needs this language, and history itself has determined that the objective process of communication develops on the basis of the language of the biggest nation."[61]

The common element in various aspects of Gorbachev's nationality policy is balance: balance between the needs of the country as a whole and the national republics in terms of resource allocation, and balance between adoption of Russian as the common language and a new emphasis on the importance of nationality languages. The emphasis on balance is very strong in the revised Party Program. While stressing that the problems "remaining from the past" have been essentially resolved and retaining the previous goals of the "blossoming" (*rastsvet*) of national cultures and eventual "rapprochement" (*sblizhenie*) of all nationalities, the Party Program states that neither "artificial urging" nor "restraints of objective tendencies of development" will be countenanced. The final goal of the "complete unity of nations" is retained, but this must not be forced. Implicitly, it is a very long-term goal.

The need for balance is also evident in the CPSU's commitment to "fight against any manifestations of localism or national exclusivity" while simultaneously promoting an increased role for each nationality and national republic. Most important, progress is to be made on the basis of "Leninist principles of socialist federalism and democratic centralism." Similarly, the Party Program promises further development of the economic and cultural potential of each nationality "within the framework of a unified economic system." Again, the interests of the center are balanced against the interests of the republics. Finally, as a key aspect of cultural policy, the program provides for "the free development and equal use of their native language" for all Soviet citizens. The program also requires a commitment to master Russian, which has been "voluntarily accepted by the Soviet people as the means to internationality communication."[62]

Gorbachev thus advocates a moderate course of action toward the nationalities, first to discuss problems openly and then to make decisions that take into account the needs of the republics as well as the needs of the state. He apparently hopes that this more reasonable approach to a highly emotional issue area, combined with his commitment to improve the economic and political situation for all Soviet citizens, will defuse the latent hostility among many Soviet nationality groups. So far, however, his nationality policy has been more "word" than "deed," and he has established only broad guidelines for future action. The problems of uneven economic development and inadequate language policy have been noted in the past, but little concrete action was taken. "As a result," according to one specialist, "hope was generated in public opinion, but it was not realized in practice."[63]

Gorbachev has been tested several times since the Party Congress. Nationality unrest has occurred in the Baltic republics, Kazakhstan, and the Transcaucasus region.[64] In addition, the Crimean Tatars have petitioned to return to their homeland, and environmental movements have been established in several republics. These events share a common basis in Gorbachev's reform efforts. Nationality spokesmen have used the expanded boundaries of public debate to articulate a broad array of demands. These have been deliberately couched in terms of glasnost and democratization, representing a growing challenge to the leadership and threatening to undermine the reform program.

Gorbachev seems willing to take risks, however, to demonstrate that his approach is in fact a departure from what Soviet citizens have come to expect. In terms of his larger goals, he may believe it necessary to allow nationality demonstrations and even to accede to some of their demands (with the exception of redrawing republic boundaries) to establish the party credibility that was lost through too many years of pretending nothing was wrong. If he can in fact deal with outbreaks of nationality dissatisfaction with little cost to central authority and no threat to the integrity of the union, he will have indeed gained a substantial victory. But in the meantime he is engaged in a substantial gamble, staking his political fortunes against his ability to douse long-smoldering fires of nationality resentment. The outcome is still in doubt, and further problems can bring intense pressure from party conservatives to apply more traditional forms of control. The leadership debate is likely to be rekindled at the long-awaited Central Committee plenum on the nationalities, now scheduled for mid-1989.

What is clear is that Gorbachev's ideology and policy are consistent with his overall strategy of restoring the authority of the CPSU by demonstrating the leadership ability to deal with the "problems that life creates."

Political Participation

Political mobilization is an essential component of Gorbachev's economic and political reform program. "The essence of perestroika," he has written, "lies in the fact that *it unites socialism with democracy* and revives the Leninist concept of socialist construction both in theory and practice."[65] Through "democratization," actively involving Soviet citizens in the administration of governmental and other public organizations, he hopes to enhance his overall reform agenda by giving ordinary citizens a greater stake in determining their future while simultaneously increasing their commitment to regime goals.

The mobilizational aspect of Gorbachev's reform program was evident in his first speech as General Secretary. He told the April 1985 plenum that, "Socialist democracy cannot be understood abstractly. It has been and remains an instrument for the development of the economy, for the growth of individual activity, and for the communist education of the masses."[66] He emphasized this message in his speech to the Twenty-seventh Party Congress: "In a socialist society, especially in contemporary conditions, administration cannot be the privilege of a narrow circle of professionals. We know, not only from theory but from our own years of experience, that socialist order develops successfully only when the people actively administer their own affairs, and when millions of people participate in political life."[67]

Gorbachev's approach is a combination of those employed by Khrushchev and Brezhnev. Like the Khrushchevian model, it encourages wide participation by the masses in many activities. But like Brezhnev, Gorbachev shuns Khrushchev's spontaneous participation and underscores the role of the Communist Party in coordinating and directing the participation process. He placed this policy in an idelological context when he told the January 1987 plenum, "We now understand better than before the profundity of Lenin's thought about the vital, inner link between socialism and democracy."[68]

Gorbachev's program for revitalizing socialist democracy consists of three major elements: activation of the soviets and the mass public organizations such as the trade unions and the komsomol; glasnost; and "direct democracy," which refers most of all to meaningful elections of economic and political leaders.

Mobilizing the soviets and other organizations is of course not original with Gorbachev. Brezhnev made a concerted effort to revitalize the soviets in the mid-1960s (see Chapter 5), and pointed out that the party typically activates the soviets at each new stage of societal development. Gorbachev concurred in his Party Congress speech that the soviets "have withstood the test of time."[69] But he complained that decision-making authority had become overly centralized, resulting in a decline in the authority of local soviet bodies. This loss of authority, he asserted in *Perestroika*, was compounded by reliance on the command economy. When decisions were made without consulting the soviets, their significance began to erode. Although attempts were made to restore their authority, such as the issuance of fourteen resolutions between 1973–

1987, "the issue never got off the ground because the economic, political, and ideological environment of the braking mechanism [i.e. the Brezhnev period] fully resisted a greater role for the soviets. . . ." Gorbachev added that, "We have underused the capabilities of the soviets to benefit the people." Besides eroding socialist democracy, this also led to the increasing involvement of the party in activities that should have been performed by the soviets.[70]

Glasnost is directly related to democratization. Gorbachev told the Party Congress that, "Without glasnost there is not and cannot be democratization, political creativity of the masses, or their participation in administration." He called glasnost the "point of departure for the psychological restructuring of our cadres."[71]

One of the objectives of glasnost is to garner support of the population in the fight against mid-level bureaucrats who have resisted the reform program. Glasnost, which is perhaps most effectively translated as "criticism," provides the instrument for articulating societal demands. But Gorbachev's overall goal is much broader. His reference to the "psychological restructuring" of cadres suggests he hopes that by encouraging the unfettered discussion of almost any topic, including many that were previously taboo, a kind of mass psychological therapy will occur. As he wrote in *Perestroika*, "One of the main political tasks of the restructuring effort, if not the main one, is to revive and consolidate in the Soviet people a sense of responsiblity for the country's destiny. A certain alienation, caused by weakened ties between state and economic bodies, work collectives, and rank-and-file workers, and by their underestimation of their role in the development of socialist society, still has a disturbing effect."[72]

The third element of Gorbachev's democratization process—elections—is the most novel. He did not mention the subject in his Party Congress speech, although he did speak of the need for "direct democracy." This was a new theme in Soviet discussions of political participation. Gorbachev applied it especially to the participation of workers in the decision-making process at their enterprises. The need for improvement in this regard was due to "forces of inertia" among economic managers who continued to ignore workers' suggestions for change.[73]

Gorbachev first addressed the election concept in January 1987. Echoing his earlier call for improvements in social democracy, he said it was necessary to consider direct elections of heads of enterprises, factories, workshops, departments, sectors, farms, and teams. These elections were crucial to perestroika since the profits of an enterprise—and thus the wages and salaries of its workers—now depend on the abilities of its managers. Workers should thus have a say in determining who manages the organization. Underscoring the radical departure his proposal represented, Gorbachev added: "This, as you understand, means a qualitatively new situation, a fundamentally different form of working people's participation in production management, an essential enhancement of the role and responsiblity of the collective for the results of its activities."[74]

Gorbachev has also called for substantial improvements in the election of soviet deputies. The goal of this effort is "to rid the voting procedure of formalism and to see to it that the election campaign . . . be held in an atmosphere of broader democracy with the interested participation of the people."[75] At the same time, he has demanded greater accountability of deputies to their electorate. For the soviets and related organizations, Gorbachev promises the widest possible participation, "giving each citizen a real chance to actively influence the development of administrative decisions, to check on their implementation, and to receive essential information about the activities of the apparat."[76]

Gorbachev's ideas on political participation were incorporated into policy at the June 1988 Party Conference. He described past policies that had created an ineffective political system and led to the replacement of democratic centralism by "bureaucratic" centralism, shutting off access to the political process by most Soviet citizens. To counter this trend, he proposed seven principles to guide reform of the political system. These included: taking actions to involve the masses in the political process; ensuring self-regulation and self-government to the maximum extent possible; perfecting the unfettered expression and aggregation of interests; guaranteeing the free development of each ethnic group and its participation in the political system; improving socialist legality to prevent the abuse of power; delineating the functions of party and state organs; and ensuring the effective renewal of party and government leaders. The ultimate goal of these reforms is the "comprehensive enrichment of human rights and enhancement of the social activity of the Soviet people."

Specific proposals Gorbachev put forth at the conference were in line with this goal. His major innovations concerned the soviets. At the highest level, Gorbachev proposed replacing the existing Supreme Soviet with a new organ of supreme state power, the Congress of People's Deputies. This would consist of 1,500 representatives elected on the territorial principle plus 750 from the national congresses or plenums of the central organs of the party, trade union, scientific, cooperative, Komsomol, women's, veteran's, and other organizations. All representatives would be elected for five-year terms. The Congress would elect from its ranks a bicameral Supreme Soviet of 400–450 members that would be a permanently functioning supreme body answerable only to the Congress. The functions of the two chambers would be clearly defined with the Soviet of Nationalities taking a more forceful role on ethnic issues than it had in the past. Finally, the Congress would elect, by secret ballot, a Chairman who would chair the Defense Council, nominate the Chairman of the Council of Ministers, decide key issues of economic and defense policy, and chair the Presidium of the new Supreme Soviet. This would essentially combine the posts of General Secretary of the CPSU with the Chairman of the Presidium of the Supreme Soviet, giving the holder of the office both a policy and ceremonial portfolio. Elections to the Congress of People's Deputies were held in March 1989, just as this book was going to press.

At lower levels, local soviets would be strengthened in several ways. Financially they would be given access to income in the form of taxes on enterprises in their area and on the local population. Politically they would gain by making the corresponding party first secretary the soviet chairman. The party secretary would be exempt from the executive committee, and this body would be brought under direct control of the soviet. Besides strengthening the soviets, this would provide an indirect measure of popular control over the party secretary. As Gorbachev put it, if a person were nominated to the party secretary post who was not supported by the soviet, the party would "have to draw appropriate conclusions," about the suitability of that person to be a party secretary.

In addition to these changes, Gorbachev also proposed limiting state officials to two consecutive five-year terms. He left open the possibility of a third term for leaders at the highest levels. Elections in all state organizations would be from among several candidates and conducted by secret ballot.

The resolutions passed by the Party Conference did not support all of Gorbachev's proposals, particularly in the definition of responsiblities of the Chairman of the Supreme Soviet Presidium—a post most observers believe will be taken by Gorbachev himself. But neither were the resolutions radically different in most respects. The end result was a strong endorsement of the overall direction of reform suggested by Gorbachev. Moreover, the resolutions were much stronger than the theses published several weeks prior to the conference, suggesting that Gorbachev had gained political ground during the conference itself.[77]

Gorbachev's most radical proposals have been for the direct elections of party officials, including party secretaries at district, raion, city, regional, and territorial party organizations. At least part of the motivation for party elections is to provide an example. As politburo member Lev Zaykov told a meeting of Czech party representatives: "We cannot conceive of a situation in which the senior officials in state agencies, enterprises, institutions, and social organizations are elected in a democratic way, but in the party apparatus everything remains unchanged."[78]

Despite his many innovations, Gorbachev has retained the key ingredient in Brezhnev's approach to participation—the central role of the Communist Party. Consistent with the tenets of developed socialism, Gorbachev has repeatedly emphasized the party's leading role over the entire political system. In some ways, he has expanded that role. This is clear especially in the revised Party Program, in which the description of social democracy contains a much more visible role for the party than the equivalent sections of the 1961 Party Program. In the new version, the party has supplanted the state as the guiding force in developing socialist democracy and has gained explicit recognition (consistent with the wording in the 1977 Constitution) as the "nucleus" of the Soviet political system and the "leading force" in the expansion of socialist democracy. Significantly, while maintaining the characterization of the "all-people's state," the revised Party Program contains no discussion of the withering of the state. The current goal—the "development and strengthening of the Soviet socialist state"—is termed a "key issue of party policy."[79]

Gorbachev has also retained Brezhnev's emphasis on People's Control. In his Party Congress speech, he included People's Control as one of the "instruments providing each citizen the possibility of actively influencing administrative decisions."[80] This is spelled out more fully in the 1986 Party Program where participation in People's Control is now considered for Soviets "an important form of the development of their political maturity and activity in defense of the people's interest."[81] More recent discussion has concentrated on the "difficult test" perestroika represents for People's Control. In contrast to the past practice of submitting long reports on the shortcomings of administrators, People's Control is now asked to focus on more "practical" measures. These include verifying that contractual commitments are met and state orders are filled. The most important role for People's Control in perestroika is "to prevent and resolutely cut short any negligence or indiscipline, to combat any manifestations of local favoritism and narrow departmental interests, and to declare a merciless war on bureaucracy, parasitic attitudes, and any attempt to steal from the state purse."[82]

Gorbachev's political participation agenda thus focuses on the interaction between guarantees of greater democracy by the party and state and a demand for greater responsibility from the population. He has defined socialist democracy as "an organic combination of democracy and discipline, of independence and responsibility, of the rights and duties of officials and of every citizen." It "has nothing in common with permissiveness, irresponsibility, and anarchy."[83] This mutually beneficial approach appears to be a characteristic Gorbachev formula. Like his strategy in incentives and nationalities policy, in political participation he offers more in the way of responsibility and authority, but demands more in return.

Whether Gorbachev can succeed in a way that will overcome the growing alienation of the population and traditional inertia of the political system is a question that remains unanswered. If he can maintain momentum in this area, his total reform effort stands a chance of succeeding. But he faces a tremendous challenge in attempting to change the course of Soviet political development of the past seventy years. He may have to settle for less than complete realization of his goals. If he compromises too much, however, and political reform is halted before it has any meaningful impact, the fate of his economic reforms will be threatened as well.

In striving for balance between regime needs and the needs of the population, Gorbachev faces a delicate balancing act of his own. In expanding participative opportunities, he must avoid any reduction of the party's role. Although he has expressed support for the continued dominance of the political system by the CPSU, his campaign for an expanded election process both within the party and other organizations can be interpreted by party conservatives as a threat. He must convince these leaders that the party can maintain control by different means, even if it entails a reduction of some of the traditional perquisites of party membership. Gorbachev is clearly aware of the dilemma he faces in trying to expand the boundaries of political participation in a Leninist system controlled by an elitist party organization.[84] He is also aware of the risk posed to his own political future if he pushes too fast and alienates key party leaders. But he evidently belives he must take this risk to restore the party's authority, credibility, and overall leadership. The alternative, in his view, is the continuing decline of party authority that would eventually lead to even more dangerous questions about the party's legitimacy and continued dominance.

CPSU Policy

Like his policies in the areas of incentives and political participation, Gorbachev's policy towards the CPSU is essential to his reform program. He must be able to rely on dependable cadres and a strong party organization committed to his plan for reshaping the Soviet economy and political system. But his cadres policy extends beyond this objective. Consistent with the need for party reform expressed by Andropov and Chernenko, Gorbachev's goal is to overcome the stagnation and corruption of the late Brezhnev period and restore the party's authority and vitality.

Predictably, much of Gorbachev's CPSU policy has been based on a rejection of Brezhnev's policy. In his speech to the January 1987 plenum, he pointed out the connection between deficient cadres policy and the overall stagnation of the late Brezhnev era. "Leading party bodies," he said, "failed to timely and critically appraise the danger of the growing negative tendencies in society and in the conduct of some communists, and to take decisions which life was imperatively demanding." Specifically, party organizations at all levels had failed to deal with permissiveness, drunkenness, complacency, and other negative phenomena. A further problem was the loss of collective leadership that was evident in the declining emphasis on meetings and conferences.

Gorbachev listed five "lessons of the past" that can be considered points of departure for his own cadres policy. First, the lack of movement among party leaders led to stagnation at the top of the party apparatus. New leaders with new ideas were prevented from attaining key positions because of Brezhnev's policy of retaining leading cadres indefinitely. Second, insufficient ideological training led to excessive involvement by party workers in economic activity which pulled them away from the political functions that should have been their primary duty. Third, although there was little movement in the party's upper echelons, there was excessive movement (and thus lack of continuity) at lower levels, especially in such critical areas as the primary party organizations in the economic sector. Fourth, the party had been lax in demanding responsibility and accountability on the part of its members. This resulted in an influx of members interested only in their own personal gain, to the detriment of the party's authority and overall capabilities. Fifth, the excessive growth of party executive bodies at the expense of elective bodies had the effect of further distancing the party from the people and eroding intra-party democracy. Gorbachev concluded from these lessons that it was neccessary to radically update party cadres policy and link it directly to the broader goals of improving the socioeconomic situation.[85]

Gorbachev's response has been to implement a series of organizational measures and to orchestrate a large-scale turnover in party personnel. The organizational measures include: adopting a systematic approach to the selection and transfer of cadres (in contrast to the formalistic and sometimes subjective approach of the past); placing more emphasis on ideology and providing a theoretical basis for cadres turnover; ensuring improvements in the morals of party members; enhancing the understanding of perestroika; ensuring that all levels of party leaders are held accountable for their actions; and emphasizing the prompt resolution of all cadres questions.[86] Gorbachev has also stressed the need to remove the party from the daily management of economic and administrative activity and restore it to a position of political leadership. He has attacked the "phrase-mongering" and "false idealization" of the past, and has

demanded that the party deal with the problems created by the complacency evident in the mid-1970s by cutting through bureaucracy to
adopt a more "business-like" approach.[87] These measures are more far-
reaching and sophisticated than Brezhnev's organizational measures of
the mid-1960s. Whereas Brezhnev emphasized discipline, party leadership, and scientific management (see Chapter 6), Gorbachev has gone
beyond these modest steps to advocate a policy that is more comprehensive
and more direct. His call for a rationalized approach to the selection
and transfer of cadres suggests that he is committed to a more effective
mechanism for personnel transfer that is based on the needs of the
individual as well as the needs of the party.

Despite these departures from Brezhnev's policy, Gorbachev has retained Brezhnev's definition of the party's leading role in the Soviet
political system. The description of the party as the main integrative
force for coordinating competing interests in the economy, as well as
its functions of establishing goals, providing necessary corrections, and
selecting key personnel are virtually identical to the description that
was codified in the doctrines of developed socialism. As the 1986 Party
Program indicates, the role of the CPSU has not changed in the current
period of socialist development. The party's importance has in fact
increased because of the growing complexity of the modern world and
the tasks of perestroika.[88]

The main thrust of Gorbachev's efforts has been in the replacement
of cadres. This has occurred both at the party's lowest and highest
levels. In the first two years after becoming General Secretary, Gorbachev
conducted a sweeping turnover of party leaders. He also orchestrated a
major reversal in party recruitment policy and removed thousands of
members who presumably joined in the late-1970s and early 1980s when
recruitment standards were less stringent. The extent of Gorbachev's
effort on all levels of the party is so great that it can justifiably be
termed a systematic purge.

Gorbachev's replacement of many of the party's top leaders has been
extensively analyzed. Beginning soon after his selection as General
Secretary, he made an astounding number of replacements in the Politburo,
Central Committee Secretariat, republican party organizations, oblast
party organizations, the Council of Ministers, and the military. As several
Western observers have pointed out, it took Khrushchev and Brezhnev
two or three times as long to attain the scope of leadership change
Gorbachev achieved in his first two years in power. Until recently,
Gorbachev had not been as successful in replacing members of the
Central Committee. Estimates are that only forty percent of this body
was dependent on Gorbachev for their appointments, although Gorbachev
was elected by the Central Committee in 1985 and must therefore have

had more support than this number suggests.[89] Gorbachev greatly strengthened his control over the Central Committee at the April 1989 plenum, when more than one-third of the members were removed and many of his supporters were promoted to full membership.

Gorbachev telegraphed his moves against party leaders in his first major speech as General Secretary in April 1985. Discussing the need to resolve "urgent cadres issues," he said that the Politburo considered it "of principle importance" to facilitate the continued stability of party leadership. He pointed out that party members had written letters to the Central Committee complaining that many party leaders who had remained in their positions for a long time had become reconciled with problems and had lost sight of the need for change. "This gives us something to think about," said Gorbachev, "to seek ways of more actively moving our leading cadres."[90]

Gorbachev's words were followed by decisive action. Yegor Ligachev, Nikolai Ryzhkov, and Viktor Chebrikov were elected to the Politburo at the April plenum. These appointments were followed in July 1985 by the transfer of Andrei Gromyko to the chairmanship of the Presidium of the Supreme Soviet and his replacement as Foreign Minister by Eduard Shevardnadze. Lev Zaykov was added to the Politburo in March 1986. There was even greater movement in the Central Committee Secretariat. Viktor Nikonov was added in April 1985, followed by Zaykov in July. Four more new secretaries were appointed in 1986, including Aleksandra Biriukova, Anatolii Dobrynin, Vadim Medvedev, Georgii Razumovskii, and Aleksandr Yakovlev. Anatolii Luk'ianov and Nikolai Sliun'kov were added in 1987. Medvedev was made a full member and Aleksandr Vlasov an alternate of the Politburo at the September 1988 plenum, while Chebrikov was given a Central Committee secretaryship. At the same time, Gromyko and Mikhail Solomentsev were removed from the Politburo and Central Committee and Vladimir Dolgikh and Dobrynin were relieved of their duties as Central Committee secretaries. These changes dramatically changed the membership of the party's two most important decision-making bodies.[91]

The number of replacements has not been as dramatic among republic party organizations, although a significant turnover has occurred here, too. Seven of the fourteen republic party first secretaries have been replaced (the RSFSR has no republic party organization), and in cases where the first secretaries remained, the second secretaries have generally been replaced.[92] The most publicized aspect of Gorbachev's cadres policy in his campaign against the former leadership has been his crackdown on the republican party organizations in Central Asia, where he has used his powers of appointment to focus attention on the criminal activity and corruption that developed in the republican party apparatus under Brezhnev. The most disturbing aspect of the situation, Gorbachev told the Twenty-seventh Party Congress, is that no one did anything about it even though Central Committee members and others had visited the area and could not help but have noticed the problems. Letters were received in the party's central organs describing the situation, but still nothing was done. Although he was referring to Uzbekistan, it was clear that his message applied to other republics as well. The reason for inaction, he added, was that "at some level" certain republics, krais, oblasts, and cities had been exempted from criticism. It was thus essential to understand that "in the party there are no and can be no organizations outside control and closed to criticism. And there are no and can be no leaders protected from party accountability."[93]

Gorbachev has frequently emphasized the type of leaders he wants in the party, as well as in government and public organizations. In *Perestroika*, for example, he stressed the need for leaders who are "resourceful, thinking and dynamic people capable of self-critically appraising a situation, of getting rid of formalism and dogmatic approaches in work, and of finding new, unorthodox solutions, people who can and want to move forward boldly and who know how to achieve success."[94] A slightly different set of traits is described in the 1986 Party Program, which calls for leaders who "have a sense of the new, are close to the people, have a readiness to accept responsibility and the desire to learn to work better, have the ability to learn the political sense of management, and possess exactingness towards themselves and others."[95] These are people who will exhibit a more business-like approach, be more inclined to collegial management, and will have the courage to deal with the problems of implementing perestroika. The decisive criterion for promoting cadres to leadership positions, however, is their attitude towards perestroika. Only those who take an active part in the reform program and who provide leadership to achieve its goals will be promoted to leadership positions.[96]

Although less publicized than his actions regarding party leaders, Gorbachev has also supervised a major cadres turnover at the party's lowest levels. Like Brezhnev, Gorbachev inherited a bloated party organization containing many members who were able to join when standards were relaxed. He told the Twenty-seventh Party Congress that the party had grown by almost 1.6 million members in the five years since the previous congress.[97] He also noted that many party organizations had "forced the growth" of party ranks. This resulted in members joining for "careerist" reasons, a practice made worse by the lack of exactingness by party organizations towards their members. He called for improvements in party recruitment practices and promised to cleanse party ranks of "those who compromise the title of communist."[98]

TABLE 8.1
CPSU Net Growth, 1984–1988* (thousands)

	1	2	3 Rate of Growth (percent)	4	5 Net Growth (percent)	6
	CPSU Members and Candidates[a]	Net Growth		Full Members		Rate of Growth
1984	na	—	—	—	—	—
1985	na	—	—	—	—	—
1986	19,004,378[b]	263,337	1.4	na	—	—
1987	19,267,715[c]	201,071	1.07	18,566,787[d]	—	—
1988	19,468,768[d]	—	—	—	—	—

na = Not available.

[a]As of 1 January.
[b]Derived from a table in *Partiinaia Zhizn'* (Uzbekistan), 10, 1986, p. 18.
[c]*Partiinaia Zhizn*, 21, 1987, p. 6.
[d]*Pravda*, 14 April 1988.
*Modeled after a table by Aryeh L. Unger, "Soviet Communist Party Membership under Brezhnev: A Comment," *Soviet Studies*, April 1977, p. 307.

Many of Gorbachev's criticisms were repeated in a 1987 CPSU Central Committee resolution on the Tashkent Obkom. The resolution described the obkom's longstanding policy of forcing membership growth. This had resulted in a number of drunks, careerists, and other undesirables entering the party. In addition, the obkom had paid little attention to ideological training and had made "serious distortions and omissions" in the candidate selection process. The resolution stipulated that "The most important criteria for joining the party's ranks must be a person's attitude to perestroika, glasnost, criticism and self-criticism, the process of democratization, and personal involvement in implementing these concepts." It also directed obkom leaders to pay more attention to the activities of local party organizations.[99]

The Tashkent resolution signalled that a crackdown had begun and that a more restrictive cadres policy had been put into effect. Table 8.1 shows that the net growth in party membership slowed dramatically in 1986–1987. While the annual net growth for virtually every year since 1974 (figures for 1984–1985 are not available) averaged approximately 350,000, the net growth for 1986 and 1987 was only 263,337 and 201,071, respectively. These numbers are even more significant when viewed as a percentage of party membership at the beginning of each year. The growth rate percentages of 1.4 and 1.0, respectively (based on the 1 January membership number each year), represent the lowest rate of growth in at least the past 30 years. (See Table 6.1 for the years 1960–1982.) Moreover, and perhaps most significant, the *Pravda* article (14 April 1988) that provided the membership figures for 1987 did not

TABLE 8.2
Average Yearly CPSU Admissions (1962-1987)

Years	Admitted as Candidates	Admitted as Full Members
1962-1965 (22nd-23rd Party Congress)	761,616	734,528
1966-1970 (23rd-24th Party Congress)	597,562	597,648
1971-1975 (24th-25th Party Congress)	518,765	494,715
1976-1980 (25th-26th Party Congress)	632,474	589,130
1981-1985 (26th-27th Party Congress)	661,191	628,334
1986 (actual)	663,070	640,719
1987 (actual)	na	585,000

na = Non available.

Source: Data for 1962-1986 derived from a table in *Partiinaia Zhizn'*, 21, 1987, p. 7. Number for 1987 is from *Pravda*, 14 April 1988.

mention the total number of candidate members. This is a departure from past practice, and may indicate a high failure rate for candidates. If so, the most likely reason would be a tougher set of standards for acceptance into full membership.

Table 8.2 shows the average number of annual admissions to the CPSU, based on averages for the periods between the 25th-26th and 26th-27th Party Congresses (actual numbers for 1986 and 1987). These numbers are important for two reasons. First, they illustrate the problem of accelerated growth Gorbachev has complained about. The trend for the ten years ending in 1986 was clearly upward, although it slowed in 1986 and was actually reversed in 1987 as Gorbachev's policies began to take hold. Second, and more important, these figures provide the basis for deriving a rough estimate of the dimensions of the purge of party ranks conducted since Gorbachev came to power.[100]

If the number of members comprising the net increase for 1986 (from Table 8.1) is subtracted from the number of candidates accepted, it turns out that almost 400,000 members were purged (or died, or retired) in that year.[101] I suggest that most were purged. Although it is dangerous to draw conclusions from incomplete data, I suggest that the equivalent number for 1987 (and possibly for 1985) will be the same or perhaps higher. If this number of members, or something close to it, was in fact purged each year, the message that Gorbachev is serious about clamping down on admissions and maintaining high standards will by now have reverberated throughout party ranks.[102]

A strongly worded Central Committee resolution published in late 1988 provides some evidence that the party has in fact undergone a purge. Describing the stringent screening process for candidates and the intensified effort to enforce party rules, the resolution points out that, "Party organizations are more decisively ridding themselves of people whose behavior compromises the title of communist." After discussing the deficienct recruitment practices of some party organizations and affirming the principle that one's attitude toward perestroika is the most important selection factor, the resolution calls on party organizations to "decisively purge *(ochishchat')* party ranks of those who oppose perestroika" or in other ways sully the image of party member.[103]

Beyond asserting his control over party membership, Gorbachev has shaken up the apparat by calling for the election of party leaders. According to most proposals, party members would have the right to submit as many candidates as they wished. Elections would be by secret ballot. While most of the emphasis has been on lower party organs, Gorbachev noted at the January 1987 plenum that the Politburo believed it worthwhile to consider election of the party's leaders. He added that the voting principle should be extended to the leading cadres in other national organizations. Such elections, according to Gorbachev, would "greatly increase the responsibility of secretaries to the party committees who elected them," and "promote greater unity and cohesion of the party's ranks." They would also act as "a safeguard against a repetition of the errors of the past." The only condition is that elections in party organizations not alter the principle of democratic centralism, in which decisions of higher party bodies are binding on lower party bodies. This includes the powers of appointment, presumably in case lower organizations did not elect a candidate considered fit by higher echelons of party leadership.[104]

By the time of the June 1988 Party Conference, Gorbachev had refined his thoughts on reforming the party. His most important suggestions— ending the quota system in recruitment, enhancing the role of the Central Committee in policy decisions, multicandidate elections to party posts through the Central Committee level, and limiting elected officials to two five-year terms—were endorsed in the conference resolutions, sometimes in language stronger than Gorbachev's. Moreover, the resolutions exceeded Gorbachev's proposals in denouncing the nomenklatura system of appointments in favor of elections, in demanding a reorganization and reduction of the party apparat, and in calling for party conferences every two-three years with powers to replace up to twenty percent of the Central Committee.

In spite of his impressive accomplishments, Gorbachev does not view cadres replacement as an end in itself, as some analysts claim.[105] He is rather using this traditional lever of the General Secretary's position to ensure his control over the cadres and to demonstrate his commitment to a strong party. To make perestroika work, he needs party representatives who are unafraid to talk to the masses, to explain why things need to be done differently and to show them the way. Most important, he needs cadres who believe in perestroika. Whether he can succeed is the key question, and one only time can answer. If he continues as he has begun, he will restructure the party in a very short period. This will provide a more solid power base for his position as General Secretary and a more significant base of support for implementing his reform policies. If he fails, one of the best indicators will be the direction taken in cadres policy. A sudden increase in party membership, similar to the late Khrushchev period or the years between Brezhnev and Gorbachev, will likely signal a weakened General Secretary and a corresponding reassertion of the power of local party officials.

Notes

1. Ligachev's speech was published in *Pravda*, 2 July 1988, and in FBIS, *Daily Report: Soviet Union*, (hereafter, FBIS) on 5 July 1988, pp. 101–104.

2. Speech to the Twenty-seventh CPSU Congress in M. S. Gorbachev, *Izbrannye Rechi i Stat'i*, (hereafter, *Rechi*) 3 vols. (Moscow: Politicheskaia Literatura, 1987), vol. 3, p. 181.

3. Mikhail Gorbachev, *Perestroika: New Thinking for Our Country and the World* (New York: Harper & Row, 1987), p. 54.

4. Throughout his tenure as regional first secretary in Krasnodar, Gorbachev stressed the need for the party to stay close to the masses by working with them directly and by acting on the many letters they sent to party and government organs. In 1978, for example, he noted that more than 20 resolutions had been promulgated by the Stavropol' kraikom in response to citizens' letters. He added that regular seminars were conducted in the kraikom to discuss issues raised in such letters. Subsequent events have demonstrated that Gorbachev built much of his agenda for change in response to the expression of the concerns expressed in these letters: the need for more and better housing, an adequate food supply, improvements in the quality of consumer goods, and others. See Gorbachev, *Rechi*, vol. 1, p. 161.

5. See, for example, Thane Gustafson and Dawn Mann, "Gorbachev's First Year: Building Power and Authority," *Problems of Communism* 35 (May-June 1986), pp. 1–19, and William E. Odom, "How Far Can Soviet Reform Go?," *Problems of Communism* 36 (November-December 1987), pp. 18–33.

6. Gorbachev, *Rechi*, vol. 2, pp. 78–79. For the text of the 1979 and 1983 Central Committee resolutions, see *Kommunist*, 7/1979, pp. 10–20, and 9/1983, pp. 39–46.

7. Gorbachev, *Rechi*, vol. 3, p. 268.

8. Ibid., p. 276 (emphasis added).

9. The revised Party Program states that the efforts of the Soviet people and successes of the Soviet economy, science, and culture "opened the stage of developed socialism." Interestingly, the Party Program does not state that the stage of developed socialism has been completed. *Programma Kommunisticheskoi Partii Sovetskogo Soiuza: Novaia Redaktsiia* (Moscow: Politicheskaia Literatura,

1986), p. 9. The text of the revised Program is also in the stenographic record of the Twenty-seventh Party Congress. See *XXVII S"ezd Kommunisticheskoi Partii Sovetskogo Soiuza: Stenograficheskii Otchet* (Moscow: Politicheskaia Literatura, 1986), vol. 1, pp. 554–623.

10. Gorbachev, *Perestroika*, p. 29. Two of Gorbachev's principal advisers on ideology, Aleksandr Yakovlev and Georgii Smirnov, have provided even more damning interpretations of developed socialism. Yakovlev, without mentioning developed socialism by name, emphatically condemned the concept in his statement that, "some Leninist tenets of socialism were treated in an oversimplified fashion, and their theoretical depth and significance were emasculated." He went on to say that this led in the 1970s to the use of "farfetched formulas and designs" so that "we entered the eighties not only with the serious practical oversights and miscalculations that are well known today, but also with a theoretical consciousness largely still at the level of the thirties." See A. N. Yakovlev, "Dostizhenie Kachestvennogo Novogo Sostoianiia Sovetskogo Obshchestva i Obshchestvennye Nauki," *Kommunist*, 8/1987, pp. 3–22. Georgii Smirnov was more direct in his criticism of developed socialism. Like Yakovlev, he believed theory had been oversimplified by the "one-sided" use of developed socialism only to laud successes while many urgent problems were ignored. For this reason, developed socialism had "not only not represented the true situation, but distorted it" and led to a disorientation of policy. See G. Smirnov, "Tvorcheskaia Teoriia Razvivaiushchegosia Sotsializma," *Kommunist*, 12/1987, pp. 19–32. For an important Western view on the demise of developed socialism, see Alfred E. Evans, Jr., "The Decline of Developed Socialism?: Some Trends in Recent Soviet Ideology," *Soviet Studies* 34 (January 1986), pp. 1–23.

11. Brezhnev's overture to China was contained in his Tashkent speech of 22 March 1982. See the text in *Kommunist*, 6/1982, pp. 14–21.

12. Gorbachev, *Rechi*, vol. 3, pp. 253–255. Gorbachev included similar statements in his speeches to the June, 1987 Central Committee Plenum and on the 70th anniversary of the revolution, and in *Perestroika*. The theme of recognizing diverse paths to communism is emphasized several times in the revised Party Program. See *Programma* (1986), pp. 11–13, 61–64 and 71–74.

13. *Pravda*, 29 July 1986.

14. *Pravda*, 14 February 1987.

15. For a more detailed summary of these events, see the articles by Celestine Bohlen in the *Washington Post*, 23 January and 25 March 1987, and by Philip Taubman in the *New York Times*, 15 March 1987. For good, representative examples of anti-Stalin pieces in the Soviet press, see the articles by A. B. Kobiakov in *Literaturnaia Gazeta*, 2 December 1987, and A. M. Samsonov in *Argumenty i Fakty*, 18/1988, pp. 4–5. Both articles were translated in FBIS, 17 December 1987 and 5 May 1988, respectively.

16. *Pravda*, 19 February 1988. In urging caution about the reappraisal of Stalin, Gorbachev was acknowledging the concerns of not only conservative Party leaders, but also the military. See, for example, the long article by retired Colonel A. Khorov in *Krasnaia Zvezda*, 12 March 1988.

17. This is especially important because many Soviets understand Lenin only from their reading of Stalin's works, *Questions of Leninism* and his *Short Course*

on the history of the CPSU. See the interview with writer Mikhail Alekseev in *Literaturnaia Gazeta*, 25 November 1987, translated in FBIS, 27 November 1987. Gorbachev has delineated the repercussions of Stalin's violations of socialist legality in *Perestroika*, pp. 106–107.

18. Professor Iurii Krasin, for example, head of the Social Sciences Institute of the CPSU Central Committee, has written that, "During the years of stagnation the very idea of a new understanding of the works of Lenin was considered a revisionist crime, an encroachment on ideological foundations. . . ." He, and other ideological spokesmen, have justified reliance on Lenin's ideas on the basis of the complexity of the current situation and the need for radical change. What is needed, he writes, is a "breakthrough in theory compatible perhaps with the one done by Lenin early in this century, which is demanded by the newly emerging reality." See his article in *Moscow News*, 15 November 1987, p. 5. For similar views, see the articles by N. Kim in *Pravda*, 5 February 1988, and S. Dzarasov in *Sotsialisticheskaia Industriia*, 8 December 1987. See also the interview with Fedor Burlatskii in *Borba* (Belgrade), 3 November 1987, translated in FBIS, 24 December 1987.

19. An alternative view is offered by Vladimir Shlapentokh, "The XXVII Congress—A Case Study of the Shaping of a New Party Ideology," *Soviet Studies* 40 (January 1988), pp. 1–20. Shlapentokh argues that, in developing its own ideology "the new leadership only gradually shows its cards, pretending for a while that it is not in direct conflict with the previously dominant party ideology." (p. 1) He adds that, "During the January [1987] meeting, Gorbachev and his supporters at the highest echelons of power took the considerable risk of almost completely revealing the new ideology, one that is sharp contrast with its predecessor under Brezhnev." (p. 20) The first point is clearly erroneous; Gorbachev (like Brezhnev) wasted no time in describing what was wrong with previous ideological formulations. Moreover, in contrast to Shlapentokh's second point, the theoretical aspects of Gorbachev's reforms have been evident from the beginning. The "new ideology" Shlapentokh is referring to is a revised ideological formulation that will express Gorbachev's theory. As discussed below, such a formulation is still being developed by party theorists. Thus, there was no "risk" taken by Gorbachev at the party congress. If the new formulation had been worked out, he certainly would have used it as part of his rejection of developed socialism. Aside from this difference in interpretation, the elements of what Shlapentokh describes as Gorbachev's ideology and what I have termed Gorbachev's ideological values are very similar. Moreover, his term "party ideology" is close to what I have described as "official" ideology.

20. Gorbachev, *Rechi*, vol. 3, pp. 268–274. In *Perestroika*, Gorbachev writes: "In politics and ideology we are seeking to revive the living spirit of Leninism. Many decades of being mezmerized by dogma, by a rulebook approach have had their effect. Today we want to inject a genuinely creative spirit into our theoretical work. This is difficult, but it must be done." Gorbachev, *Perestroika*, p. 66.

21. For a thorough discussion of Gorbachev's economic reforms and the background of previous reforms, see Ed A. Hewett, *Reforming the Soviet Economy*

(Washington: The Brookings Institution, 1988). Much useful information is also contained in the two-volume compendium, *Gorbachev's Economic Plans* (Washington: U.S. Congress, Joint Economic Committee, Government Printing Office, 1987).

22. The theses can be found in *Pravda*, 27 May 1988. The conference resolutions are in *Pravda*, 5 July 1988.

23. Both speeches were published in *Pravda*, 2 July 1988.

24. Gorbachev, *Perestroika*, pp. 141 and 143. The change to official ideology represented by "new thinking" was the result of several years discussion among the leadership. See the insightful article by Martin Walker, "Gorbachev Speech a Major Change in Soviet Ideology," *Manchester Guardian Weekly*, 1 March 1987, p. 8. The Soviet view is that new thinking represents not a change to ideology but rather is "Marxism-Leninism's contemporary stance on fundamental general human problems." See, for example, the report on a Moscow ideological conference in *Sovetskaia Kul'tura*, 17 December 1987, pp. 2–6, translated in FBIS, 30 December 1987, pp. 9–16.

25. Gorbachev, *Perestroika*, p. 148. Compare the definitions of "class struggle" in the 1961 and 1986 editions of the *Party Program*.

26. FBIS, 5 August 1988.

27. *Vestnik Ministerstva Inostrannykh Del SSSR*, 15/88, translated in FBIS, 22 September 1988, p. 8. Aleksandr Yakovlev responded to Ligachev's speech a week later with the statement that the "founders of socialism" considered "common human interests from the viewpoint of the history and future development of all mankind, not only individual countries or classes, peoples or social groups." Ibid., 17 August 1988.

28. See the report on Medvedev's address to an ideological conference in *Sovetskaia Kul'tura*, 17 December 1987, translated in FBIS, 30 December 1987. A problem developed over "peaceful coexistence" at the Moscow summit when Gorbachev proposed a joint statement that would obligate both sides to refrain from using military solutions to international conflicts and to agree that peaceful coexistence is a "universal principle of international relations." See the *Washington Post*, 3 June 1988.

29. FBIS, 22 September 1988, p. 10.

30. *Kommunist*, 5/1988, pp. 3–11.

31. Gorbachev, *Perestroika*, p. 65.

32. The issue of the periodization of Soviet experience is again being debated by Soviet specialists. In a roundtable discussion in late 1987, two revised periodizations were offered. Maksim Kim, a member of the USSR Academy of Sciences and a specialist on nationalities, suggested three major "boundaries" between 1917–1987: the transitional period from capitalism to socialism (1917–World War II), the completion of the building of socialism (World War II–1985), and the gradual shift to communism (1985–present). V. Drobizhev, in contrast, suggested four stages: transitional period (1917–mid-1930s), mid-1930s–mid-1950s, mid-1950s–1985, and 1986–present. Like the earlier versions of such periodizations (see Chapter 2), the break with Stalin represented by 1956 is the most contentious point. Also similar is the effort to credit the new leader with

initiating a new stage of development. Kim, for example, terms the Gorbachev era as a new stage, while Drobizhev places the first year of Gorbachev's regime in the same stage with Khrushchev and Brezhnev. See "Osnovnye Ehtapy Razvitiia Sovetskogo Obshchestva," *Kommunist*, 12/1987, pp. 66–79.

33. Smirnov made these remarks in a roundtable discussion on the role of the social sciences in restructuring, carried by Moscow television on 12 October 1987. See FBIS, 22 October 1987, p. 60.

34. O. T. Bogomolov, "Mir Sotsializma—Na Puti Perestroiki," *Kommunist*, 16/1987, pp. 92–102.

35. *Literaturnaia Gazeta*, 20 April 1988, p. 2.

36. See Hewett, *Reforming the Soviet Economy*, Chapter 7, for an excellent discussion of Gorbachev's economic reform strategy. The principles of Gorbachev's overall program, as Hewett points out, are spelled out most clearly in the "Basic Principles for Radical Restructuring of Economic Management" adopted at the June 1987 Central Committee Plenum. See *Pravda*, 27 June 1987 for the text of the basic principles. In his speech to the Twenty-seventh Party Congress, Gorbachev defined "acceleration" as an increase in the tempo of economic growth and a new "quality of growth," which includes a universal intensification of production on the basis of scientific-technical progress, a structural reorganization of the economy, and effective norms for management, organization, and incentives. See Gorbachev, *Rechi*, vol. 3, p. 199.

37. *Pravda*, 26 June 1987, translated in FBIS, 26 June 1987.

38. Mikhail Gorbachev, "Reorganization and the Party's Personnel Policy" (speech to the January 1987 plenum of the CPSU Central Committee), (Moscow: Novosti Press Agency Publishing House, 1987), pp. 11–14. Gorbachev has explicitly renounced wage leveling. In the same speech, he said: "We have taken a resolute course for abandoning wage-leveling and are consistently adhering to the socialist principle of distribution in accordance with the quantity and quality of one's work." See ibid., p. 20.

39. Gorbachev, *Perestroika*, p. 96.

40. Ibid., p. 100. See also Gorbachev's June 1987 plenum speech.

41. On the new wage system, see *Pravda*, 17 February 1987. This article discusses the shortcomings of the wage scales introduced in 1972–1975, which contained insufficient wage differentials according to a worker's skill level. The complex system of wage increments, bonuses, and other supplements obscured the differentials that had existed between manual workers and the most highly trained specialists. See also the interview with Boris Gavrilov, deputy chairman of the USSR State Committee for Labor and Social Problems, in FBIS, 11 December 1987, pp. 72–73.

42. See the discussion in Gorbachev's Party Congress speech in *Rechi*, vol. 3, pp. 225-226.

43. Brian D. Silver, "Political Beliefs of the Soviet Citizen: Sources of Support for Regime Norms," in James R. Millar, ed., *Politics, Work, and Daily Life in the USSR* (Cambridge: Cambridge University Press, 1987), pp. 122–131. The distinction between "subjective" and "objective" material satisfaction is important. As James Millar and Elizabeth Clayton argue, the SIP respondents who were

in fact receiving proportionally the highest material rewards under Brezhnev were also the most dissatisfied. See their essay, "Quality of Life: Subjective Measures of Relative Satisfaction," in ibid., pp. 31–57. In a related study based on SIP data, Aaron Vinokur and Gur Offer suggest that income inequality actually grew in the 1970s, despite Soviet claims (and Brezhnev's policy preferences) that incomes became more equal. See their essay in ibid., pp. 171–202.

44. Elizabeth Teague, "Gorbachev's 'Human Factor' Policies," in U.S. Congress, Joint Economic Committee, *Gorbachev's Economic Plans* (Washington: Government Printing Office, 1987), vol. 2, pp. 224–239.

45. *Literaturnaia Gazeta*, 18 February 1987. For an example of Gorbachev's promise about more consumer goods, see his Party Congress speech in *Rechi*, vol. 3, p. 215.

46. For a pessimistic analysis about Gorbachev's ability to fulfill his promise of increased and better consumer goods, see Walter D. Connor, "Social Policy Under Gorbachev," *Problems of Communism*, 35 (July–August 1986), pp. 31–46.

47. See, for example, Gorbachev's speech to a joint session of the Karachaevo-Cherkesskii Obkom and Oblispolkom in January 1972, his article published in *Stavropol'skaia Pravda* in February 1973, his speech in Vilnius in June 1980, and others in volume one of *Rechi.*

48. M. S. Gorbachev, *Rechi*, vol. 3, p. 233.

49. Gorbachev, *Perestroika*, pp. 118–119. For a full analysis of the problems of the past and an overall discussion of Soviet nationality policy in the context of "new political thinking," see the article by E. V. Tadevosian in *Voprosy Istorii KPSS*, 3/1988, pp. 18–33.

50. One of the most well publicized replacements was that of Dinmukhamed Kunaev in Kazakhstan. Kunaev used his influential position to siphon off money to support an opulent life style, which included exclusive hunting lodges and other luxuries. In Uzbekistan, Sharaf Rashidov encouraged the false reporting of statistics for cotton production, and turned a blind eye to the nepotism that became the predominant principle of cadre promotion in Uzbekistan in the late Brezhnev period. Rashidov died before he could be removed; Kunaev was replaced by Gennadii Kolbin after the Alma-Ata riots in late 1986, and has since been vilified by the central party apparatus.

51. *Izvestiia*, 23 April 1988, and Iulian V. Bromlei, "Improving National Relations in the USSR," *Kommunist*, 8/86, translated in *Soviet Law and Government*, 26/2 (Fall 1987), pp. 37–49.

52. See, for example, *Krasnaia Zvezda*, 12 and 17 March 1987, 7 May 1987, and 2 April 1988. The 12 March article includes a statement that Russian officers need to study the problems of the nationalities represented in their units. This a rare admission that the majority of officers are Russian; it is rarer still to admit a need to learn about the nationality problem. The Russian language problem in the military had been noted in the Brezhnev period as well. See Chapter 4, fn. 40.

53. Gorbachev, "Reorganization and the Party's Personnel Policy," p. 41.

54. Gorbachev, *Rechi*, vol. 3, p. 234.

55. In Kazakhstan, for example, cadres have been replaced not only in the party apparatus, but also in the government and militia. Gennadii Kolbin reported

that two of nineteen oblasts and fourteen ministries have been abolished, resulting in a cutback of 33,000 (of 132,000) administrative workers. This was necessary, according to Kolbin, because of the distortions that occurred in "Leninist cadre policy, when family ties and the attendant vestiges of the past began to be used everywhere." Under the new approach to selecting cadres, "a leader's ability to foster a spirit of internationalism in people is now defnitely taken into account during the certification procedure and the renewal of his character reference." See the interview with Kolbin in *Pravda*, 24 April 1988. See also his report to the March 1987 plenum of the Kazakh Central Committee in *Kazakhstanskaia Pravda*, 15 March 1987, translated in FBIS, 1 April 1987. Similar cuts in personnel, although evidently not as drastic, occurred in the Ukraine in 1987. Obkom first secretaries in Voroshilovgrad, Dnepropetrovsk, and Lvov were replaced, and non-party members were appointed to a significant number of administrative posts. See V. Shcherbitskii's report to the March 1987 plenum of the Ukrainian Central Commitee in *Pravda Ukrainy*, 25, 26, and 29 March 1987, translated in FBIS, 7, 10, and 13 April 1987. In Tadzhikistan, more than 60% of raikom and gorkom first secretaries were replaced by the end of 1987. See the article on the plenum of the Tadzhik CP Central Committee in *Pravda*, 30 December 1987, translated in FBIS, 31 December 1987.

56. Gorbachev, "Reorganization and the Party's Personnel Policy," p. 43. This message has been repeated by prominent academic specialists as well. Iulian Bromlei asserts that there has been no serious study of the nationalities situation since the "late 1960s." Bromlei, "Improving National Relations in the USSR," pp. 48–49. In his *Izvestiia* interview, Bromlei added that the concept "nation" still needs to be developed and amplified. The 1960s debate on this subject, he says, ended with essentially a reproduction of the Stalinist definition of the concept. Nationalities specialist Eduard Bagramov has also called for more significant research on the nationalities problem. He has cited particularly the "relationship between the union and the local, the international and the national" as areas in need of further work. See his article in *Pravda*, 14 August 1987.

57. Gorbachev, *Rechi*, pp. 211 and 216. Academician Bromlei has cited two specific examples of how this policy will apply. Machine building will be accelerated in the Transcaucasus (in part to offset lost income as a result of mandated cutbacks in winemaking), and Uzbekistan's cotton industry will be intensified with the addition of processing plants to handle the raw material produced in the republic. Bromlei, "Improving National Relations in the USSR," p. 40.

58. Gorbachev, *Rechi*, pp. 233–234.

59. Gorbachev, *Perestroika*, p. 120.

60. Two resolutions were passed in Kazakhstan in March 1987, one calling for improvements in language education in Kazakh and the other calling for improvements in training in Russian. See FBIS, 5 March 1987. A resolution of the Ukrainian CP Central Committee stated concerns about "the narrowing sphere in which the Ukrainian language may be used, to the sinking level of teaching in this language and of learning it, to the violation of the language status of Ukrainian theaters, and to the fall in the number of motion pictures

circulated in Ukrainian." This decision also called for improvements in the teaching of Russian in addition to improving training for instructors in Ukrainian. See FBIS, 20 August 1987. In late 1988, the Baltic languages were raised to the status of official languages of their respective republics. See FBIS, 12 and 27 October and 4 November 1988. Part of the official concern with nationality languages stems from surveys conducted by the Soviet Academy of Sciences. One of these, conducted between 1971–1982, revealed that "language remains a stable basis for national identity among all nationalities." See the essay by L. M. Drobizheva published in *Sovetskaia Etnografiia*, 5/85, and translated in *Soviet Law and Government* 25/1 (Summer 1986), pp. 51–73.

61. Gorbachev, *Perestroika*, p. 121. There have been recent signs that Russians are disturbed about the growing trend towards use of nationality languages. Commenting on the demand for making Estonian the state language of that republic, *Izvestiia* complained that there was no mention of Russian as the language of interethnic communication. The overall tone of the article is quite defensive. *Izvestiia*, 19 October 1988.

62. The language of the revised Program is much more specific on these points than the 1961 program. The earlier Program speaks of the need for the economic development of the republics, "correctly combining the interests of the whole state with the interests of each republic." But it also promises that more resources will be given "those regions of the country that need faster development." On language policy, the 1961 Program allows only for the right of all citizens to "raise and teach their children" in the language of their choice. It says nothing about the "free and equal development" of native languages. Compare *Programma* (1961), pp. 312–315 with *Programma* (1986), pp. 43–45. For an excellent summary of Gorbachev's nationality policy that stresses the importance of balance, see the article by Eduard Bagramov in *Pravda*, 14 August 1987. Also see the *Pravda* editorial of 30 December 1987.

63. See the article by Academician A. Zharnikov in *Pravda*, 18 April 1988.

64. The most striking aspect of the regime's response to these incidents has been the degree of candor—unexpected even under glasnost—in providing the reasons for the disturbances. Latvian First Secretary Pugo, for example, in discussing the demonstrations in summer and fall, 1987, blamed "subversive activity by Western special services" for inciting the incidents. This was a pre-glasnost statement. But he then described those who responded to these provocations as "people who suffered of whose relatives suffered damage in the forties because of their social and material position." He also said that "a role was played by a certain underestimation of the effect of certain problems in the study of Latvian history which emerged during the period of the Stalin personality cult." Most surprising of all, however, was his admission that at least part of the motivation for the demonstrations were "shortcomings in the supply of housing, food, and other mass consumer goods." *Pravda*, 4 December 1987. In another example of unusual candor, Gennadii Kolbin attributed the sources of the Alma Ata riots in December 1986 to "the distortion of Leninist cadre policy, when family ties and the attendant vestiges of the past began to be used everywhere." *Pravda*, 24 April 1988.

65. Gorbachev, *Perestroika*, p. 35 (emphasis in original).

66. Gorbachev, *Rechi*, vol. 2, p. 165. Doctor of Philosophical Sciences V. Zotov and other specialists have underscored the relationship between economic and political reform in the context of Gorbachev's rejection of Brezhnev's policies. Zotov asserts that, "It would be incorrect to imagine that the braking mechanism developed somehow apart from the state and political system as a whole. This process of applying the brakes was rooted in serious shortcomings in the functioning of the institutions of socialist democracy and in the conservative management mechanism." See his article in *Pravda*, 20 November 1987.

67. Gorbachev, *Rechi*, p. 235.

68. Gorbachev, "Reorganization and the Party's Personnel Policy," p. 26.

69. Gorbachev, *Rechi*, p. 236.

70. Gorbachev, *Perestroika*, pp. 111–112.

71. Gorbachev, *Rechi*, p. 241.

72. Gorbachev, *Perestroika*, pp. 102–103.

73. Gorbachev, *Rechi*, vol. 3, pp. 239–241.

74. Gorbachev, "Reorganization of the Party's Personnel Policy," pp. 30–31. For an excellent discussion of worker participation under Gorbachev, see Russell Bova, "The Role of Workplace Participation," *Problems of Communism*, 36 (July–August 1987), pp. 76–86. Bova is certainly correct in his assertion that the goal of changes in worker participation is "to use participatory mechanisms to mold workers who are economically productive and politically acquiescent" (p. 79).

75. Gorbachev, "Reorganization and the Party's Personnel Policy," pp. 32–33.

76. Gorbachev, *Rechi*, p. 238. See the discussion of the soviets on pp. 236–237. For a discussion of soviet elections, see *Pravda*, 29 March and 7 April 1987.

77. The theses for the Party Conference are in *Pravda*, 27 May 1988; the conference resolutions were published in ibid., 5 July 1988. Gorbachev's report to the conference was broadcast on Soviet television on 28 June 1988, and translated in FBIS, 29 June 1988, pp. 1–35.

78. See the 5 March 1987 edition of *Bratislava Pravda*. Zaykov's speech is translated in FBIS, 11 March 1987.

79. Compare the section on "Tasks of the Party in the Area of State Organization and the Further Development of Social Democracy" in the 1961 Program with the section "Development of the Political System of Soviet Society" in the 1986 version. The 1986 revision is consistent with the earlier version in establishing as the ultimate goal the establishment of "communist self-administration," and describes the eventual disappearance of the "political character" of state (*gosudarstvo*) activities. See *Programma* (1986), p. 23.

80. Gorbachev, *Rechi*, vol. 3, p. 238.

81. *Programma* (1986), p. 48.

82. See the editorial in *Pravda*, 5 February 1988, translated in FBIS, 16 February 1988. See also the article by E. V. Shorina in *Sovetskoe Gosudarstvo i Pravo*, 1/86, translated in *Soviet Law and Government* 25, nr. 2 (Fall 1986), pp. 42–54. Shorina indicates that as of late 1986 there were approximately ten million

people's controllers active in 1.3 million groups. The number of people active in People's Control has grown by only 500,000 since 1978 (see Chapter 5). Although further study is necessary to examine this low net growth, it may be due to the establishment of more stringent entry requirements or even a purge of People's Control consistent with Gorbachev's toughened stance on cadres, addressed in the next section of this chapter. It may also indicate that People's Control has stagnated since the late 1970s, with few new members and many dropouts.

83. Gorbachev, "Reorganization and the Party's Personnel Policy," pp. 38–39.

84. Zbigniew Brzezinski, "The Crisis of Communism: The Paradox of Political Participation," *Washington Quarterly*, vol. 10, nr. 4 (Autumn, 1987), pp. 167–174. Brzezinski compares the experiences of the Soviet Union, China, and Poland, concluding that "all have so far been unable to solve the problem of participation" because of this dilemma. He adds that a solution of the political participation problem is essential if the Soviet Union expects to remain competitive in the post-industrial world.

85. Gorbachev, "Reorganization and the Party's Personnel Policy," pp. 15–16 and 44–51.

86. "O Perestroike i Kadrovoi Politike Partii," *Kommunist*, 3/1987, pp. 53–64. Many of these measures apply to non-party leaders as well.

87. See, for example, Gorbachev's speech to the April 1985 plenum in Gorbachev, *Rechi*, vol. 2, pp. 162–165.

88. See the definition of the party's functions in *Perestroika*, p. 122, and in *Programma* (1986), p. 75. The expanded definition of the party's role can be seen by comparing the wording of the revised program with the wording in the 1961 edition. In describing the reasons for the growing role of the party, both editions discuss the higher level of political leadership required by the increased scale and complexity of the tasks of communist construction. They also mention the growing involvement of the population in the administration of affairs and the growing significance of scientific communism in overcoming the prejudices of the past. The 1986 edition adds to these reasons two new ones: the need for intensifying cooperation with other socialist countries and for ensuring unity in the face of bourgeois propaganda; and the increasing complexity of international relations. Both of these are Gorbachevian ideological themes, and both suggest that the need for a strong, unified party will continue indefinitely. See *Programma* (1961), p. 331 for the earlier iteration of the reasons for the party's growth. Gorbachev also addressed the growing role of the party in his speech to a Central Committee conference in November 1987. See *Pravda*, 21 November 1987.

89. See the excellent articles by Thane Gustafson and Dawn Mann ("Gorbachev's Next Gamble," pp. 1–20), Jerry F. Hough ("Gorbachev Consolidating Power," pp. 21–43) and Dale R. Herspring ("Gorbachev, Yazov, and the Military," pp. 99–107) in *Problems of Communism*, 36 (July-August 1987).

90. Gorbachev, *Rechi*, vol. 2, pp. 164–165.

91. Many of Gorbachev's appointments have come from among people he worked with over the years. The three main networks he used were: contacts

he made in Stavropol' and adjacent regions while he was a regional secretary; students who graduated from Moscow University at about the same time he did; and people who worked in the Komsomol organization in the late 1950s and early 1960s, a period when Gorbachev was also active in the organization. See Hough, "Gorbachev Consolidating Power," p. 30.

92. Gustafson and Mann, "Gorbachev's Next Gamble," p. 14. The seventh was Karl Vayno of Estonia, who was replaced in June 1988 by V. I. Vyalyas.

93. Gorbachev, *Rechi*, p. 263.

94. Gorbachev, *Perestroika*, p. 123.

95. *Programma* (1986), p. 76.

96. "O Perestroike i Kadrovoi Politike Partii."

97. Gorbachev was certainly referring to the party's net growth. The actual number of members added during the period between the 26th and 27th Congresses was 3,141,671. In addition, a total of 3,305,956 candidates joined during the same period. *Partiinaia Zhizn'*, 21/1987, p. 7. See the discussion below.

98. Gorbachev, *Rechi*, pp. 264–265. This theme was addressed in the revised Party Program as well. Calling for the end of accepting members who have only careerist motives, the Program stated, "Belonging to the party provides no privileges. It means only greater responsibility for everything that happens in the country, for the fate of communist construction, and for social progress." See *Programma* (1986), p. 77. Gorbachev also discussed "deviations from recruitment practices" in his speech to the January 1987 plenum. See "Reorganization and the Party's Personnel Policy," p. 16.

99. *Kommunist*, 10/1987, pp. 73–76.

100. I have been unable to locate the total membership number as of 1 January for either 1984 or 1985 and thus cannot calculate the party's net growth for those two years. Since 1985 was Gorbachev's first year as General Secretary, however, I doubt that the number purged for that year was as high as the two subsequent years.

101. The equivalent number cannot be derived for 1987 because we still don't know how many candidates were accepted that year. We cannot draw any conclusions about 1985 either, because the membership numbers for that year are not yet available in any of the sources I consulted.

102. Gorbachev is still displeased with some party elements for not instituting stricter standards. The *Pravda* article that contained the membership numbers for 1987 pointed out that necessary measures were not being taken everywhere to ensure standards were maintained. Some of the problems noted in certain party organizations included tolerance of apolitical attitudes, unscrupulousness, and nationalistic quirks (*vyvikhi*), instances of drunkenness, and general misbehavior. See *Pravda*, 14 April 1988.

103. *Partiinaia Zhizn'*, 9/1988, pp. 4–6.

104. Gorbachev, "Reorganization and the Party's Personnel Policy," pp. 33–34. For a discussion of party elections, see *Pravda*, 10 February 1987. Werner Hahn has pointed out that Gorbachev's election proposals were probably patterned on similar efforts in Poland, Hungary, and other communist countries. Like

those efforts, the goal of Gorbachev's approach is to narrow the gap between the political leaders and the population by making the leaders more accountable for their actions. Providing some measure of choice in the election process is also part of Gorbachev's overall effort to forge a new relationship between the leaders and the led. Hahn's analysis of the reasons behind Gorbachev's political reforms is consistent with my own, and his comparative approach is particularly convincing. There are pitfalls to the election process, as Hahn points out in his description of the evolution of party elections in Poland. However, Gorbachev is certain to build in safeguards based on the Polish experience and his own sense of what is possible in the Soviet system. His reference to the continuing validity of democratic centralism seems to be the main guarantee that party elections won't get out of hand. See Werner Hahn, "Electoral Choice in the Soviet Bloc," *Problems of Communism*, 36 (March-April 1987), pp. 29–39.

105. William Odom suggests that a purge of party officials is Gorbachev's main goal. While Odom may be correct that Gorbachev is not seeking systemic change and his insights into the unintended consequences of reform are valuable, his argument that Gorbachev's main goal is to replace party officials with those supportive of his efforts is unconvincing. It does not explain the far-reaching aspects of Gorbachev's economic reforms, the extent of his democratization program, or the startling changes in Soviet foreign policy such as the withdrawal of forces from Afghanistan or the intrusive verification measures allowed under the INF treaty. If all Gorbachev wanted was cadres changes, he could certainly have accomplished this much more easily and with much less risk to his status and power. See William E. Odom, "How Far Can Soviet Reform Go?," *Problems of Communism*, 36 (November-December 1987), pp. 18–33.

Bibliography

Allworth, Edward, ed. *Ethnic Russia in the USSR*. New York: Pergamon Press, 1980.

———. *Soviet Nationality Problems*. New York: Columbia University Press, 1971.

Bailes, Kendall E. *Technology and Society Under Lenin and Stalin*. Princeton: Princeton University Press, 1978.

Bandera, V. N., and Melnyk, Z. L. *The Soviet Economy in Regional Perspective*. New York: Praeger, 1971.

Bialer, Seweryn. *The Domestic Context of Soviet Foreign Policy*. Boulder: Westview Press, 1981.

Bilinsky, Yaroslav. *The Second Soviet Republic: The Ukraine After World War II*. New Brunswick: Rutgers University Press, 1964.

Bloembergen, Samuel. "The Union Republics: How Much Autonomy?" *Problems of Communism*. 16 (September-October, 1967): 27–35.

Bochenski, Joseph. "The Three Components of Soviet Thought." *Studies in Soviet Thought II*. 1 (March 1962): 7–11.

Bova, Russell. "The Role of Workplace Participation." *Problems of Communism*. 36 (July-August 1987): 76–86.

Breslauer, George. *Khrushchev and Brezhnev as Leaders: Building Authority in Soviet Politics*. London: George Allen & Unwin, 1982.

Brezhnev, L. I. *Leninskim Kursom*. Eight volumes. Moscow: Politicheskaia Literatura, 1970–1981.

———. *Report of the Central Committee of the CPSU to the XXVI Congress of the Communist Party of the Soviet Union and the Immediate Tasks of the Party in Home and Foreign Policy*. Moscow: Novosti Press Agency, 1981.

Brown, Archie, and Kaser, Michael, eds. *Soviet Policy for the 1980s*. Bloomington: Indiana University Press, 1982.

Brzezinski, Zbigniew K. "The Crisis of Communism: The Paradox of Political Participation." *Washington Quarterly*. 10 (Autumn 1987): 167–174.

———. *The Soviet Bloc: Unity and Conflict*. Revised ed. Cambridge, Massachusetts: Harvard University Press, 1967.

———, and Huntington, Samuel P. *Political Power: USA/USSR*. New York: The Viking Press, 1965.

Cherkovets, V. N., ed. *Problemy Razvitogo Sotsializma v Politicheskoi Ehkonomiki*. Moscow: Nauka, 1977.

Chotiner, Barbara Ann. *Khrushchev's Party Reform*. Westport, Connecticut: Greenwood Press, 1984.

Clem, Ralph S., ed. *The Soviet West: Interplay Between Nationality and Social Organization*. New York: Praeger Publishers, 1975.

Cocks, Paul, Daniels, Robert V., and Heer, Nancy Whittier, eds. *The Dynamics of Soviet Politics*. Cambridge, Massachusetts: Harvard University Press, 1976.

Cohen, Stephen F., Rabinowitch, Alexander, and Sharlet, Robert, eds. *The Soviet Union Since Stalin*. Bloomington: Indiana University Press, 1980.

Connor, Walker. *The National Question in Marxist-Leninist Theory and Strategy*. Princeton: Princeton University Press, 1984.

Connor, Walter D. "Social Policy Under Gorbachev." *Problems of Communism*. 35 (July-August 1986): 31–46.

_____ . *Socialism, Politics, and Equality*. New York: Columbia University Press, 1979.

Conquest, Robert. *The Harvest of Sorrow: Soviet Collectivization and the Terror-Famine*. New York: Oxford University Press, 1986.

_____ . *Soviet Deportation of Nationalities*. London: Bodley Head, 1970.

_____ . *Soviet Nationalities Policy in Practice*. London: The Bodley Head, 1967.

Churchward, L. G. "Contemporary Soviet Theory of the Soviet State." *Soviet Studies*. 12 (April 1961): 404–419.

Dallin, Alexander, and Larson, Thomas B., eds. *Soviet Politics Since Khrushchev*. Englewood Cliffs: Prentice Hall, 1968.

Daniels, Robert V. "The State and Revolution: A Case Study in the Genesis and Transformation of Communist Ideology." *American Slavic and East European Review*. 12 (February 1953): 22–43.

d'Encausse, Hélène Carrère. *Decline of an Empire*. New York: Harper Colophon Books, 1981.

_____ . "Party and Federation in the USSR." *Government and Opposition*. 13 (Spring 1978): 133–150.

Domes, Juergen. *China After the Cultural Revolution*. Berkeley: University of California Press, 1977.

Dunham, Vera S. *In Stalin's Time: Middleclass Values in Soviet Fiction*. Cambridge, England: Cambridge University Press, 1976.

Evans, Alfred B., Jr. "The Decline of Developed Socialism? Some Trends in Recent Soviet Ideology." *Soviet Studies*. 34 (January 1986): 1–23.

_____ . "Developed Socialism in Soviet Ideology," *Soviet Studies* 24 (July 1977): 409–428.

_____ . "Social Transformation in Developed Socialism: Recent Trends in Soviet Ideology," *Co-existence*. 17 (April 1980): 58–81.

Fainsod, Merle. *How Russia is Ruled*. Revised edition. Cambridge, Massachusetts: Harvard University Press, 1963.

Field, Mark G., ed. *Social Consequences of Modernization*. Baltimore: Johns Hopkins Press, 1976.

Friedgut, Theodore H. *Political Participation in the USSR*. Princeton: Princeton University Press, 1979.

Friedrich, Carl J., and Brzezinski, Zbigniew K. *Totalitarian Dictatorship and Autocracy*. Second edition. Revised by Carl J. Friedrich. New York: Frederick A. Praeger, 1965.

Friend, J. W. "The Roots of Autonomy in West European Communism." *Problems of Communism.* 29 (September-October 1980): 28–43.

Gati, Charles, ed. *The International Politics of Eastern Europe.* New York: Praeger Publishers, 1976.

Glezerman, G. E., and Reingol'd, O., eds. *Razvitoe Sotsialisticheskoe Obshchestvo: Sushchnost', Kriterii Zrelosti, Kritika Revizionistskikh Kontseptsii.* Moscow: Mysl', 1979.

Goodman, Elliot R. "Nationalities, Nations, and the Soviet World State: Khrushchev's Ambitions and Frustrations." *Orbis.* 9 (September 1965): 459–471.

Gorbachev, Mikhail. *Izbrannye Rechi i Stat'i.* Three volumes. Moscow: Politicheskaia Literatura, 1987.

_____ . *Perestroika: New Thinking for Our Country and the World.* New York: Harper & Row, 1987.

Goure, Leon. *The Military Indoctrination of Soviet Youth.* New York: National Strategy Information Center, 1973.

Griffith, William E. *The Sino-Soviet Rift.* Cambridge, Massachusetts: MIT Press, 1964.

Gustafson, Thane, and Mann, Dawn. "Gorbachev's First Year: Building Power and Authority." *Problems of Communism.* 35 (May-June 1986): 1–19.

_____ . "Gorbachev's Next Gamble." *Problems of Communism.* 36 (July-August 1987): 1–20.

Hahn, Werner. "Electoral Choice in the Soviet Bloc." *Problems of Communism.* 36 (March-April 1987): 29–39.

Harding, Neil, ed. *The State in Socialist Society.* Albany: State University of New York Press, 1984.

Herspring, Dale R. "Gorbachev, Yazov, and the Military." *Problems of Communism.* 36 (July-August 1987): 99–107.

Hewett, Ed A. *Reforming the Soviet Economy.* Washington: The Brookings Institution, 1988.

Hill, Ronald J., and Frank, Peter. *The Soviet Communist Party.* London: George Allen & Unwin, 1981.

Hodnet, Grey. "The Debate Over Soviet Federalism." *Soviet Studies.* 18 (April 1967): 458–481.

_____ . "What's in a Nation." *Problems of Communism.* 16 (September-October 1967): 2–15.

Hoffman, Erik P., and Laird, Robbin F. *The Politics of Economic Modernization in the Soviet Union.* Ithaca: Cornell University Press, 1982.

Hough, Jerry F. "Andropov's First Year." *Problems of Communism.* 32 (November-December 1983): 49–64.

_____ . "Gorbachev Consolidating Power." *Problems of Communism.* 36 (July-August 1987): 21–43.

_____ . *Soviet Leadership in Transition.* Washington: The Brookings Institution, 1980.

_____ . *The Soviet Union and Social Science Theory.* (Cambridge, Massachusetts: Harvard University Press, 1977.

_____ , and Fainsod, Merle. *How the Soviet Union is Governed.* Cambridge, Massachusetts: Harvard University Press, 1979.

Huntington, Samuel P., and Moore, Clement H., eds. *Authoritarian Politics in Modern Society: The Dynamics of One-Party Systems.* New York: Basic Books, 1970.

Hutchings, Robert L. *Soviet-East European Relations: Consolidation and Conflict, 1968–1980.* Madison: University of Wisconsin Press, 1983.

Istoriia Kommunisticheskoi Partii Sovetskogo Soiuza. Moscow: Politicheskaia Literatura, 1976.

Jacob, Philip E., and Toscano, James V., eds. *The Integration of Political Communities.* Philadelphia: J. B. Lippincott Company, 1964.

Kanet, Roger E. *Soviet Foreign Policy in the 1980s.* New York: Praeger, 1982.

_____ . "The All-People's State: Recent Changes in the Soviet Theory of the State," *Soviet Studies.* 20 (July 1968): 81–93.

Kapitonov, K. V., ed. *Voprosy Organizatsionno-Partiinoi Raboty KPSS.* Moscow: Politicheskaia Literatura, 1978.

Karinskii, S. S. *Pooshchreniia za Doblestnii Trud po Sovetskomu Zakonodatel'stvu.* Moscow: Znanie, 1956.

Kelley, Donald R. *The Politics of Developed Socialism: The Soviet Union as a Post-Industrial State.* New York: Greenwood Press, 1986.

Kim, M. P., ed. *Sovetskii Narod—Novaia Istoricheskaia Obshchnost' Liudei.* Moscow: Nauka, 1975.

Krawciw, Bohdan. "Progressive Russification of the Ukrainian SSR." *Ukrainian Quarterly.* 29 (Summer 1973): 137–145.

Liber, George. "Language, Literacy, and Book Publishing in the Ukrainian SSR, 1923–1928." *Slavic Review.* 41 (Winter, 1982): 673–685.

Linden, Carl A. *Khrushchev and the Soviet Leadership.* Baltimore: Johns Hopkins Press, 1966.

_____ . *The Soviet Party-State: The Politics of Ideocratic Despotism.* New York: Praeger Publishers, 1983.

Lowenthal, Richard. "Development vs. Utopia in Communist Policy." In *Change in Communist Systems.* Edited by Chalmers Johnson. Stanford: Stanford University Press, 1970.

_____ . *World Communism: The Disintegration of a Secular Faith.* New York: Oxford University Press, 1964.

MacFarquhar, Roderick. *The Origins of the Cultural Revolution.* Two volumes. New York: Columbia University Press, 1974 and 1983.

Mannheim, Karl. *Ideology and Utopia.* New York: Harcourt, Brace, and Company, 1936.

Matthews, Mervyn. *Privilege in the Soviet Union.* London: George Allen & Unwin, 1978.

Medvedev, Roy A. *On Socialist Democracy.* New York: W. W. Norton, 1975.

Meyer, Alfred G. "The Functions of Ideology in the Soviet Political System." *Soviet Studies.* 17 (January 1966): 273–285.

_____ . *Leninism.* Cambridge, Massachusetts: Harvard University Press, 1957.

McNeal, Robert H. *Stalin: Man and Ruler.* New York: New York University Press, 1988.

Mickiewicz, Ellen. "Regional Variation in Female Recruitment and Advancement in the Communist Party of the Soviet Union." *Slavic Review.* 36 (September 1977): 441–454.

Millar, James R., ed. *Politics, Work, and Daily Life in the USSR: A Survey of Former Soviet Citizens.* Cambridge, England: Cambridge University Press, 1987.

Mujal-Leon, Eusebio. "Cataluna, Carrillo, and Eurocommunism." *Problems of Communism.* 30 (March-April 1981): 25–47

_____ . "The PCE in Spanish Politics." *Problems of Communism.* 27 (July-August 1978): 15–37.

Murphy, Paul J. *Brezhnev: Soviet Politician.* Jefferson, N.C.: McFarland & Company, 1981.

Nove, Alec. *The Soviet Economic System.* London: George Allen & Unwin, 1977.

Odom, William E. "How Far Can Soviet Reform Go?" *Problems of Communism.* 36 (November-December 1987): 18–33.

Oliner, Samuel P. "The Non-Russian Peoples in the USSR: An Unsolved Problem." *Ukrainian Quarterly.* 32 (Autumn 1976): 261–285.

Pipes, Richard. *The Formation of the Soviet Union.* New York: Athenum, 1974.

Poliakov, Iu. A., ed. *Konstitutsiia Razvitogo Sotsializma.* Moscow: Nauka, 1981.

Programma Kommunisticheskoi Partii Sovetskogo Soiuza. Moscow: Politizdat, 1986.

Putnam, Robert D. "Studying Elite Political Culture: The case of 'Ideology.'" *American Political Science Review.* 65 (September 1971): 651–681.

Pye, Lucian W., and Verba, Sidney, eds. *Political Culture and Political Development.* Princeton: Princeton University Press, 1965.

Reshetar, John S. *The Soviet Polity: Government and Politics in the USSR.* Second edition. New York: Harper & Row, 1978.

Rigby, T. H. *Communist Party Membership in the USSR, 1917–1967.* Princeton: Princeton University Press, 1968.

_____ . "Soviet Communist Party Membership Under Brezhnev." *Soviet Studies.* 28 (July 1976): 317–337.

_____ . "The Soviet Regional Leadership: The Brezhnev Generation." *Slavic Review.* 37 (March 1978): 1–24.

Rodionov, P. A., ed. *Vozrastanie Rukovodiashchei Roli KPSS v Stroitel'stve Sotsializma i Kommunizma.* Moscow: Politicheskaia Literatura, 1979.

Ryavec, Karl W., ed. *Soviet Society and the Communist Party.* Amherst: Unversity of Massachusetts Press, 1978.

Scanlan, James P. *Marxism in the USSR: A Critical Survey of Current Soviet Thought.* Ithaca: Cornell University Press, 1985.

Schroeder, Gertrude. "Industrial Wage Differentials in the USSR." *Soviet Studies.* 17 (January 1966): 303–317.

Schurman, Franz. *Ideology and Organization in Communist China.* Berkeley, California: University of California Press, 1966.

Seroka, Jim, and Simon, Maurice D., eds. *Developed Socialism in the Soviet Bloc: Political Theory and Political Reality.* Boulder, Colorado: Westview Press, 1982.

Sharlet, Robert. *The New Soviet Constitution of 1977.* Brunswick, Ohio: King's Court Communications, 1978.

Sheehy, Ann. "Language Problems in the Soviet Armed Forces." *Radio Liberty Research Bulletin.* 196/78, September 1978.

Sherlock, Thomas. "Politics and History Under Gorbachev." *Problems of Communism.* 37 (May-August 1988): 16–42.

Shlapentokh, Vladimir. "The XXVII Congress—A Case Study of the Shaping of a New Party Ideology." *Soviet Studies.* 40 (January 1988): 1–20.

Sikorskii, V. M. *KPSS Na Ehtape Razvitogo Sotsializma.* Minsk: BGU, 1975.

Solchanyk, Roman. "Russian Language and Soviet Politics." *Soviet Studies.* 34 (January 1982): 23–42.

Suslov, M. A. *Na Putiakh Stroitel'stva Kommunizma.* 2 vols. Moscow: Politicheskaia Literatura, 1977.

Tatu, Michel. *Power in the Kremlin: From Khrushchev to Kosygin.* New York: The Viking Press, 1969.

Terry, Sarah Meiklejohn, ed. *Soviet Policy in Eastern Europe.* New Haven: Yale University Press, 1984.

Thornton, Richard C. *China: A Political History, 1917–1980.* Boulder, Colorado: Westview Press, 1982.

Tucker, Robert C. *Stalinism: Essays in Historical Interpretation.* New York: W. W. Norton, 1977.

———. "Swollen State, Spent Society: Stalin's Legacy to Brezhnev's Russia." *Foreign Affairs* 60 (Winter 1981/1982): 414–435.

Ulam, Adam. *Expansion and Coexistence: Soviet Foreign Policy 1917–1973.* Second edition. New York: Praeger Publishers, 1974.

———. *Stalin: The Man and His Era.* New York: Viking Press, 1973.

Unger, Aryeh L. "Soviet Communist Party Membership Under Brezhnev: A Comment." *Soviet Studies.* 29 (April 1977): 306–316.

U.S. Congress, Joint Economic Committee. *East European Economic Assessment.* Washington: Government Printing Office, 1981.

———. *Gorbachev's Economic Plans.* Washington: Government Printing Office, 1987.

———. *Soviet Economy in a Time of Change.* Washington: Government Printing Office, 1979.

———. *Soviet Economy in the 1980s: Problems and Prospects.* Washington: Government Printing Office, 1982.

XXII S"ezd Kommunisticheskoi Partii Sovetskogo Soiuza: Stenograficheskii Otchet. Moscow: Politicheskaia Literatura, 1961.

XXIII S"ezd Kommunisticheskoi Partii Sovetskogo Soiuza: Stenograficheskii Otchet. Moscow: Politizdat, 1966.

XXIV S"ezd Kommunisticheskoi Partii Sovetskogo Soiuza, 30 Marta–9 Aprel'ia 1971 g.: Stenograficheskii Otchet. Two volumes. Moscow: Politizdat, 1971.

XXV S"ezd KPSS: Edinstvo Teorii i Praktiki. Moscow: Politicheskaia Literatura, 1977.

Zimmerman, William. *Soviet Perspectives on International Relations, 1956–1967.* Princeton: Princeton University Press, 1973.

Zlotnick, Marc D. "Chernenko Succeeds." *Problems of Communism.* 33 (March-April 1984): 17–31.

Zwick, Peter. "Intrasystem Inequality and the Symmetry of Socioeconomic Development in the USSR." *Comparative Politics.* 8 (July 1976): 501–524.

Index